# 2009
## A BRAND-NEW YEAR—
## A PROMISING NEW START

With expert readings and forecasts, you can chart a course to romance, adventure, good health, or career opportunities while gaining valuable insight into yourself and others. Offering a daily outlook for 18 full months, this fascinating guide shows you:

- The important dates in your life
- What to expect from an astrological reading
- How the stars can help you stay healthy and fit
  And more!

Let this sound advice guide you through a year of heavenly possibilities—for today and for every day of 2009!

## SYDNEY OMARR'S® DAY-BY-DAY
## ASTROLOGICAL GUIDE FOR

**ARIES**—March 21–April 19
**TAURUS**—April 20–May 20
**GEMINI**—May 21–June 20
**CANCER**—June 21–July 22
**LEO**—July 23–August 22
**VIRGO**—August 23–September 22
**LIBRA**—September 23–October 22
**SCORPIO**—October 23–November 21
**SAGITTARIUS**—November 22–December 21
**CAPRICORN**—December 22–January 19
**AQUARIUS**—January 20–February 18
**PISCES**—February 19–March 20

## IN 2009

# SYDNEY OMARR'S®

## DAY-BY-DAY ASTROLOGICAL GUIDE FOR

# PISCES

### FEBRUARY 19–MARCH 20

# 2009

by Trish MacGregor
with Carol Tonsing

A SIGNET BOOK

SIGNET
Published by New American Library, a division of
Penguin Group (USA) Inc., 375 Hudson Street,
New York, New York 10014, USA
Penguin Group (Canada), 90 Eglinton Avenue East, Suite 700, Toronto,
Ontario M4P 2Y3, Canada (a division of Pearson Penguin Canada Inc.)
Penguin Books Ltd., 80 Strand, London WC2R 0RL, England
Penguin Ireland, 25 St. Stephen's Green, Dublin 2,
Ireland (a division of Penguin Books Ltd.)
Penguin Group (Australia), 250 Camberwell Road, Camberwell, Victoria 3124,
Australia (a division of Pearson Australia Group Pty. Ltd.)
Penguin Books India Pvt. Ltd., 11 Community Centre, Panchsheel Park,
New Delhi - 110 017, India
Penguin Group (NZ), 67 Apollo Drive, Rosedale, North Shore 0632,
New Zealand (a division of Pearson New Zealand Ltd.)
Penguin Books (South Africa) (Pty.) Ltd., 24 Sturdee Avenue,
Rosebank, Johannesburg 2196, South Africa

Penguin Books Ltd., Registered Offices:
80 Strand, London WC2R 0RL, England

First published by Signet, an imprint of New American Library,
a division of Penguin Group (USA) Inc.

First Printing, June 2008
10  9  8  7  6  5  4  3  2  1

# CONTENTS

 INTRODUCTION

# Accessible Astrology

At a recent New York exhibit honoring the life of Princess Grace of Monaco (the former Hollywood star Grace Kelly) there was a surprise for astrology fans. A glass display case was filled with her astrological memorabilia: a jeweled Scorpio pendant, meticulous handwritten horoscopes of loved ones, and invitations to a gala Scorpio-theme birthday party. Even the catalogue of the exhibit prominently mentioned her sun sign. Like many of the rich and famous of her era, Princess Grace had access to astrologers, and she consulted them regularly.

At the time of Princess Grace's death in 1982, astrology was becoming widely available to the general public via books and horoscope magazines. Today, astrology is more accessible than ever to anyone who wishes to gain self-knowledge or to help make better life choices. As you approach the challenges and opportunities of 2009, let this guide help you discover and use all the tools astrology provides. You'll learn the important dates in your life this year, in addition to how the stars can help you improve relationships, find the right career, get organized, or support ecological programs. For those who are new to astrology or would like to know more about it, there are easy techniques to start putting astrology to work for you every day. You'll learn about your sun sign and how to decipher the mysterious symbols on a horoscope chart. Then you can use the convenient tables in this book to look up other planets in your horoscope, each of which sheds light on a different facet of your personal life.

Will the passion last, is Aries or Capricorn "the one," and where will you meet the perfect partner? Astrology is an age-old mating and dating coach. In our chapters, you'll

1

find answers to your burning questions about romance and tips about how to seduce every sign. We illustrate each sun-sign combination with famous pairs so you can visualize how some couples kept the flame of love burning and some fizzled out.

Whether it's money matters, fashion tips, or ways to sustain the planet, we'll provide guidance you can use every day. Can't decide whether to go to Italy or Mexico for this year's vacation? Try your sun sign's favored vacation spot. Most people have access to the Internet, where there's a mind-boggling variety of astrology sites. We've edited them down to the best sites where you can get free horoscopes, connect with other astrology fans, buy astrology software, and even find an accredited college that specializes in astrological studies.

There are so many ways to put astrology into your life. Before giving yourself or your home a makeover, consult your sun sign's special colors and styles to create a harmonious environment. Get in the best shape ever with a fitness program designed for your sign.

To make the most of each day, there are eighteen months of on-target daily horoscopes. So here's hoping you use your star power wisely and well to make 2009 a productive and happy year!

## CHAPTER 1

# The Top Trends of 2009: A New Balancing Act

Astrologers judge the trends of a year by following the slow-moving planets, from Jupiter through Pluto. A change in sign indicates a new cycle, with new emphasis. The farthest planets (Uranus, Neptune, and Pluto) which stay in a sign for at least seven years, cause a very significant change in the atmosphere when they change signs. Shifts in Jupiter, which changes every year, and Saturn, every two years, are more obvious in current events and daily lives. Jupiter generally brings a fortunate, expansive emphasis to its new sign, while Saturn's two-year cycle is a reality check, bringing tests of maturity, discipline, and responsibility.

## The Power of Little Pluto

Though astronomers have demoted tiny Pluto from being a full-fledged planet to a dwarf planet, astrologers have been tracking its influence since Pluto was discovered in 1930 and have witnessed that this minuscule celestial body has a powerful effect on both a personal and global level. So Pluto, which moved into the sign of Capricorn last year, will still be called a "planet" by astrologers and will be given just as much importance as before.

# Down-to-Earth Capricorn Is Balanced with Forward-Looking Aquarius

Last year, the emphasis was on the earth signs of Capricorn and Virgo, which still continues for most of this year. Until 2024, Pluto will exert its influence in this practical, building, healing earth sign. Capricorn relates to structures, institutions, order, mountains and mountain countries, mineral rights, issues involving the elderly and growing older—all of which will be emphasized in the coming years. It is the sign of established order, corporations, big business—all of which will be accented. Possibly, it will fall to business structures to create a new sense of order in the world.

You should now feel the rumblings of change in the Capricorn area of your horoscope and in the world at large. The last time Pluto was in Capricorn was the years up to and during the Revolutionary War; therefore this should be an important time in the U.S. political scene, as well as a reflection of the aging and maturing of American society in general. Both the rise and the fall of the Ottoman Empire happened under Pluto in Capricorn.

# The Aquarius Factor

This year, Jupiter moves from conservative Capricorn to more liberal, experimental, humanitarian Aquarius. During the year that Jupiter remains in a sign, the fields associated with that sign are the ones that currently arouse excitement and enthusiasm, usually providing excellent opportunities for expansion, fame, and fortune.

Jupiter in Aquarius promotes freedom-loving, liberal influences, which should balance the more conservative serious Capricorn-Virgo atmosphere. As it joins and expands the influence of Neptune, also in Aquarius, there should be many artistic and scientific breakthroughs. International politics also comes under this influence, as Neptune in Aquarius raises issues of global boundaries and political structures not being as solid as they seem. This could continue to produce rebellion and chaos in the environment. However, with the generally benevolent force of Jupiter backing up the creative side of Neptune, it is possible that highly original and effective solutions to global problems will be found, which could transcend the current social and cultural barriers.

Another place we notice the Jupiter influence is in fashion, which should veer into a more original and experimental mode, perhaps reminiscent of the 1960s, with brighter colors and more high-tech fabrics.

Those born under Aquarius should have many opportunities during the year. However, the key is to keep your feet on the ground. The flip side of Jupiter is that there are no limits. You can expand off the planet under a Jupiter transit, which is why the planet is often called the "Gateway to Heaven." If something is going to burst (such as an artery) or overextend or go over the top in some way, it could happen under a supposedly lucky Jupiter transit, so beware.

Those born under Leo may find their best opportunities working with partners this year, as Jupiter will be transiting their seventh house of relationships.

# Saturn in Virgo: The Maturing of the Baby Boomers, Reforms in Care and Maintenance

Saturn, the planet of limitation, testing, and restriction, will be transiting Virgo for most of the year. This is a time when Virgo issues—health care and maintenance, education, and moral standards and controls—will come to the fore. For most of this year, we will be adjusting the structures of our lives, making changes so that we can function at an optimal efficient level. That means making game plans and to-do lists, clearing out clutter, and organizing and simplifying our lives. We'll be challenged with a reality check in areas where we have been too optimistic or expansive.

# Saturn in Libra

Saturn moves into Libra on October 29. This is one of Saturn's best positions, where it can steady the scales of justice and promote balanced, responsible judgment. There should be much deliberation over duty, honor, and fairness, which will be ongoing for the next two years. Far-reaching new legislation and diplomatic moves are possible, perhaps resolving difficult international standoffs. Because this placement works well with the humanitarian Aquarius influence of Jupiter and Neptune, there should be new hope of resolving conflicts. Previously, Saturn was in Libra during the early 1920s, the early 1950s, and again in the early 1980s.

# Continuing Trends

Uranus and Neptune continue to do a kind of astrological dance called a "mutual reception." This is a supportive relationship where Uranus is in Pisces, the sign ruled by Neptune, while Neptune is in Aquarius, the sign ruled by Uranus. When this dance is over in 2011, it is likely that we will be living under very different political and social circumstances.

# Uranus in Pisces

Uranus, known as the Great Awakener, tends to cause both upheaval and innovation in the sign it transits. During previous episodes of Uranus in Pisces, great religions and spiritual movements have come into being, most recently Mormonism and Christian Fundamentalism. In its most positive mode, Pisces promotes imagination and creativity, the art of illusion in theater and film, and the inspiration of great artists.

A water sign, Pisces is naturally associated with all things liquid—such as oceans, oil, and alcohol—and with those creatures that live in the water—fish, the fishing industry, fish habitats, and fish farming. Currently there is a great debate going on about overfishing, contamination of fish, and fish farming. The underdogs, the enslaved, and the disenfranchised should also benefit from Uranus in Pisces. Since Uranus is a disruptive influence that aims to challenge the status quo, the forces of nature that manifest now will most likely be in the Pisces area— the oceans, seas, and rivers. We have so far seen unprecedented rainy seasons, floods, mud slides, and disastrous hurricanes. Note that 2005's devastating Hurricane Katrina hit an area known for both the oil and fishing industries.

Pisces is associated with the prenatal phase of life, which is related to regenerative medicine. The controversy over embryonic stem cell research will continue to be debated, but recent developments may make the arguments moot. Petroleum issues, both in the oil-producing countries and offshore oil drilling, will come to a head. Uranus in Pisces suggests that development of new hydroelectric sources may provide the power we need to continue our current power-thirsty lifestyle.

As in previous eras, there should continue to be a flourishing of the arts. We are seeing many new artistic forms developing now, such as computer-created actors and special effects. The sky's the limit on this influence.

Those who have problems with Uranus are those who resist change, so the key is to embrace the future.

# Neptune in Aquarius

Neptune is a planet of imagination and creativity, but also of deception and illusion. Neptune is associated with hospitals, which have been the subject of much controversy. On the positive side, hospitals are acquiring cutting-edge technology. The atmosphere of many hospitals is already changing from the intimidating and sterile environment of the past to that of a health-promoting spa. Alternative therapies, such as massage, diet counseling, and aromatherapy, are becoming commonplace, which expresses this Neptune trend. New procedures in plastic surgery, also a Neptune glamour field, and antiaging therapies are giving the illusion of youth.

However, issues involving the expense and quality of health care, medication, and the evolving relationship between doctors, drug companies, and HMOs reflect a darker side of this trend.

# Eclipses Are Movers and Shakers

Six eclipses this year, more than usual, could shake up the financial markets and rock your world in January, July, and late December. The three eclipses in July are the ones to watch, especially the total solar eclipse at the time of the new moon on July 22, which is sandwiched between two lunar eclipses on July 7 and August 5. As several recent studies have shown the stock market to be linked to the lunar cycle, it might be wise to track investments more carefully during this time.

# What About the New Planets?

Our solar system is getting crowded, as astronomers continue to discover new objects circling the sun. In addition to the familiar planets, there are dwarf planets, comets, cometoids, asteroids, and strange icy bodies in the Kuiper Belt beyond Neptune. A dwarf planet christened Eris, discovered in 2005, is now being observed and analyzed by astrologers. Eris was named after a goddess of discord and strife. In mythology, she was a troublemaker who made men think their opinions were right and others wrong. What an appropriate name for a planet discovered during a time of discord in the Middle East and elsewhere! Eris has a companion moon named Dysnomia for her daughter, described as a demon spirit of lawlessness. With mythological associations like these, we wonder what the effect of this mother-daughter duo will be. Once

Eris's orbit is established, astrologers will track the impact of this planet on our horoscopes. Eris takes about 560 years to orbit the sun, which means its emphasis in a given astrological sign will affect several generations.

# CHAPTER 2

# How Astrology Works: The Basics

It's hard to believe, but once the inner workings of astrology were a mystery accessible only to a select few scholars. Now it's easy to pick up enough basic knowledge to go beyond the realm of your sun sign into the deeper areas of this fascinating subject, which combines science, art, spirituality, and psychology. In this chapter, we'll show you how astrology works. You'll be able to define a sign and figure out why astrologers say what they do about each sign. As you look at your astrological chart, you'll have a good idea of what's going on in each portion of the horoscope. Let's get started.

## Know the Difference Between Signs and Constellations

Most readers know their signs, but many often confuse them with constellations. *Signs* are actually a type of celestial real estate, located on the *zodiac*, an imaginary 360-degree belt circling the earth. This belt is divided into twelve equal 30-degree portions, which are the *signs*. There's a lot of confusion about the difference between the *signs* and the *constellations* of the zodiac, patterns of stars which originally marked the twelve divisions, like signposts. Though a *sign* is named after the *constellation* that once marked the same area, the constellations are no longer in the same place relative to the earth that they were many centuries ago. Over hundreds of years, the earth's orbit has shifted, so that from our point of view here on earth, the constellations seem to have moved. However, the signs remain in place. (Most Western astrology uses the twelve-equal-part division of the zodiac, though there are some other methods of astrology that still use the constellations instead of the signs.)

Most people think of themselves in terms of their sun sign. A *sun sign* refers to the sign the sun is orbiting through at a given moment (from our point of view here on earth). For instance, if someone says, "I'm an Aries," the sun was passing through Aries when that person was born. However, there are nine other planets (plus asteroids, fixed stars, and sensitive points) that also form our total astrological personality, and some or many of these will be located in other signs. No one is completely "Aries," with all their astrological components in one sign! (Please note that, in astrology, the sun and moon are usually referred to as "planets," though of course they're not. Though there is some controversy over Pluto, it is still called a "planet" by astrologers.)

As we mentioned before, the sun signs are *places* on the zodiac. They do not *do* anything (the planets are the doers). However, they are associated with many things, depending on their location on the zodiac.


# How Do We Define a Sign's Characteristics?

The definitions of the signs evolved systematically from four interrelated components: a sign's element, its quality, its polarity or sex, and its order in the progression of the zodiac. All these factors work together to tell us what the sign is like.

The system is magically mathematical: the number 12—as in the twelve signs of the zodiac—is divisible by 4, by 3, and by 2. There are four elements, three qualities, and two polarities, which follow one another in sequence around the zodiac.

The four elements (earth, air, fire, and water) are the building blocks of astrology. The use of an element to describe a sign probably dates from man's first attempts to categorize what he saw. Ancient sages believed that all things were composed of combinations of these basic elements—

earth, air, fire, and water. This included the human character, which was fiery/choleric, earthy/melancholy, airy/sanguine, or watery/phlegmatic. The elements also correspond to our emotional (water), physical (earth), mental (air), and spiritual (fire) natures. The energies of each of the elements were then observed to related to the time of year when the sun was passing though a certain segment of the zodiac.

Those born with the sun in fire signs—Aries, Leo, Sagittarius—embody the characteristics of that element. Optimism, warmth, hot tempers, enthusiasm, and "spirit" are typical of these signs. Taurus, Virgo, and Capricorn are "earthy"—more grounded, physical, materialistic, organized, and deliberate than fire sign people. Air sign people—Gemini, Libra, and Aquarius—are mentally oriented communicators. Water signs—Cancer, Scorpio, and Pisces—are emotional, sensitive, and creative.

Think of what each element does to the others: water puts out fire or evaporates under heat. Air fans the flames or blows them out. Earth smothers fire, drifts and erodes with too much wind, and becomes mud or fertile soil with water. Those are often perfect analogies for the relationships between people of different sun-sign elements. This astrochemistry was one of the first ways man described his relationships. Fortunately, no one is entirely "air" or "water." We all have a bit, or a lot, of each element in our horoscopes. It is this unique mix that defines each astrological personality.

Within each element, there are three qualities that describe types of behavior associated with the sign. Those of cardinal signs are activists, go-getters. These four signs—Aries, Cancer, Libra, and Capricorn—begin each season. Fixed signs, which happen in the middle of the season, are associated with builders and stabilizers. You'll find that Taurus, Leo, Scorpio, and Aquarius are usually gifted with concentration, stamina, and focus. Mutable signs—Gemini, Virgo, Sagittarius, and Pisces—fall at the end of each season and thus are considered catalysts for change. People born under mutable signs are flexible and adaptable.

The polarity of a sign is either its positive or negative "charge." It can be masculine, active, positive, and yang, like air or fire signs, or it can be feminine, reactive, negative, and yin, like the water and earth signs. The polarities alternate, moving energy around the zodiac like the poles of a battery.

Finally, we consider the sign's place in the order of the zodiac. This is vital to the balance of all the forces and the transmission of energy moving through the signs. You may have noticed that your sign is quite different from your neighboring sign on either side. Yet each seems to grow out of its predecessor like links in a chain and transmits a syntheses of energy gathered along the "chain" to the following sign, beginning with the fire-powered positive charge of Aries.

## *How the Signs Add Up*

| SIGN | ELEMENT | QUALITY | POLARITY | PLACE |
|------|---------|---------|----------|-------|
| Aries | fire | cardinal | masculine | first |
| Taurus | earth | fixed | feminine | second |
| Gemini | air | mutable | masculine | third |
| Cancer | water | cardinal | feminine | fourth |
| Leo | fire | fixed | masculine | fifth |
| Virgo | earth | mutable | feminine | sixth |
| Libra | air | cardinal | masculine | seventh |
| Scorpio | water | fixed | feminine | eighth |
| Sagittarius | fire | mutable | masculine | ninth |
| Capricorn | earth | cardinal | feminine | tenth |
| Aquarius | air | fixed | masculine | eleventh |
| Pisces | water | mutable | feminine | twelfth |

13

# Each Sign Has a Special Planet

Each sign has a "ruling" planet that is most compatible with its energies. Mars adds its fiery assertive characteristics to Aries. The sensual beauty and comfort-loving side of Venus rules Taurus, whereas the idealistic side of Venus rules Libra. Quick-moving Mercury rules two mutable signs, Gemini and Virgo. Its mental agility belongs to Gemini while its analytical side is best expressed in Virgo. The changeable emotional moon is associated with Cancer, while the outgoing Leo personality is ruled by the sun. Scorpio originally shared Mars, but when Pluto was discovered in this century, its powerful magnetic energies were deemed more suitable to the intense vibrations of the fixed water sign Scorpio. Though Pluto has, as of this writing, been downgraded, it is still considered by astrologers to be a powerful force in the horoscope. Disciplined Capricorn is ruled by Saturn, and expansive Sagittarius by Jupiter. Unpredictable Aquarius is ruled by Uranus and creative, imaginative Pisces by Neptune. In a horoscope, if a planet is placed in the sign it rules, it is sure to be especially powerful.

# The Layout of a Horoscope Chart

A horoscope chart is a map of the heavens at a given moment in time. It looks like a wheel with twelve spokes. In between each of the "spokes" is a section called a *house*.

Each house deals with a different area of life and is influenced by a special sign and a planet. Astrologers look at the houses to tell in what area of life an event is happening or about to happen.

The house is governed by the sign passing over the spoke (or cusp of the house) at that particular moment. Though the first house is naturally associated with Aries and Mars, it would also have an additional Capricorn influence if that sign was passing over the house cusp at the time the chart was cast. The sequence of the houses starts with the first house located at the left center spoke (or the number 9 position, if you were reading a clock). The houses are then read *counterclockwise* around the chart, with the fourth house at the bottom of the chart, the tenth house at the top or twelve o'clock position.

Where do the planets belong? Around the horoscope, planets are placed within the houses according to their location at the time of the chart. That is why it is so important to have an accurate time; with no specific time, the planets have no specific location in the houses and one cannot determine which area of life they will apply to. Since the signs move across the houses as the earth turns, planets in a house will naturally intensify the importance of that house. The house that contains the sun is naturally one of the most prominent.

## The First House: Self

The sign passing over the first house at the time of your birth is known as your ascendant, or rising sign. The first house is the house of "firsts"—the first impression you make, how you initiate matters, the image you choose to project. This is where you advertise yourself, where you project your personality. Planets that fall here will intensify the way you come across to others. It is the home of Aries and the planet Mars.

## The Second House: The Material You

This house is where you experience the material world, what you value. Here are your attitudes about money, possessions, and finances, as well as your earning and spending capacity. On a deeper level, this house reveals your sense of self-worth, the inner values that draw wealth in various forms. It is the natural home of Taurus and the planet Venus.

## The Third House: Your Thinking Process

This house describes how you communicate with others, how you reach out to others nearby and interact with the immediate environment. It shows how your thinking process works and the way you express your thoughts. Are you articulate or tongue-tied? Can you think on your feet? This house also shows your first relationships, your experiences with brothers and sisters, as well as how you deal with people close to you, such as your neighbors or pals. It's where you take short trips, write letters, or use the telephone. It shows how your mind works in terms of left-brain logical and analytical functions. It is the home of Gemini and the planet Mercury.

## The Fourth House: Your Home Life

The fourth house shows the foundation of life, the psychological underpinnings. Located at the bottom of the chart, this house shows how you are nurtured and made to feel secure—your roots! It shows your early home environment and the circumstances at the end of your life (your final "home"), as well as the place you call home now. Astrologers look here for information about the parental nurturers in your life. It is the home of Cancer and the moon.

## The Fifth House: Your Self-Expression

The Leo house is where the creative potential develops. Here you express yourself and procreate, in the sense that children are outgrowths of your creative ability. But this house most represents your inner childlike self, who delights in play. If your inner security has been established by the time you reach this house, you are now free to have fun, romance, and love affairs and to give of yourself. This is also the place astrologers look for playful love affairs, flirtations, and brief romantic encounters (rather than long-term commitments). It is the home of Leo and the sun.

## The Sixth House: Care and Maintenance

The sixth house has been called the "care and maintenance" department. This house shows how you take care of your body and organize yourself to perform efficiently in the world. Here is where you get things done, where you look after others and fulfill service duties, such as taking care of pets. Here is what you do to survive on a day-to-day basis. The sixth house demands order in your life; otherwise there would be chaos. The house is your "job" (as opposed to your career, which is the domain of the tenth house), your diet, and your health and fitness regimens. It is the home of Virgo and the planet Mercury.

## The Seventh House: Your Relationships

This house shows your attitude toward your partners and those with whom you enter commitments, contracts, or agreements. Here is the way your relate to others, as well as your close, intimate, one-on-one relationships (including open enemies—those you "face off" with). Open hostilities, lawsuits, divorces, and marriages happen here. If the first house represents the "I," the seventh or opposite house is the "not I"—the complementary partner you attract by the way you come across. If you are having trouble with partnerships, consider what you are attracting by the energies of your first and seventh house. It is the home of Libra and the planet Venus.

## The Eighth House: Your Power House

The eighth house refers to how you merge with something or someone, and how you handle power and control. This is one of the most mysterious and powerful houses, where your energy transforms itself from "I" to "we." As you give up power and control by uniting with something or someone, two kinds of energies merge and become something greater, leading to a regeneration of the self on a higher level. Here are your attitudes toward sex, shared resources, and taxes (what you share with the government). Because this house involves what belongs to others, you face issues of control and power struggles, or undergo a deep psychological transformation as you bond with another. Here you transcend yourself through dreams, drugs, and occult or psychic experiences that reflect the collective unconscious. It is the home of Scorpio and the planet Pluto.

17

# The Ninth House: Your Worldview

The ninth house shows your search for wisdom and higher knowledge: your belief system. As the third house represents the "lower mind," its opposite on the wheel, the ninth house, is the "higher mind," the abstract, intuitive, spiritual mind that asks "big" questions, like "Why we are here?" After the third house has explored what was close at hand, the ninth stretches out to broaden you mentally with higher education and travel. Here you stretch spiritually with religious activity. Since you are concerned with how everything is related, you tend to push boundaries and take risks. Here is where you express your ideas in a book or thesis, where you pontificate, philosophize, or preach. It is the home of Sagittarius and the planet Jupiter.

# The Tenth House: Your Public Life

The tenth house is associated with your public life and high-profile activities. Located directly overhead at the "high noon" position on the horoscope wheel, this is the most "visible" house in the chart, the one where the world sees you. It deals with your career (but not your routine "job") and your reputation. Here is where you go public, take on responsibilities (as opposed to the fourth house, where you stay home). This will affect the career you choose and your "public relations." This house is also associated with your father figure or the main authority figure in your life. It is the home of Capricorn and the planet Saturn.

# The Eleventh House: Your Social Concerns

The eleventh house is where you extend yourself to a group, a goal, or a belief system. This house is where you define what you really want: the kinds of friends you have, your political affiliations, and the kind of groups you identify with as an equal. Here is where you become concerned with "what other people think" or where you rebel against social conventions. It's where you become a socially conscious humanitarian or a partying social butterfly. It's where you look to others to stimulate you and discover your kinship to the rest of humanity. The sign on this house can help you understand what you gain and lose from friendships. It is the home of Aquarius and the planet Uranus.

# The Twelfth House: Where You Become Selfless

Old-fashioned astrologers used to put a rather negative spin on this house, calling it the "house of self-undoing." When we "undo ourselves," we surrender control, boundaries, limits, and rules. The twelfth house is where the boundaries between yourself and others become blurred and you become selfless. But instead of being self-undoing, the twelfth house can be a place of great creativity and talent. It is the place where you can tap into the collective unconscious, where your imagination is limitless.

In your trip around the zodiac, you've gone from the "I" of self-assertion in the first house to the final house, which symbolizes the dissolution that happens before rebirth. The twelfth house is where accumulated experiences are processed in the unconscious. Spiritually oriented astrologers look to this house for evidence of past lives and karma. Places where we go for solitude or to do spiritual or reparatory work belong here, such as retreats, religious institutions, or hospitals. Here is also where we withdraw from society voluntarily or involuntarily, and where we are put in prison because of antisocial activity. Selfless giving through charitable acts is part of this house, as is helpless receiving or dependence on charity.

In your daily life, the twelfth house reveals your deepest intimacies, your best-kept secrets, especially those you hide from yourself and repress deep in the unconscious. It is where we surrender a sense of a separate self to a deep feeling of wholeness, such as selfless service in religion or any activity that involves merging with the greater whole. Many sports stars have important planets in the twelfth house, which enable them to play in the zone, finding an inner, almost mystical, strength that transcends their limits. The twelfth house is the home of Pisces and the planet Neptune.

# Which Are the Most Powerful Houses?

Houses are stronger or weaker depending on how many planets are inhabiting them. If there are many planets in a given house, it follows that the activities of that house will be especially important in your life. If the planet that rules the house is also located there, this too adds power to the house. The most powerful houses are the first, fourth, seventh, and tenth. These are the houses on "the angles" of a horoscope.

# CHAPTER 3

# Access All Your Planets

Did you know that astrology offers you not one but ten opportunities to get to know yourself (and others) better? Of course, you know your sun sign, which gives you some very useful generic information. But there are nine other members of your planetary team, each of which has a specific role to play in your total astrological personality. It's the way all these planets express themselves through their sign and their relationship to one another that makes your horoscope unique. The complete horoscope chart then lights up with colorations from many different signs and planets.

If you know all the planets (including the sun and moon), you'll be more capable of predicting how the subject of the chart will act in a given situation. If you want to know what turns someone on, consult his Venus. How about mastering a fear? Look up Saturn. Does someone anger easily? Check their Mars.

The planets are the doers of the horoscope, each representing a basic force in life. The sign and house where the planet is located indicate how and where its force will operate. For a moment, think of the horoscope as real estate. Prime property is close to the rising sign or at the top of the chart. If two or more planets are grouped together in one sign, they usually operate like a team, playing off each other, rather than expressing their energy singularly. But a loner, a planet that stands far away from the others, is usually outstanding and often calls the shots.

The sign of a planet also has a powerful influence. In some signs, the planet's energies are very much at home and can easily express themselves. In others, the planet has to work harder and is slightly out of sorts. The sign that most corresponds to the planet's energies is said to be ruled by that planet and obviously is the best place for that planet to be. The next best place is a sign where it is exalted, or especially harmonious. On the other hand, there are places in the horoscope where a planet has to stretch itself to play its role, such as the sign opposite a planet's rulership, which embodies the opposite area of life, and the sign opposite its exaltation. However, a planet that must work harder can also be more complete, because it must grow to meet the challenges of living in a more difficult sign. Like world leaders who've had to struggle for greatness, this planet may actually develop strength and character.

Here's a list of the best places for each planet to be. Note that, as new planets were discovered in this century, they replaced the traditional rulers of signs which best complemented their energies.

ARIES—Mars
TAURUS—Venus, in its most sensual form
GEMINI—Mercury, in its communicative role
CANCER—the moon
LEO—the sun
VIRGO—also Mercury, this time in its more critical capacity
LIBRA—also Venus, in its more aesthetic, judgmental form
SCORPIO—Pluto, co-ruled by Mars
SAGITTARIUS—Jupiter
CAPRICORN—Saturn
AQUARIUS—Uranus, replacing Saturn, its original ruler
PISCES—Neptune, replacing Jupiter, its original ruler

Those who have many planets in exalted signs are lucky indeed, for here is where the planet can accomplish the most and be its most influential and creative.

SUN—exalted in Aries, where its energy creates action
MOON—exalted in Taurus, where instincts and reactions operate on a highly creative level
MERCURY—exalted in Aquarius, where it can reach analytical heights

22

VENUS—exalted in Pisces, a sign whose sensitivity encourages love and creativity

MARS—exalted in Capricorn, a sign that puts energy to work productively

JUPITER—exalted in Cancer, where it encourages nurturing and growth

SATURN—at home in Libra, where it steadies the scales of justice and promotes balanced, responsible judgment

URANUS—powerful in Scorpio, where it promotes transformation

NEPTUNE—especially favored in Cancer, where it gains the security to transcend to a higher state

PLUTO—exalted in Pisces, where it dissolves the old cycle, to make way for transition to the new

# The Personal Planets: Mercury, Venus, and Mars

These planets work in your immediate personal life.

Mercury affects how you communicate and how your mental processes work. Are you a quick study who grasps information rapidly, or do you learn more slowly and thoroughly? How is your concentration? Can you express yourself easily? Are you a good writer? All these questions can be answered by your Mercury placement.

Venus shows what you react to. What turns you on? What appeals to you aesthetically? Are you charming to others? Are you attractive to look at? Your taste, your refinement, your sense of balance and proportion are all Venus-ruled.

Mars is your outgoing energy, your drive and ambition. Do you reach out for new adventures? Are you assertive? Are you motivated? Self-confident? Hot-tempered? How you channel your energy and drive is revealed by your Mars placement.

# Mercury Shows How Your Mind Works

Since Mercury never travels far from the sun, read Mercury in your sun sign, and then the signs preceding and following it. Then decide which reflects the way you think.

## Mercury in Aries

Your mind is very active and assertive. It approaches a plan aggressively. You never hesitate to say what you think, never shy away from a battle. In fact, you may relish a verbal confrontation. Tact is not your strong point, so you may have to learn not to trip over your tongue.

## Mercury in Taurus

This is a much more cautious Mercury. Though you may be a slow learner, you have good concentration and mental stamina. You want to make your ideas really happen. You'll attack a problem methodically and consider every angle thoroughly, never jumping to conclusions. You'll stick with a subject until you master it.

## Mercury in Gemini

You are a wonderful communicator with great facility for expressing yourself both verbally and in writing. You love gathering all kinds of information. You probably finish other people's sentences and express yourself with eloquent hand gestures. You can talk to anybody anytime and probably have phone and E-mail bills to prove it. You read anything from sci-fi to Shakespeare and might need an extra room just for your book collection. Though you learn fast, you may lack focus and discipline. Watch a tendency to jump from subject to subject.

## Mercury in Cancer

You rely on intuition more than logic. Your mental processes are usually colored by your emotions, so you may seem shy or hesitant to voice your opinions. However, this placement gives you the advantage of great imagination and empathy in the way you communicate with others.

## Mercury in Leo

You are enthusiastic and very dramatic in the way you express yourself. You like to hold the attention of groups and could be a great public speaker. Your mind thinks big, so you'd prefer to deal with the overall picture rather than with the details.

## Mercury in Virgo

This is one of the best places for Mercury. It should give you critical ability, attention to details, and thorough analysis. Your mind focuses on the practical side of things. This type of thinking is very well suited to being a teacher or editor.

## Mercury in Libra

You're either a born diplomat who smoothes over ruffled feathers or a talented debater. Many lawyers have this placement. However, since you're forever weighing the pros and cons of a situation, you may vacillate when making decisions.

## Mercury in Scorpio

This is an investigative mind that stops at nothing to get the answers. You may have a sarcastic, stinging wit, a gift for the cutting remark. There's always a grain of truth to your verbal sallies, thanks to your penetrating insight.

# Mercury in Sagittarius

You are a super salesman with a tendency to expound. Though you are very broad-minded, you can be dogmatic when it comes to telling others what's good for them. You won't hesitate to tell the truth as you see it, so watch a tendency toward tactlessness. On the plus side, you have a great sense of humor. This position of Mercury is often considered by astrologers to be at a disadvantage because Sagittarius opposes Gemini, the sign Mercury rules, and squares off with Virgo, another Mercury-ruled sign. What often happens is that Mercury in Sagittarius oversteps its bounds and loses sight of the facts in a situation. Do a reality check before making promises that you may not be able to deliver.

# Mercury in Capricorn

This placement endows good mental discipline. You have a love of learning and a very orderly approach to your subjects. You will patiently plod through the facts and figures until you have mastered the tasks. You grasp structured situations easily, but may be short on creativity.

# Mercury in Aquarius

An independent, original thinker, you'll have more cutting-edge ideas than the average person. You'll be quick to check out any unusual opportunities. Your opinions are so well-researched and grounded that once your mind is made up, it is difficult to change.

# Mercury in Pisces

You have the psychic intuitive mind of a natural poet. Learn to make use of your creative imagination. You may think in terms of helping others, but check a tendency to be vague and forgetful of details.

# Venus Is the Popularity Planet

Venus tells how you relate to others and to your environment. It shows where you receive pleasure and what you love to do. Find your Venus placement on the chart in this book by looking for the year of your birth in the left-hand column. Then follow the line of that year across the page until you reach the time period of your birthday. The sign heading that column will be your Venus. If you were born on a day when Venus was changing signs, check the signs preceding or following that day to determine if that feels more like your Venus nature.

## Venus in Aries

You can't stand to be bored, confined, or ordered around. But a good challenge, maybe even a rousing row, turns you on. Confess—don't you pick a fight now and then just to get someone stirred up? You're attracted by the chase, not the catch, which could cause some problems in your love life, if the object of your affection becomes too attainable. You like to wear red and can spot a trend before anyone else.

## Venus in Taurus

All your senses work in high gear. You love to be surrounded by glorious tastes, smells, textures, sounds, and visuals—austerity is not for you. Neither is being rushed. You like time to enjoy your pleasures. Soothing surroundings with plenty of creature comforts are your cup of tea. You like to feel secure in your nest, with no sudden jolts or surprises. You like familiar objects—in fact, you may hate to let anything or anyone go.

## Venus in Gemini

You are a lively, sparkling personality who thrives in a situation that affords a constant variety and a frequent change of scenery. A varied social life is important to you,

27

with plenty of mental stimulation and a chance to engage in some light flirtation. Commitment may be difficult, because playing the field is so much fun.

## Venus in Cancer

An atmosphere where you feel protected, coddled, and mothered is best for you. You love to be surrounded by children in a cozy, homelike situation. You are attracted to those who are tender and nurturing, who make you feel secure and well provided for. You may be quite secretive about your emotional life or attracted to clandestine relationships.

## Venus in Leo

First-class attention in large doses turns you on, and so does the glitter of real gold and the flash of mirrors. You like to feel like a star at all times, surrounded by your admiring audience. The side effect is that you may be attracted to flatterers and tinsel, while the real gold requires some digging.

## Venus in Virgo

Everything neatly in its place? On the surface, you are attracted to an atmosphere where everything is in perfect order, but underneath are some basic, earthy urges. You are attracted to those who appeal to your need to teach, be of service, or play out a Pygmalion fantasy. You are at your best when you are busy doing something useful.

## Venus in Libra

Elegance and harmony are your key words. You can't abide an atmosphere of contention. Your taste tends toward the classic, with light harmonies of color—nothing clashing, trendy, or outrageous. You love doing things with a partner and should be careful to pick one who is decisive, but patient enough to let you weigh the pros and cons. And steer clear of argumentative types.

## Venus in Scorpio

Mysteries intrigue you—in fact, anything that is too open and aboveboard is a bit of a bore. You surely have a stack of whodunits by the bed, along with an erotic magazine or two. You like to solve puzzles. You may also be fascinated with the occult, crime, or scientific research. Intense, all-or-nothing situations add spice to your life, and you love to ferret out the secrets of others. But you could get burned by your flair for living dangerously. The color black, spicy food, dark wood furniture, and heady perfume put you in the right mood.

## Venus in Sagittarius

If you are not actually a world traveler, your surroundings are sure to reflect your love of faraway places. You like a casual outdoor atmosphere and a dog or two to pet. There should be plenty of room for athletic equipment and suitcases. You're attracted to kindred souls who love to travel and who share your freedom-loving philosophy of life. Athletics and spiritual or New Age pursuits could be other interests.

## Venus in Capricorn

No fly-by-night relationships for you! You want substance in life, and you are attracted to whatever will help you get where you are going. Status objects turn you on. And so do those who have a serious responsible, businesslike approach, or who remind you of a beloved parent. It is characteristic of this placement to be attracted to someone of a different generation. Antiques, traditional clothing, and dignified behavior are becoming to you.

## Venus in Aquarius

This Venus wants to make friends, to be "cool." You like to be in a group, particularly one pushing a worthy cause. You feel quite at home surrounded by people, and could even court fame, yet all the while, you tend to remain detached from intense commitment. Original ideas and unpredictable people fascinate you. You prefer spontaneity and delightful surprises, rather than a well-planned schedule of events.

## Venus in Pisces

This Venus loves to give of yourself, and you find plenty of takers. Stray animals and people appeal to your heart and your pocketbook, but be careful to look at their motives realistically once in a while. You are extremely vulnerable to sob stories of all kinds. Fantasy, the arts (especially film, dance, and theater), and psychic or spiritual activities also speak to you.

# Mars: The Action Hero

Mars is the mover and shaker in your life. It shows how you pursue your goals, whether you have energy to burn or proceed in a slow, steady pace. It will also show how you get angry. Do you explode, or do a slow burn, or hold everything inside and then get revenge later?

To find your Mars, turn to the chart on pages 64–73. Then find your birth year in the left-hand column and trace the line across horizontally until you come to the column headed by the month of your birth. There you will find an abbreviation of your Mars sign. If the description of your Mars sign doesn't ring true, read the description of the signs preceding and following it. You might have been born on a day when Mars was changing signs, in which case your Mars might fall into the adjacent sign.

# Mars in Aries

In the sign it rules, Mars shows its brilliant fiery nature. You have an explosive temper and can be quite impatient. On the other hand, you have tremendous courage, energy, and drive. You'll let nothing stand in your way as you race to be first! Obstacles are met head-on and broken through by force. However, problems that require patience and persistence to solve can have you exploding in rage. You're a great starter, but not necessarily around for the finish.

# Mars in Taurus

Slow, steady, concentrated energy gives you the power to last until the finish line. You've great stamina, and you never give up. Your tactic is to wear away obstacles with your persistence. Often you come out a winner because you've had the patience to hang in there. When angered, you do a slow burn.

# Mars in Gemini

You can't sit still for long. This Mars craves variety. You often have two or more things going on at once—it's all an amusing game to you. Your life can get very complicated, but that only adds spice and stimulation. What drives you into a nervous, hyper state? Boredom, sameness, routine, and confinement. You can do wonderful things with your hands, and you have a way with words.

# Mars in Cancer

You rarely attack head-on. Instead, you'll keep things to yourself, make plans in secret, and always cover your actions. This might be interpreted by some as manipulative, but you are only being self-protective. You get furious when anyone knows too much about you. But you do like to know all about others. Your mothering and feeding instincts can be put to good use, if you work in the food, hotel, or child-care related businesses. You may have to overcome your fragile sense of security, which prompts you not to take risks and to get physically upset when criticized. Don't take things so personally!

## Mars in Leo

You have a very dominant personality that takes center stage—modesty is not one of your traits, nor is taking a back seat. You prefer giving the orders and have been known to make a dramatic scene if they are not obeyed. Properly used, this Mars confers leadership ability, endurance, and courage.

## Mars in Virgo

You are the faultfinder of the zodiac, who notices every detail. Mistakes of any kind make you very nervous. You may worry, even if everything is going smoothly. You may not express your anger directly, but you sure can nag. You have definite likes and dislikes, and you are sure you can do the job better than anyone else. You are certainly more industrious and detail-oriented than other signs. Your Mars energy is often most positively expressed in some kind of teaching role.

## Mars in Libra

This Mars will have a passion for beauty, justice, and art. Generally, you will avoid confrontations at all costs. You prefer to spend your energy finding diplomatic solutions or weighing pros and cons. Your other techniques are passive aggression or exercising your well-known charm to get people to do what you want.

## Mars in Scorpio

This is a powerful placement, so intense that it demands careful channeling into worthwhile activities. Otherwise, you could become obsessed with your sexuality or might use your need for power and control to manipulate others. You are strong-willed, shrewd, and very private about your affairs, and you'll usually have a secret agenda behind your actions. Your great stamina, focus, and discipline would be excellent assets for careers in the military or medical fields, especially research or surgery. When angry, you don't get mad—you get even!

## Mars in Sagittarius

This expansive Mars often propels people into sales, travel, athletics or philosophy. Your energies function well when you are on the move. You have a hot temper and are inclined to say what you think before you consider the consequences. You shoot for high goals—and talk endlessly about them—but you may be weak on groundwork. This Mars needs a solid foundation. Watch a tendency to take unnecessary risks.

## Mars in Capricorn

This is an ambitious Mars with an excellent sense of timing. You have an eye for those who can be of use to you, and you may dismiss people ruthlessly when you're angry. But you drive yourself hard and deliver full value. This is a good placement for an executive. You'll aim for status and a high material position in life, and keep climbing despite the odds. A great Mars to have!

## Mars in Aquarius

This is the most rebellious Mars. You seem to have a drive to assert yourself against the status quo. You may enjoy provoking people, shocking them out of traditional views. Or this placement could express itself in an offbeat sex life. Somehow you often find yourself in unconventional situations. You enjoy being a leader of an active group, which pursues forward-looking studies, politics, or goals.

## Mars in Pisces

This Mars is a good actor who knows just how to appeal to the sympathies of others. You create and project wonderful fantasies or use your sensitive antennae to crusade for those less fortunate. You get what you want through creating a veil of illusion and glamour. This is a good Mars for someone in the creative and imaginative fields—a dancer, a performer, a photographer, or an actor. Many famous film stars have this placement. Watch a tendency to manipulate by making others feel sorry for you.

# Jupiter Is the Optimist

This big, bright, swirling mass of gases is associated with abundance, prosperity, and the kind of windfall you get without too much hard work. You're optimistic under Jupiter's influence, when anything seems possible. You'll travel, expand your mind with higher education, and publish to share your knowledge widely. On the other hand, Jupiter's influence is neither discriminating nor disciplined. It represents the principle of growth without judgment. Therefore, if not kept in check, it could result in extravagance, weight gain, laziness, and carelessness.

Be sure to look up your Jupiter in the tables in this book. When the current position of Jupiter is favorable, you may get that lucky break. This is a great time to try new things, take risks, travel, or get more education. Opportunities seem to open up easily, so take advantage of them.

Once a year, Jupiter changes signs. That means you are due for an expansive time every twelve years, when Jupiter travels through your sun sign. You'll also have periods every four years when Jupiter is in the same element as your sun sign.

## Jupiter in Aries

You are the soul of enthusiasm and optimism. Your luckiest times are when you are getting started on an exciting project or selling an ideal that you really believe in. You may have to watch a tendency to be arrogant with those who do not share your enthusiasm. You follow your impulses, often ignoring budget or other commonsense limitations. To produce real, solid benefits, you'll need patience and the will to follow though wherever this Jupiter falls in your horoscope.

## Jupiter in Taurus

You'll spend money on beautiful material things, especially those that come from nature—items made of rare woods, natural fabrics, or precious gems, for instance. You can't have too much comfort or too many sensual pleasures. Watch a tendency to overindulge in good food, or to over-pamper yourself with nothing but the best. Spartan living is not for you! You may be especially lucky in matters of real estate.

## Jupiter in Gemini

You are the great talker of the zodiac, and you may be a great writer too. But restlessness could be your weak point. You jump around and talk too much; you could be a jack-of-all-trades. Keeping a secret is especially difficult, so you'll also have to watch a tendency to spill the beans. Since you love to be at the center of a beehive of activity, you'll have a vibrant social life. Your best opportunities will come through your talent for language; speaking, writing, communicating, and selling.

## Jupiter in Cancer

You are luckiest in situations where you can find emotional closeness or deal with basic security needs, such as food, nurturing, or shelter. You may be a great collector, and you may simply love to accumulate things—you are the one who stashes things away for a rainy day. You probably have a very good memory and love children—in fact, you may have many children to care for. The food, hotel, child-care, and shipping businesses hold good opportunities for you.

## Jupiter in Leo

You are a natural showman who loves to live in a larger-than-life way. Yours is a personality full of color that always finds its way into the limelight. You can't have too much attention. Showbiz is a natural place for you, and so is any area where you can play to a crowd. Exercising your flair for drama, your natural playfulness, and your romantic nature brings you good fortune. But watch a tendency to be overextravagant or to monopolize center stage.

## Jupiter in Virgo

You actually love those minute details others find boring. To you, they make all the difference between the perfect and the ordinary. You are the fine craftsman who spots every flaw. You expand your awareness by finding the most efficient methods and by being of service to others. Many will be drawn to medical or teaching fields. You'll also have luck in publishing, crafts, nutrition, and service professions. Watch out for a tendency to overwork.

## Jupiter in Libra

This is an other-directed Jupiter that develops best with a partner, for the stimulation of others helps you grow. You are also most comfortable in harmonious, beautiful situations, and you work well with artistic people. You have a great sense of fair play and an ability to evaluate the pros and cons of a situation. You usually prefer to play the role of diplomat rather than that of adversary.

## Jupiter in Scorpio

You love the feeling of power and control, of taking things to their limit. You can't resist a mystery, and your shrewd, penetrating mind sees right through to the heart of most situations and people. You have luck in work that provides for solutions to matters of life and death. You may be drawn to undercover work, behind-the-scenes intrigue, psychotherapy, the occult, and sex-related ventures. Your challenge will be to develop a sense of moderation and tolerance for other beliefs. You may have luck in handling other people's money—insurance, taxes, and inheritance can bring you a windfall.

# Jupiter in Sagittarius

Independent, outgoing, and idealistic, you'll shoot for the stars. This Jupiter compels you to travel far and wide, both physically and mentally, via higher education. You may have luck while traveling in an exotic place. You also have luck with outdoor ventures, exercise, and animals, particularly horses. Since you tend to be very open about your opinions, watch a tendency to be tactless and to exaggerate. Instead, use your wonderful sense of humor to make your point.

# Jupiter in Capricorn

Jupiter is much more restrained in Capricorn, the sign of rules and authority. Here, Jupiter can make you overwork and heighten any ambition or sense of duty you may have. You'll expand in areas that advance your position, putting you higher up the social or corporate ladder. You are lucky working within the establishment in a very structured situation, where you can show off your ability to organize and reap rewards for your hard work.

# Jupiter in Aquarius

This is another freedom-loving Jupiter, with great tolerance and originality. You are at your best when you are working for a humanitarian cause and in the company of many supporters. This is a good Jupiter for a political career. You'll relate to all kinds of people on all social levels. You have an abundance of original ideas, but you are best off away from routine and any situation that imposes rigid rules. You need mental stimulation!

# Jupiter in Pisces

You are a giver whose feelings and pocketbook are easily touched by others, so choose your companions with care. You could be the original sucker for a hard-luck story. Better find a worthy hospital or charity to appreciate your selfless support. You have a great creative imagination and may attract good fortune in fields related to oil, perfume, pharmaceuticals, petroleum, dance, footwear, and alcohol. But beware not to overindulge in alcohol—focus on a creative outlet instead.

# Saturn Puts on the Brakes

Jupiter speeds you up with lucky breaks, and then along comes Saturn to slow you down with the disciplinary brakes. It is the planet that can help you achieve lasting goals. Saturn has unfairly been called a malefic planet, one of the bad guys of the zodiac. On the contrary, Saturn is one of our best friends—the kind who tells you what you need to hear, even if it's not good news. Under a Saturn transit, we grow up, take responsibility for our lives, and emerge from whatever test this planet has in store as far wiser, more capable, and mature human beings. After all, it is when we are under pressure that we grow stronger.

When Saturn hits a critical point in your horoscope, you can count on an experience that will make you slow up, pull back, and reexamine your life. It is a call to eliminate what is not working and to shape up. By the end of its twenty-eight-year trip around the zodiac, Saturn will have tested you in all areas of your life. The major tests happen in seven-year cycles, when Saturn passes over the angles of your chart—your rising sign, the top of your chart or midheaven, your descendant, and the nadir or bottom of your chart. This is when the real life-changing experiences happen. But you are also in for a testing period whenever Saturn passes a planet in your chart or stresses that planet from a distance. Therefore, it is useful to check your planetary positions with the timetable of Saturn to prepare in advance, or at least to brace yourself.

When Saturn returns to its location at the time of your birth, at approximately age twenty-eight, you'll have your first Saturn return. At this time, a person usually takes stock or settles down to find his mission in life and assumes full adult duties and responsibilities.

Another way Saturn helps us is to reveal the karmic lessons from previous lives and give us the chance to overcome them. So look at Saturn's challenges as much-needed opportunities for self-improvement. Under a Jupiter influence, you'll have more fun, but Saturn gives you solid, long-lasting results.

Look up your natal Saturn in the tables in this book for clues on where you need work.

## Saturn in Aries

Saturn here puts the brakes on Aries's natural drive and enthusiasm. There is often an angry side to this placement. You don't let anyone push you around and you know what's best for yourself. Following orders is not your strong point, nor is diplomacy. You tend to be quick to go on the offensive in relationships, attacking first, before anyone attacks you. Because no one quite lives up to your standards, you often wind up doing everything yourself. You'll have to learn to cooperate and tone down any self-centeredness. Pat Buchanan has this Saturn.

## Saturn in Taurus

A big issue is getting control of the cash flow. There will be lean periods that can be frightening, but you have the patience and endurance to stick them out and the methodical drive to prosper in the end. Learn to take a philosophical attitude like Ben Franklin, who also had this placement, and who said, "A penny saved is a penny earned."

## Saturn in Gemini

You are a serious student of life, who may have difficulty communicating or sharing your knowledge. You may be shy, speak slowly, or have fears about communicating, like Eleanor Roosevelt. You dwell in the realms of science, theory, or abstract analysis, even when you are dealing with the emotions, like Sigmund Freud, who also had this placement.

## Saturn in Cancer

Your tests come with establishing a secure emotional base. In doing so, you may have to deal with some very basic fears centering on your early home environment. Most of your Saturn tests will have emotional roots in those early-childhood experiences. You may have difficulty remaining objective in terms of what you try to achieve, so it will be especially important for you to deal with negative feelings such as guilt, paranoia, jealousy, resentment, and suspicion. Galileo and Michelangelo also navigated these murky waters.

## Saturn in Leo

This is an authoritarian Saturn—a strict, demanding parent who may deny the pleasure principle in your zeal to see that rules are followed. Though you may feel guilty about taking the spotlight, you are very ambitious and loyal. You have to watch a tendency toward rigidity, also toward overwork and holding back affection. Joseph Kennedy and Billy Graham share this placement.

## Saturn in Virgo

This is a cautious, exacting Saturn, intensely hard on yourself. Most of all, you give yourself the roughest time with your constant worries about every little detail, often making yourself sick. You may have difficulties setting priorities and getting the job done. Your tests will come in learning tolerance and understanding of others. Charles de Gaulle, Mae West, and Nathaniel Hawthorne had this meticulous Saturn.

## Saturn in Libra

Saturn is exalted here, which makes this planet an ally. You may choose very serious, older partners in life, perhaps stemming from a fear of dependency. You need to learn to stand solidly on your own before you commit to another. Since you are extremely cautious, you deliberate every involvement—with good reason. It is best that you find an occupation that makes good use of your sense of duty and honor. Steer clear of fly-by-night situations. Both Khrushchev and Mao Tse-tung had this placement.

## Saturn in Scorpio

You have great staying power. This Saturn tests you in situations involving the control of others. You may feel drawn to some kind of intrigue or undercover work, like J. Edgar Hoover. Or there may be an air of mystery surrounding your life and death, like Marilyn Monroe and Robert Kennedy, who both had this placement. There are lessons to be learned from your sexual involvements. Often sex is used for manipulation or is somehow out of the ordinary. The Roman emperor Caligula and the transsexual Christine Jorgensen are extreme cases.

## Saturn in Sagittarius

Your challenges and lessons will come from tests of your spiritual and philosophical values, as happened to Martin Luther King Jr. and Gandhi. You are high-minded and sincere with this reflective, moral placement. Uncompromising in your ethical standards, you could become a benevolent despot.

## Saturn in Capricorn

With the help of Saturn at maximum strength, your judgment will improve with age. And, like Spencer Tracy's screen image, you'll be the gray-haired hero with a strong sense of responsibility. You advance in life slowly but steadily, always with a strong hand at the helm and an eye for the advantageous situation. Like Pat Robertson, you're likely to stand for conservative values. Negatively, you may be a loner, prone to periods of melancholy.

## Saturn in Aquarius

Your tests come from relationships with groups. Do you care too much about what others think? Do you feel like an outsider, like Greta Garbo? You may fear being different from others and therefore slight your own unique, forward-looking gifts. Or like Lord Byron and Howard Hughes, you may take the opposite tack and rebel in the extreme. You can apply discipline to accomplish great humanitarian goals, as Albert Schweitzer did.

## Saturn in Pisces

Your fear of the unknown and the irrational may lead you to the safety and protection of an institution. You may go on the run like Jesse James to avoid looking too deeply inside. Or you might go in the opposite, more positive direction and develop a disciplined psychoanalytic approach, which puts you more in control of your feelings. Some of you will take refuge in work with hospitals, charities, or religious institutions. Queen Victoria, who had this placement, symbolized an era when institutions of all kinds were sustained. Discipline applied to artistic work, especially poetry and dance, or spiritual work, such as yoga or meditation, might be helpful.

# How Uranus, Neptune, and Pluto Influence Your Generation

These three planets remain in signs such a long time that a whole generation bears the imprint of the sign. Mass movements, great sweeping changes, fads that characterize a generation, and even the issues of the conflicts and wars of the time are influenced by these outer three planets. When one of these distant planets changes signs, there is a definite shift in the atmosphere, the feeling of the end of an era.

Since these planets are so far away from the sun—too distant to be seen by the naked eye—they pick up signals from the universe at large. These planetary receivers literally link the sun with distant energies, and then perform a similar function in your horoscope by linking your central character with intuitive, spiritual, transformative forces from the cosmos. Each planet has a special domain and will reflect this in the area of your chart where it falls.

# Uranus Is the Surprise Ingredient

Uranus is the surprise ingredient that sets you and your generation apart. There is nothing ordinary about this quirky green planet that seems to be traveling on its side, surrounded by a swarm of moons. Is it any wonder that astrologers assigned it to Aquarius, the most eccentric and gregarious sign? Uranus seems to wend its way around the sun, marching to its own tune.

Significantly, Uranus follows Saturn, the planet of limitations and structures. Often we get caught up in the structures we have created to give ourselves a sense of security. However, if we lose contact with our spiritual roots in the process, Uranus is likely to jolt us out of our comfortable rut and wake us up.

Uranus energy is electrical, happening in sudden flashes. It is not influenced by karma or past events, nor does it regard tradition, sex, or sentiment. Uranus's key words are surprise and awakening. Suddenly, there's that flash of inspiration, that bright idea, or that totally new approach that revolutionizes whatever scheme you were undertaking. A Uranus event takes you by surprise, for better or for worse. The Uranus place in your life is where you awaken and become your own person, leaving the structures of Saturn behind. And it is probably the most unconventional place in your chart.

Look up the sign of Uranus at the time of your birth and see where you follow your own tune.

## Uranus in Aries

Birth Dates:
  March 31, 1927–November 4, 1927
  January 13, 1928–June 6, 1934

October 10, 1934–March 28, 1935

Your generation is original, creative, and pioneering. It developed the computer, the airplane, and the cyclotron. You let nothing hold you back from exploring the unknown, and you have a powerful mixture of fire and electricity behind you. Women of your generation were among the first to be liberated. You were the unforgettable style setters. You have a surprise in store for everyone. As with Yoko Ono, Grace Kelly, and Jacqueline Onassis, your life may be jolted by sudden and violent changes.

## Uranus in Taurus

Birth dates:
    June 6, 1934–October 10, 1934
    March 28, 1935–August 7, 1941
    October 5, 1941–May 15, 1942

The great territorial shakeups of World War II began during your generation. You're independent; you're probably self-employed or you would like to be. You have original ideas about making money, and you brace yourself for sudden changes of fortune. This Uranus can cause shakeups, particularly in finances, but it can also make you a born entrepreneur, like Martha Stewart.

## Uranus in Gemini

Birth dates:
    August 7, 1941–October 5, 1941
    May 15, 1942–August 30, 1948
    November 12, 1948–June 10, 1949

You were the first children to be influenced by television, and in your adult years, your generation stocks up on answering machines, cell phones, computers, and fax machines—any new way you can communicate. You have an inquiring mind, but your interests may be rather short-lived. This Uranus can be easily fragmented if there is no structure and focus.

# Uranus in Cancer

Birth date:
    August 30–November 12, 1948
    June 10, 1949–August 24, 1955
    January 28, 1956–June 10, 1956

This generation came at a time when divorce was becoming commonplace, so your home image is unconventional. You may have an unusual relationship with your parents, or come from a broken home or an unconventional one. You'll have unorthodox ideas about parenting, intimacy, food, and shelter. You may also be interested in dreams, psychic phenomena, and memory work.

# Uranus in Leo

Birth date:
    August 24, 1955–January 28, 1956
    June 10, 1956–November 1, 1961
    January 10, 1962–August 10, 1962

This generation understood how to use electronic media. Many of your group are now leaders in the high-tech industries, and you also understand how to use the new media to promote yourself. Like Isadora Duncan, you may have a very eccentric kind of charisma and a life that is sparked by unusual love affairs. Your children may have traits that are out of the ordinary. Where this planet falls in your chart, you'll have a love of freedom, be a bit of an egomaniac, and show the full force of your personality in a unique way, like tennis great Martina Navratilova.

# Uranus in Virgo

Birth dates:
    November 1, 1961–January 10, 1962
    August 10, 1962–September 28, 1968
    May 20, 1969–June 24, 1969 .

You'll have highly individual work methods, and many will be finding newer, more practical ways to use computers. Like Einstein, who had this placement, you'll break the rules brilliantly. Your generation came at a time of student rebellions, the civil rights movement, and the general acceptance of health foods. Chances are, you're concerned about pollution and cleaning up the environment. You may also be involved with nontraditional healing methods.

## Uranus in Libra

Birth dates:
  September 28, 1968–May 20, 1969
  June 24, 1969–November 21, 1974
  May 1, 1975–September 8, 1975

Your generation will be always changing partners. Born during the era of women's liberation, you may have come from a broken home and may have no clear image of what a marriage entails. There will be many sudden splits and experiments before you settle down. Your generation will be much involved in legal and political reforms and in changing artistic and fashion looks.

## Uranus in Scorpio

Birth dates:
  November 21, 1974–May 1, 1975
  September 8, 1975–February 17, 1981
  March 20, 1981–November 16, 1981

Interest in transformation, meditation, and life after death signaled the beginning of New Age consciousness. Your generation recognizes no boundaries, no limits, and no external controls. You'll have new attitudes toward death and dying, psychic phenomena, and the occult. Like Mae West and Casanova, you'll shock 'em sexually.

## Uranus in Sagittarius

Birth date:
  February 17, 1981–March 20, 1981
  November 16, 1981–February 15, 1988
  May 27, 1988–December 2, 1988

Could this generation be the first to travel in outer space? The new generation with this placement included Charles Lindbergh and a time when the first zeppelins and the Wright Brothers were conquering the skies. Uranus here forecasts great discoveries, mind expansion, and long-distance travel. Like Galileo and Martin Luther, those born in these years will generate new theories about the cosmos and man's relation to it.

## Uranus in Capricorn

Birth Dates:
  December 20, 1904–January 30, 1912
  September 4, 1912–November 12, 1912
  February 15, 1988–May 27, 1988
  December 2, 1988–April 1, 1995
  June 9, 1995–January 12, 1996

This generation, now reaching adulthood, will challenge traditions. In these years, we got organized with the help of technology put to practical use. The Internet was born after the great economic boom of the 1990s. Great leaders who were movers and shakers of history, like Julius Caesar and Henry VIII, were born under this placement.

## Uranus in Aquarius

Birth Dates:
  January 30, 1912–September 4, 1912
  November 12, 1912–April 1, 1919
  August 16, 1919–January 22, 1920
  April 1, 1995–June 9, 1995
  January 12, 1996–March 10, 2003
  September 15, 2003–December 30, 2003

Uranus in Aquarius is the strongest placement for this planet. Recently, we've had the opportunity to witness the full force of its power of innovation, as well as its sudden wake-up calls and insistence on humanitarian values. This was a time of high-tech development, when home computers became as ubiquitous as television. It was a time of globalization, surprise attacks (9/11), and underdeveloped countries demanding attention. The last generation with this placement produced great innovative minds, such as Leonard Bernstein and Orson Welles. The next will become another radical breakthrough generation, much concerned with global issues that involve all humanity.

## Uranus in Pisces

Birth Dates:
  April 1, 1919–August 16, 1919
  January 22, 1920–March 31, 1927
  November 4, 1927–January 12, 1928
  March 10, 2003–September 15, 2003
  December 30, 2003–May 28, 2010

Uranus is now in Pisces, ushering in a new generation. In the past century, Uranus in Pisces focused attention on the rise of electronic entertainment—radio and the cinema—and the secretiveness of Prohibition. This produced a generation of idealists exemplified by Judy Garland's theme, "Somewhere over the Rainbow." Uranus in Pisces also hints at stealth activities, at hospital and prison reform, at high-tech drugs and medical experiments, at shake-ups in and new locations for Pisces-ruled off-shore petroleum drilling. Issues regarding the water and oil supply, water-related storm damage (Hurricaine Katrina), sudden hurricanes, droughts, and floods demand our attention.

# Neptune Is the Magic Solvent

Neptune is often maligned as the planet of illusions that dissolves reality, enabling you to escape the material world. Under Neptune's influence, you see what you want to see. But Neptune also encourages you to create. It embodies glamour, subtlety, mystery, and mysticism, and governs anything that takes you beyond the mundane world, including out-of-body experiences.

Neptune breaks through and transcends your ordinary perceptions to take you to another level, where you experience either confusion or ecstasy. Its force can pull you off course only if you allow this to happen. Those who use Neptune wisely can translate their daydreams into poetry, theater, design, or inspired moves in the business world, avoiding the tricky con artist side of this planet.

Find your Neptune listed below:

# Neptune in Cancer

Birth Dates:
  July 19, 1901–December 25, 1901
  May 21, 1902–September 23, 1914
  December 14, 1914–July 19, 1915
  March 19, 1916–May 2, 1916

Dreams of the homeland, idealistic patriotism, and glamorization of the nurturing assets of women characterized this time. You who were born here have unusual psychic ability and deep insights into basic needs of others.

# Neptune in Leo

Birth Dates:
  September 23, 1914–December 14, 1914
  July 19, 1915–March 19, 1916
  May 2, 1916–September 21, 1928
  February 19, 1929–July 24, 1929

Neptune in Leo brought us the glamour and high living of the 1920s and the big spenders of that time. Neptune temptations of gambling, seduction, theater, and lavish entertaining distracted from the realities of the age. Those born in that generation also made great advances in the arts.

# Neptune in Virgo

Birth Dates:
  September 21, 1928–February 19, 1929
  July 24, 1929–October 3, 1942
  April 17, 1943–August 2, 1943

Neptune in Virgo encompassed the 1930s, the Great Depression, and the beginning of World War II, when a new order was born. This was a time of facing what didn't work. Many were unemployed and found solace at the movies, watching the great Virgo star Greta Garbo or the escapist dance films of Busby Berkley. New public services were born. Those with Neptune in Virgo later spread the gospel of health and fitness. This generation's devotion to spending hours at the office inspired the word workaholic.

## Neptune in Libra

Birth dates:
  October 3, 1942–April 17, 1943
  August 2, 1943–December 24, 1955
  March 12, 1956–October 19, 1956
  June 15, 1957–August 6, 1957
This was the time of World War II, and the immediate postwar period, when the world regained balance and returned to relative stability. Neptune in Libra was the romantic generation who would later be concerned with relating. As this generation matured, there was a new trend toward marriage and commitment. Racial and sexual equality become important issues, as they redesigned traditional roles to suit modern times.

## Neptune in Scorpio

Birth dates:
  December 24, 1955–March 12, 1956
  October 19, 1956–June 15, 1957
  August 6, 1957–January 4, 1970
  May 3, 1970–November 6, 1970
Neptune in Scorpio brought in a generation that would become interested in transformative power. Born in an era that glamorized sex, drugs, rock and roll, and Eastern religion, they matured in a more sobering time of AIDS, cocaine abuse, and New Age spirituality. As they evolve, they will become active in healing the planet from the results of the abuse of power.

## Neptune in Sagittarius

Birth dates:
  January 4, 1970–May 3, 1970
  November 6, 1970–January 19, 1984

June 23, 1984–November 21, 1984

Neptune in Sagittarius was the time when space travel became a reality. The Neptune influence glamorized new approaches to mysticism, religion, and mind expansion. This generation will take a new approach to spiritual life, with emphasis on visions, mysticism, and clairvoyance.

## Neptune in Capricorn

Birth dates:
January 19, 1984–June 23, 1984
November 21, 1984–January 29, 1998

Neptune in Capricorn brought a time when delusions about material power were glamorized in the mideighties and nineties. There was a boom in the stock market, and the Internet era spawned young tycoons who later lost all their wealth. It was also a time when the psychic and occult worlds spawned a new category of business enterprise, and sold services on television.

## Neptune in Aquarius

Birth dates:
January 29, 1998–April 4, 2011

This should continue to be a time of breakthroughs. Here the creative influence of Neptune reaches a universal audience. This is a time of dissolving barriers and globalization—when we truly become one world. During this transit of high-tech Aquarius, new kinds of entertainment media reach across cultural differences. However, the transit of Neptune has also raised boundary issues between cultures, especially in Middle Eastern countries with Neptune-ruled oil fields. As Neptune raises issues of social and political structures not being as solid as they seem, this could continue to produce rebellion and chaos in the environment. However, by using imagination (Neptune) in partnership with a global view (Aquarius), we could reach creative solutions.

Those born with this placement should be true citizens of the world, with a remarkable creative ability to transcend social and cultural barriers.

# Pluto Can Transform You

Though Pluto is a tiny, mysterious body in space, its influence is great. When Pluto zaps a strategic point in your horoscope, your life changes dramatically.

Little Pluto is the power behind the scenes; it affects you at deep levels of consciousness, causing events to come to the surface that will transform you and your generation. Nothing escapes, or is sacred, with this probing planet. Its purpose is to wipe out the past so something new can happen.

The Pluto place in your horoscope is where you have invisible power (Mars governs the visible power), where you can transform, heal, and affect the unconscious needs of the masses. Pluto tells lots about how your generation projects power and what makes it seem cool to others. And when Pluto changes signs, there is a whole new concept of what's cool. Pluto's strange elliptical orbit occasionally runs inside the orbit of neighboring Neptune. Because of its eccentric path, the length of time Pluto stays in any given sign can vary from thirteen to thirty-two years. It covered only seven signs in the last century.

## Pluto in Gemini

Late 1800s–May 26, 1914

This was a time of mass suggestion and breakthroughs in communications, when many brilliant writers, such as Ernest Hemingway and F. Scott Fitzgerald, were born. Henry Miller, D. H. Lawrence, and James Joyce scandalized society by using explicit sexual images and language in their literature. "Muckraking" journalists exposed corruption. Pluto-ruled Scorpio president Theodore Roosevelt said, "Speak softly, but carry a big stick." This generation had an intense need to communicate and made major breakthroughs in knowledge. A compulsive restlessness and a thirst for a variety of experiences characterize many of this generation.

# Pluto in Cancer

Birth Dates:

May 26, 1914–June 14, 1939

Dictators and mass media arose to wield emotional power over the masses. Women's rights were a popular issue. Deep sentimental feelings, acquisitiveness, and possessiveness characterized these times and people. Most of the great stars of the Hollywood era who embodied the American image were born during this period: Grace Kelly, Esther Williams, Frank Sinatra, and Lana Turner, to name a few.

# Pluto in Leo

Birth Dates:

June 14, 1939–August 19, 1957

The performing arts played on the emotions of the masses. Mick Jagger, John Lennon, and rock and roll were born at this time. So were baby boomers like Bill and Hillary Clinton. Those born here tend to be self-centered, powerful, and boisterous. This generation does its own thing, for better or for worse. They are quick to embrace self-transformation in the form of antiaging and plastic surgery techniques, to stay forever young and stay relevant in society.

# Pluto in Virgo

Birth Dates:

August 19, 1957–October 5, 1971

April 17, 1972–July 30, 1972

This is the yuppie generation that sparked a mass movement toward fitness, health, and career. It is a much more sober, serious, and driven generation than the fun-loving Pluto in Leo. During this time, machines were invented to process detail work efficiently. Inventions took a practical turn with answering machines, fax machines, car phones, and home-office equipment—all making the workplace far more efficient.

# Pluto in Libra

Birth Dates:
  October 5, 1971–April 17, 1972
  July 30, 1972–November 5, 1983
  May 18, 1984–August 27, 1984

A mellower generation, people born at this time are concerned with partnerships, working together, and finding diplomatic solutions to problems. Marriage is important to this generation, and they will define it by combining traditional values with equal partnership. This was a time of women's liberation, gay rights, the ERA, and legal battles over abortion—all of which transformed our ideas about relationships.

# Pluto in Scorpio

Birth Dates:
  November 5, 1983–May 18, 1984
  August 27, 1984–January 17, 1995

Pluto was in its ruling sign for a comparatively short period of time. However, this was a time of record achievements, destructive sexually transmitted diseases, nuclear power controversies, and explosive political issues. Pluto destroys in order to create new understanding—the phoenix rising from the ashes—which should be some consolation for those of you who felt Pluto's force before 1995. Sexual shockers were par for the course during these intense years, when black clothing, transvestites, body piercing, tattoos, and sexually explicit advertising pushed the boundaries of good taste.

# Pluto in Sagittarius

Birth Dates:
  January 17, 1995–April 20, 1995
  November 10, 1995–January 27, 2008
  June 13, 2008–November 26, 2008

During the most recent Pluto transit, we were pushed to expand our horizons and find deeper spiritual meaning in life.

Pluto's opposition with Saturn in 2001 brought an enormous conflict between traditional societies and the forces of change. It signaled a time when religious convictions exerted power in our political life as well.

Since Sagittarius is associated with travel, Pluto, the planet of extremes, made space travel a reality for wealthy adventurers, who paid for the privilege of travel on space shuttles. Globalization transformed business and traditional societies as outsourcing became the norm.

New dimensions in electronic publishing, concern with animal rights and the environment, and an increasing emphasis on extreme forms of religion were other signs of Pluto in Sagittarius. Charismatic religious leaders asserted themselves and questions of the boundaries between church and state arose. There were also sexual scandals associated with the church, which transformed the religious power structure.

## Pluto in Capricorn

Birth Dates:
   January 25, 2008–June 13, 2008
   November 26, 2008–January 20, 2024

As Pluto in Jupiter-ruled Sagittarius signaled a time of expansion and globalization, Pluto's entry into Saturn-ruled Capricorn last year signaled a time of adjustment, of facing reality and limitations, then finding pragmatic solutions. It will be a time when a new structure is imposed, when we become concerned with what actually works.

As Capricorn is associated with corporations and also with responsibility and duty, look for dramatic changes in business practices, hopefully with more attention paid to ethical and social responsibility as well as the bottom line. Big business will have enormous power during this transit, perhaps handling what governments have been unable to accomplish. There will be an emphasis on trimming down, perhaps a new belt-tightening regime. And, since Capricorn is the sign of Father Time, there will be a new emphasis on the aging of the population. The generation born now is sure to be a more practical and realistic one than that of their older Pluto in Sagittarius siblings.

## VENUS SIGNS 1901–2009

| | Aries | Taurus | Gemini | Cancer | Leo | Virgo |
|---|---|---|---|---|---|---|
| **1901** | 3/29–4/22 | 4/22–5/17 | 5/17–6/10 | 6/10–7/5 | 7/5–7/29 | 7/29–8/23 |
| **1902** | 5/7–6/3 | 6/3–6/30 | 6/30–7/25 | 7/25–8/19 | 8/19–9/13 | 9/13–10/7 |
| **1903** | 2/28–3/24 | 3/24–4/18 | 4/18–5/13 | 5/13–6/9 | 6/9–7/7 | 7/7–8/17 |
| | | | | | | 9/6–11/8 |
| **1904** | 3/13–5/7 | 5/7–6/1 | 6/1–6/25 | 6/25–7/19 | 7/19–8/13 | 8/13–9/6 |
| **1905** | 2/3–3/6 | 3/6–4/9 | 7/8–8/6 | 8/6–9/1 | 9/1–9/27 | 9/27–10/21 |
| | 4/9–5/28 | 5/28–7/8 | | | | |
| **1906** | 3/1–4/7 | 4/7–5/2 | 5/2–5/26 | 5/26–6/20 | 6/20–7/16 | 7/16–8/11 |
| **1907** | 4/27–5/22 | 5/22–6/16 | 6/16–7/11 | 7/11–8/4 | 8/4–8/29 | 8/29–9/22 |
| **1908** | 2/14–3/10 | 3/10–4/5 | 4/5–5/5 | 5/5–9/8 | 9/8–10/8 | 10/8–11/3 |
| **1909** | 3/29–4/22 | 4/22–5/16 | 5/16–6/10 | 6/10–7/4 | 7/4–7/29 | 7/29–8/23 |
| **1910** | 5/7–6/3 | 6/4–6/29 | 6/30–7/24 | 7/25–8/18 | 8/19–9/12 | 9/13–10/6 |
| **1911** | 2/28–3/23 | 3/24–4/17 | 4/18–5/12 | 5/13–6/8 | 6/9–7/7 | 7/8–11/18 |
| **1912** | 4/13–5/6 | 5/7–5/31 | 6/1–6/24 | 6/24–7/18 | 7/19–8/12 | 8/13–9/5 |
| **1913** | 2/3–3/6 | 3/7–5/1 | 7/8–8/5 | 8/6–8/31 | 9/1–9/26 | 9/27–10/20 |
| | 5/2–5/30 | 5/31–7/7 | | | | |
| **1914** | 3/14–4/6 | 4/7–5/1 | 5/2–5/25 | 5/26–6/19 | 6/20–7/15 | 7/16–8/10 |
| **1915** | 4/27–5/21 | 5/22–6/15 | 6/16–7/10 | 7/11–8/3 | 8/4–8/28 | 8/29–9/21 |
| **1916** | 2/14–3/9 | 3/10–4/5 | 4/6–5/5 | 5/6–9/8 | 9/9–10/7 | 10/8–11/2 |
| **1917** | 3/29–4/21 | 4/22–5/15 | 5/16–6/9 | 6/10–7/3 | 7/4–7/28 | 7/29–8/21 |
| **1918** | 5/7–6/2 | 6/3–6/28 | 6/29–7/24 | 7/25–8/18 | 8/19–9/11 | 9/12–10/5 |
| **1919** | 2/27–3/22 | 3/23–4/16 | 4/17–5/12 | 5/13–6/7 | 6/8–7/7 | 7/8–11/8 |
| **1920** | 4/12–5/6 | 5/7–5/30 | 5/31–6/23 | 6/24–7/18 | 7/19–8/11 | 8/12–9/4 |
| **1921** | 2/3–3/6 | 3/7–4/25 | 7/8–8/5 | 8/6–8/31 | 9/1–9/25 | 9/26–10/20 |
| | 4/26–6/1 | 6/2–7/7 | | | | |
| **1922** | 3/13–4/6 | 4/7–4/30 | 5/1–5/25 | 5/26–6/19 | 6/20–7/14 | 7/15–8/9 |
| **1923** | 4/27–5/21 | 5/22–6/14 | 6/15–7/9 | 7/10–8/3 | 8/4–8/27 | 8/28–9/20 |
| **1924** | 2/13–3/8 | 3/9–4/4 | 4/5–5/5 | 5/6–9/8 | 9/9–10/7 | 10/8–11/12 |
| **1925** | 3/28–4/20 | 4/21–5/15 | 5/16–6/8 | 6/9–7/3 | 7/4–7/27 | 7/28–8/21 |

| Libra | Scorpio | Sagittarius | Capricorn | Aquarius | Pisces |
|---|---|---|---|---|---|
| 8/23–9/17 | 9/17–10/12 | 10/12–1/16 | 1/16–2/9 | 2/9–3/5 | 3/5–3/29 |
|  |  |  | 11/7–12/5 | 12/5–1/11 |  |
| 10/7–10/31 | 10/31–11/24 | 11/24–12/18 | 12/18–1/11 | 2/6–4/4 | 1/11–2/6 |
|  |  |  |  |  | 4/4–5/7 |
| 8/17–9/6 | 12/9–1/5 |  |  | 1/11–2/4 | 2/4–2/28 |
| 11/8–12/9 |  |  |  |  |  |
| 9/6–9/30 | 9/30–10/25 | 1/5–1/30 | 1/30–2/24 | 2/24–3/19 | 3/19–4/13 |
|  |  | 10/25–11/18 | 11/18–12/13 | 12/13–1/7 |  |
| 10/21–11/14 | 11/14–12/8 | 12/8–1/1/06 |  |  | 1/7–2/3 |
| 8/11–9/7 | 9/7–10/9 | 10/9–12/15 | 1/1–1/25 | 1/25–2/18 | 2/18–3/14 |
|  | 12/15–12/25 | 12/25–2/6 |  |  |  |
| 9/22–10/16 | 10/16–11/9 | 11/9–12/3 | 2/6–3/6 | 3/6–4/2 | 4/2–4/27 |
|  |  |  | 12/3–12/27 | 12/27–1/20 |  |
| 11/3–11/28 | 11/28–12/22 | 12/22–1/15 |  |  | 1/20–2/4 |
| 8/23–9/17 | 9/17–10/12 | 10/12–11/17 | 1/15–2/9 | 2/9–3/5 | 3/5–3/29 |
|  |  |  | 11/17–12/5 | 12/5–1/15 |  |
| 10/7–10/30 | 10/31–11/23 | 11/24–12/17 | 12/18–12/31 | 1/1–1/15 | 1/16–1/28 |
|  |  |  |  | 1/29–4/4 | 4/5–5/6 |
| 11/19–12/8 | 12/9–12/31 |  | 1/1–1/10 | 1/11–2/2 | 2/3–2/27 |
| 9/6–9/30 | 1/1–1/4 | 1/5–1/29 | 1/30–2/23 | 2/24–3/18 | 3/19–4/12 |
|  | 10/1–10/24 | 10/25–11/17 | 11/18–12/12 | 12/13–12/31 |  |
| 10/21–11/13 | 11/14–12/7 | 12/8–12/31 |  | 1/1–1/6 | 1/7–2/2 |
| 8/11–9/6 | 9/7–10/9 | 10/10–12/5 | 1/1–1/24 | 1/25–2/17 | 2/18–3/13 |
|  | 12/6–12/30 | 12/31 |  |  |  |
| 9/22–10/15 | 10/16–11/8 | 1/1–2/6 | 2/7–3/6 | 3/7–4/1 | 4/2–4/26 |
|  |  | 11/9–12/2 | 12/3–12/26 | 12/27–12/31 |  |
| 11/3–11/27 | 11/28–12/21 | 12/22–12/31 |  | 1/1–1/19 | 1/20–2/13 |
| 8/22–9/16 | 9/17–10/11 | 1/1–1/14 | 1/15–2/7 | 2/8–3/4 | 3/5–3/28 |
|  |  | 10/12–11/6 | 11/7–12/5 | 12/6–12/31 |  |
| 10/6–10/29 | 10/30–11/22 | 11/23–12/16 | 12/17–12/31 | 1/1–4/5 | 4/6–5/6 |
| 11/9–12/8 | 12/9–12/31 |  | 1/1–1/9 | 1/10–2/2 | 2/3–2/26 |
| 9/5–9/30 | 1/1–1/3 | 1/4–1/28 | 1/29–2/22 | 2/23–3/18 | 3/19–4/11 |
|  | 9/31–10/23 | 10/24–11/17 | 11/18–12/11 | 12/12–12/31 |  |
| 10/21–11/13 | 11/14–12/7 | 12/8–12/31 |  | 1/1–1/6 | 1/7–2/2 |
| 8/10–9/6 | 9/7–10/10 | 10/11–11/28 | 1/1–1/24 | 1/25–2/16 | 2/17–3/12 |
|  | 11/29–12/31 |  |  |  |  |
| 9/21–10/14 | 1/1 | 1/2–2/6 | 2/7–3/5 | 3/6–3/31 | 4/1–4/26 |
|  | 10/15–11/7 | 11/8–12/1 | 12/2–12/25 | 12/26–12/31 |  |
| 11/13–11/26 | 11/27–12/21 | 12/22–12/31 |  | 1/1–1/19 | 1/20–2/12 |
| 8/22–9/15 | 9/16–10/11 | 1/1–1/14 | 1/15–2/7 | 2/8–3/3 | 3/4–3/27 |
|  |  | 10/12–11/6 | 11/7–12/5 | 12/6–12/31 |  |

## VENUS SIGNS 1901–2009

| | Aries | Taurus | Gemini | Cancer | Leo | Virgo |
|---|---|---|---|---|---|---|
| 1926 | 5/7–6/2 | 6/3–6/28 | 6/29–7/23 | 7/24–8/17 | 8/18–9/11 | 9/12–10/5 |
| 1927 | 2/27–3/22 | 3/23–4/16 | 4/17–5/11 | 5/12–6/7 | 6/8–7/7 | 7/8–11/9 |
| 1928 | 4/12–5/5 | 5/6–5/29 | 5/30–6/23 | 6/24–7/17 | 7/18–8/11 | 8/12–9/4 |
| 1929 | 2/3–3/7 4/20–6/2 | 3/8–4/19 6/3–7/7 | 7/8–8/4 | 8/5–8/30 | 8/31–9/25 | 9/26–10/19 |
| 1930 | 3/13–4/5 | 4/6–4/30 | 5/1–5/24 | 5/25–6/18 | 6/19–7/14 | 7/15–8/9 |
| 1931 | 4/26–5/20 | 5/21–6/13 | 6/14–7/8 | 7/9–8/2 | 8/3–8/26 | 8/27–9/19 |
| 1932 | 2/12–3/8 | 3/9–4/3 | 4/4–5/5 7/13–7/27 | 5/6–7/12 7/28–9/8 | 9/9–10/6 | 10/7–11/1 |
| 1933 | 3/27–4/19 | 4/20–5/28 | 5/29–6/8 | 6/9–7/2 | 7/3–7/26 | 7/27–8/20 |
| 1934 | 5/6–6/1 | 6/2–6/27 | 6/28–7/22 | 7/23–8/16 | 8/17–9/10 | 9/11–10/4 |
| 1935 | 2/26–3/21 | 3/22–4/15 | 4/16–5/10 | 5/11–6/6 | 6/7–7/6 | 7/7–11/8 |
| 1936 | 4/11–5/4 | 5/5–5/28 | 5/29–6/22 | 6/23–7/16 | 7/17–8/10 | 8/11–9/4 |
| 1937 | 2/2–3/8 4/14–6/3 | 3/9–4/13 6/4–7/6 | 7/7–8/3 | 8/4–8/29 | 8/30–9/24 | 9/25–10/18 |
| 1938 | 3/12–4/4 | 4/5–4/28 | 4/29–5/23 | 5/24–6/18 | 6/19–7/13 | 7/14–8/8 |
| 1939 | 4/25–5/19 | 5/20–6/13 | 6/14–7/8 | 7/9–8/1 | 8/2–8/25 | 8/26–9/19 |
| 1940 | 2/12–3/7 | 3/8–4/3 | 4/4–5/5 7/5–7/31 | 5/6–7/4 8/1–9/8 | 9/9–10/5 | 10/6–10/31 |
| 1941 | 3/27–4/19 | 4/20–5/13 | 5/14–6/6 | 6/7–7/1 | 7/2–7/26 | 7/27–8/20 |
| 1942 | 5/6–6/1 | 6/2–6/26 | 6/27–7/22 | 7/23–8/16 | 8/17–9/9 | 9/10–10/3 |
| 1943 | 2/25–3/20 | 3/21–4/14 | 4/15–5/10 | 5/11–6/6 | 6/7–7/6 | 7/7–11/8 |
| 1944 | 4/10–5/3 | 5/4–5/28 | 5/29–6/21 | 6/22–7/16 | 7/17–8/9 | 8/10–9/2 |
| 1945 | 2/2–3/10 4/7–6/3 | 3/11–4/6 6/4–7/6 | 7/7–8/3 | 8/4–8/29 | 8/30–9/23 | 9/24–10/18 |
| 1946 | 3/11–4/4 | 4/5–4/28 | 4/29–5/23 | 5/24–6/17 | 6/18–7/12 | 7/13–8/8 |
| 1947 | 4/25–5/19 | 5/20–6/12 | 6/13–7/7 | 7/8–8/1 | 8/2–8/25 | 8/26–9/18 |
| 1948 | 2/11–3/7 | 3/8–4/3 | 4/4–5/6 6/29–8/2 | 5/7–6/28 8/3–9/7 | 9/8–10/5 | 10/6–10/31 |
| 1949 | 3/26–4/19 | 4/20–5/13 | 5/14–6/6 | 6/7–6/30 | 7/1–7/25 | 7/26–8/19 |
| 1950 | 5/5–5/31 | 6/1–6/26 | 6/27–7/21 | 7/22–8/15 | 8/16–9/9 | 9/10–10/3 |
| 1951 | 2/25–3/21 | 3/22–4/15 | 4/16–5/10 | 5/11–6/6 | 6/7–7/7 | 7/8–11/9 |

58

| Libra | Scorpio | Sagittarius | Capricorn | Aquarius | Pisces |
| --- | --- | --- | --- | --- | --- |
| 10/6–10/29 | 10/30–11/22 | 11/23–12/16 | 12/17–12/31 | 1/1–4/5 | 4/6–5/6 |
| 11/10–12/8 | 12/9–12/31 | 1/1–1/7 | 1/8 | 1/9–2/1 | 2/2–2/26 |
| 9/5–9/28 | 1/1–1/3 | 1/4–1/28 | 1/29–2/22 | 2/23–3/17 | 3/18–4/11 |
|  | 9/29–10/23 | 10/24–11/16 | 11/17–12/11 | 12/12–12/31 |  |
| 10/20–11/12 | 11/13–12/6 | 12/7–12/30 | 12/31 | 1/1–1/5 | 1/6–2/2 |
|  |  |  |  |  |  |
| 8/10–9/6 | 9/7–10/11 | 10/12–11/21 | 1/1–1/23 | 1/24–2/16 | 2/17–3/12 |
|  | 11/21–12/31 |  |  |  |  |
| 9/20–10/13 | 1/1–1/3 | 1/4–2/6 | 2/7–3/4 | 3/5–3/31 | 4/1–4/25 |
|  | 10/14–11/6 | 11/7–11/30 | 12/1–12/24 | 12/25–12/31 |  |
| 11/2–11/25 | 11/26–12/20 | 12/21–12/31 |  | 1/1–1/18 | 1/19–2/11 |
|  |  |  |  |  |  |
| 8/21–9/14 | 9/15–10/10 | 1/1–1/13 | 1/14–2/6 | 2/7–3/2 | 3/3–3/26 |
|  | 10/11–11/5 | 11/6–12/4 | 12/5–12/31 |  |  |
| 10/5–10/28 | 10/29–11/21 | 11/22–12/15 | 12/16–12/31 | 1/1–4/5 | 4/6–5/5 |
|  |  |  |  |  |  |
| 11/9–12/7 | 12/8–12/31 |  | 1/1–1/7 | 1/8–1/31 | 2/1–2/25 |
| 9/5–9/27 | 1/1–1/2 | 1/3–1/27 | 1/28–2/21 | 2/22–3/16 | 3/17–4/10 |
|  | 9/28–10/22 | 10/23–11/15 | 11/16–12/10 | 12/11–12/31 |  |
| 10/19–11/11 | 11/12–12/5 | 12/6–12/29 | 12/30–12/31 | 1/1–1/5 | 1/6–2/1 |
|  |  |  |  |  |  |
| 8/9–9/6 | 9/7–10/13 | 10/14–11/14 | 1/1–1/22 | 1/23–2/15 | 2/16–3/11 |
|  | 11/15–12/31 |  |  |  |  |
| 9/20–10/13 | 1/1–1/3 | 1/4–2/5 | 2/6–3/4 | 3/5–3/30 | 3/31–4/24 |
|  | 10/14–11/6 | 11/7–11/30 | 12/1–12/24 | 12/25–12/31 |  |
| 11/1–11/25 | 11/26–12/19 | 12/20–12/31 |  | 1/1–1/18 | 1/19–2/11 |
|  |  |  |  |  |  |
| 8/21–9/14 | 9/15–10/9 | 1/1–1/12 | 1/13–2/5 | 2/6–3/1 | 3/2–3/26 |
|  | 10/11–11/5 | 11/6–12/4 | 12/5–12/31 |  |  |
| 10/4–10/27 | 10/28–11/20 | 11/21–12/14 | 12/15–12/31 | 1/1–4/5 | 4/6–5/5 |
| 11/9–12/7 | 12/8–12/31 |  | 1/1–1/7 | 1/8–1/31 | 2/1–2/24 |
| 9/3–9/27 | 1/1–1/2 | 1/3–1/27 | 1/28–2/20 | 2/21–3/16 | 3/17–4/9 |
|  | 9/28–10/21 | 10/22–11/15 | 11/16–12/10 | 12/11–12/31 |  |
| 10/19–11/11 | 11/12–12/5 | 12/6–12/29 | 12/30–12/31 | 1/1–1/4 | 1/5–2/1 |
|  |  |  |  |  |  |
| 8/9–9/6 | 9/7–10/15 | 10/16–11/7 | 1/1–1/21 | 1/22–2/14 | 2/15–3/10 |
|  | 11/8–12/31 |  |  |  |  |
| 9/19–10/12 | 1/1–1/4 | 1/5–2/5 | 2/6–3/4 | 3/5–3/29 | 3/30–4/24 |
|  | 10/13–11/5 | 11/6–11/29 | 11/30–12/23 | 12/24–12/31 |  |
| 11/1–11/25 | 11/26–12/19 | 12/20–12/31 |  | 1/1–1/17 | 1/18–2/10 |
|  |  |  |  |  |  |
| 8/20–9/14 | 9/15–10/9 | 1/1–1/12 | 1/13–2/5 | 2/6–3/1 | 3/2–3/25 |
|  | 10/10–11/5 | 11/6–12/5 | 12/6–12/31 |  |  |
| 10/4–10/27 | 10/28–11/20 | 11/21–12/13 | 12/14–12/31 | 1/1–4/5 | 4/6–5/4 |
| 11/10–12/7 | 12/8–12/31 |  | 1/1–1/7 | 1/8–1/31 | 2/1–2/24 |

# VENUS SIGNS 1901–2009

| | Aries | Taurus | Gemini | Cancer | Leo | Virgo |
|---|---|---|---|---|---|---|
| **1952** | 4/10–5/4 | 5/5–5/28 | 5/29–6/21 | 6/22–7/16 | 7/17–8/9 | 8/10–9/3 |
| **1953** | 2/2–3/3 | 3/4–3/31 | 7/8–8/3 | 8/4–8/29 | 8/30–9/24 | 9/25–10/18 |
| | 4/1–6/5 | 6/6–7/7 | | | | |
| **1954** | 3/12–4/4 | 4/5–4/28 | 4/29–5/23 | 5/24–6/17 | 6/18–7/13 | 7/14–8/8 |
| **1955** | 4/25–5/19 | 5/20–6/13 | 6/14–7/7 | 7/8–8/1 | 8/2–8/25 | 8/26–9/18 |
| **1956** | 2/12–3/7 | 3/8–4/4 | 4/5–5/7 | 5/8–6/23 | 9/9–10/5 | 10/6–10/31 |
| | | | 6/24–8/4 | 8/5–9/8 | | |
| **1957** | 3/26–4/19 | 4/20–5/13 | 5/14–6/6 | 6/7–7/1 | 7/2–7/26 | 7/27–8/19 |
| **1958** | 5/6–5/31 | 6/1–6/26 | 6/27–7/22 | 7/23–8/15 | 8/16–9/9 | 9/10–10/3 |
| **1959** | 2/25–3/20 | 3/21–4/14 | 4/15–5/10 | 5/11–6/6 | 6/7–7/8 | 7/9–9/20 |
| | | | | | 9/21–9/24 | 9/25–11/9 |
| **1960** | 4/10–5/3 | 5/4–5/28 | 5/29–6/21 | 6/22–7/15 | 7/16–8/9 | 8/10–9/2 |
| **1961** | 2/3–6/5 | 6/6–7/7 | 7/8–8/3 | 8/4–8/29 | 8/30–9/23 | 9/24–10/17 |
| **1962** | 3/11–4/3 | 4/4–4/28 | 4/29–5/22 | 5/23–6/17 | 6/18–7/12 | 7/13–8/8 |
| **1963** | 4/24–5/18 | 5/19–6/12 | 6/13–7/7 | 7/8–7/31 | 8/1–8/25 | 8/26–9/18 |
| **1964** | 2/11–3/7 | 3/8–4/4 | 4/5–5/9 | 5/10–6/17 | 9/9–10/5 | 10/6–10/31 |
| | | | 6/18–8/5 | 8/6–9/8 | | |
| **1965** | 3/26–4/18 | 4/19–5/12 | 5/13–6/6 | 6/7–6/30 | 7/1–7/25 | 7/26–8/19 |
| **1966** | 5/6–5/31 | 6/1–6/26 | 6/27–7/21 | 7/22–8/15 | 8/16–9/8 | 9/9–10/2 |
| **1967** | 2/24–3/20 | 3/21–4/14 | 4/15–5/10 | 5/11–6/6 | 6/7–7/8 | 7/9–9/9 |
| | | | | | 9/10–10/1 | 10/2–11/9 |
| **1968** | 4/9–5/3 | 5/4–5/27 | 5/28–6/20 | 6/21–7/15 | 7/16–8/8 | 8/9–9/2 |
| **1969** | 2/3–6/6 | 6/7–7/6 | 7/7–8/3 | 8/4–8/28 | 8/29–9/22 | 9/23–10/17 |
| **1970** | 3/11–4/3 | 4/4–4/27 | 4/28–5/22 | 5/23–6/16 | 6/17–7/12 | 7/13–8/8 |
| **1971** | 4/24–5/18 | 5/19–6/12 | 6/13–7/6 | 7/7–7/31 | 8/1–8/24 | 8/25–9/17 |
| **1972** | 2/11–3/7 | 3/8–4/3 | 4/4–5/10 | 5/11–6/11 | | |
| | | | 6/12–8/6 | 8/7–9/8 | 9/9–10/5 | 10/6–10/30 |
| **1973** | 3/25–4/18 | 4/18–5/12 | 5/13–6/5 | 6/6–6/29 | 7/1–7/25 | 7/26–8/19 |
| **1974** | 5/5–5/31 | 6/1–6/25 | 6/26–7/21 | 7/22–8/14 | 8/15–9/8 | 9/9–10/2 |
| **1975** | 2/24–3/20 | 3/21–4/13 | 4/14–5/9 | 5/10–6/6 | 6/7–7/9 | 7/10–9/2 |
| | | | | | 9/3–10/4 | 10/5–11/9 |
| **1976** | 4/8–5/2 | 5/2–5/27 | 5/27–6/20 | 6/20–7/14 | 7/14–8/8 | 8/8–9/1 |
| **1977** | 2/2–6/6 | 6/6–7/6 | 7/6–8/2 | 8/2–8/28 | 8/28–9/22 | 9/22–10/17 |
| **1978** | 3/9–4/2 | 4/2–4/27 | 4/27–5/22 | 5/22–6/16 | 6/16–7/12 | 7/12–8/6 |
| **1979** | 4/23–5/18 | 5/18–6/11 | 6/11–7/6 | 7/6–7/30 | 7/30–8/24 | 8/24–9/17 |

60

| Libra | Scorpio | Sagittarius | Capricorn | Aquarius | Pisces |
|---|---|---|---|---|---|
| 9/4–9/27 | 1/1–1/2 | 1/3–1/27 | 1/28–2/20 | 2/21–3/16 | 3/17–4/9 |
| | 9/28–10/21 | 10/22–11/15 | 11/16–12/10 | 12/11–12/31 | |
| 10/19–11/11 | 11/12–12/5 | 12/6–12/29 | 12/30–12/31 | 1/1–1/5 | 1/6–2/1 |
| | | | | | |
| 8/9–9/6 | 9/7–10/22 | 10/23–10/27 | 1/1–1/22 | 1/23–2/15 | 2/16–3/11 |
| | 10/28–12/31 | | | | |
| 9/19–10/13 | 1/1–1/6 | 1/7–2/5 | 2/6–3/4 | 3/5–3/30 | 3/31–4/24 |
| | 10/14–11/5 | 11/6–11/30 | 12/1–12/24 | 12/25–12/31 | |
| 11/1–11/25 | 11/26–12/19 | 12/20–12/31 | | 1/1–1/17 | 1/18–2/11 |
| | | | | | |
| 8/20–9/14 | 9/15–10/9 | 1/1–1/12 | 1/13–2/5 | 2/6–3/1 | 3/2–3/25 |
| | | 10/10–11/5 | 11/6–12/6 | 12/7–12/31 | |
| 10/4–10/27 | 10/28–11/20 | 11/21–12/14 | 12/15–12/31 | 1/1–4/6 | 4/7–5/5 |
| | | | | | |
| 11/10–12/7 | 12/8–12/31 | | 1/1–1/7 | 1/8–1/31 | 2/1–2/24 |
| 9/3–9/26 | 1/1–1/2 | 1/3–1/27 | 1/28–2/20 | 2/21–3/15 | 3/16–4/9 |
| | 9/27–10/21 | 10/22–11/15 | 11/16–12/10 | 12/11–12/31 | |
| 10/18–11/11 | 11/12–12/4 | 12/5–12/28 | 12/29–12/31 | 1/1–1/5 | 1/6–2/2 |
| 8/9–9/6 | 9/7–12/31 | | 1/1–1/21 | 1/22–2/14 | 2/15–3/10 |
| 9/19–10/12 | 1/1–1/6 | 1/7–2/5 | 2/6–3/4 | 3/5–3/29 | 3/30–4/23 |
| | 10/13–11/5 | 11/6–11/29 | 11/30–12/23 | 12/24–12/31 | |
| 11/1–11/24 | 11/25–12/19 | 12/20–12/31 | | 1/1–1/16 | 1/17–2/10 |
| | | | | | |
| 8/20–9/13 | 9/14–10/9 | 1/1–1/12 | 1/13–2/5 | 2/6–3/1 | 3/2–3/25 |
| | | 10/10–11/5 | 11/6–12/7 | 12/8–12/31 | |
| 10/3–10/26 | 10/27–11/19 | 11/20–12/13 | 2/7–2/25 | 1/1–2/6 | 4/7–5/5 |
| | | | 12/14–12/31 | 2/26–4/6 | |
| | | | | | |
| 11/10–12/7 | 12/8–12/31 | | 1/1–1/6 | 1/7–1/30 | 1/31–2/23 |
| 9/3–9/26 | 1/1 | 1/2–1/26 | 1/27–2/20 | 2/21–3/15 | 3/16–4/8 |
| | 9/27–10/21 | 10/22–11/14 | 11/15–12/9 | 12/10–12/31 | |
| 10/18–11/10 | 11/11–12/4 | 12/5–12/28 | 12/29–12/31 | 1/1–1/4 | 1/5–2/2 |
| 8/9–9/7 | 9/8–12/31 | | 1/1–1/21 | 1/22–2/14 | 2/15–3/10 |
| 9/18–10/11 | 1/1–1/7 | 1/8–2/5 | 2/6–3/4 | 3/5–3/29 | 3/30–4/23 |
| | 10/12–11/5 | 11/6–11/29 | 11/30–12/23 | 12/24–12/31 | |
| 10/31–11/24 | 11/25–12/18 | 12/19–12/31 | | 1/1–1/16 | 1/17–2/10 |
| | | | | | |
| 8/20–9/13 | 9/14–10/8 | 1/1–1/12 | 1/13–2/4 | 2/5–2/28 | 3/1–3/24 |
| | | 10/9–11/5 | 11/6–12/7 | 12/8–12/31 | |
| 10/3–10/26 | 10/27–11/19 | 11/20–12/13 | 12/14–12/31 | 3/1–4/6 | 4/7–5/4 |
| | | | 1/30–2/28 | 1/1–1/29 | |
| 11/10–12/7 | 12/8–12/31 | | 1/1–1/6 | 1/7–1/30 | 1/31–2/23 |
| | | | | | |
| 9/1–9/26 | 9/26–10/20 | 1/1–1/26 | 1/26–2/19 | 2/19–3/15 | 3/15–4/8 |
| 10/17–11/10 | 11/10–12/4 | 12/4–12/27 | 12/27–1/20/78 | | 1/4–2/2 |
| 8/6–9/7 | 9/7–1/7 | | | 1/20–2/13 | 2/13–3/9 |
| 9/17–10/11 | 10/11–11/4 | 1/7–2/5 | 2/5–3/3 | 3/3–3/29 | 3/29–4/23 |
| | | 11/4–11/28 | 11/28–12/22 | 12/22–1/16/80 | |

## VENUS SIGNS 1901–2009

| | Aries | Taurus | Gemini | Cancer | Leo | Virgo |
|---|---|---|---|---|---|---|
| **1980** | 2/9–3/6 | 3/6–4/3 | 4/3–5/12 | 5/12–6/5 | 9/7–10/4 | 10/4–10/30 |
| | | | 6/5–8/6 | 8/6–9/7 | | |
| **1981** | 3/24–4/17 | 4/17–5/11 | 5/11–6/5 | 6/5–6/29 | 6/29–7/24 | 7/24–8/18 |
| **1982** | 5/4–5/30 | 5/30–6/25 | 6/25–7/20 | 7/20–8/14 | 8/14–9/7 | 9/7–10/2 |
| **1983** | 2/22–3/19 | 3/19–4/13 | 4/13–5/9 | 5/9–6/6 | 6/6–7/10 | 7/10–8/27 |
| | | | | | 8/27–10/5 | 10/5–11/9 |
| **1984** | 4/7–5/2 | 5/2–5/26 | 5/26–6/20 | 6/20–7/14 | 7/14–8/7 | 8/7–9/1 |
| **1985** | 2/2–6/6 | 6/7–7/6 | 7/6–8/2 | 8/2–8/28 | 8/28–9/22 | 9/22–10/16 |
| **1986** | 3/9–4/2 | 4/2–4/26 | 4/26–5/21 | 5/21–6/15 | 6/15–7/11 | 7/11–8/7 |
| **1987** | 4/22–5/17 | 5/17–6/11 | 6/11–7/5 | 7/5–7/30 | 7/30–8/23 | 8/23–9/16 |
| **1988** | 2/9–3/6 | 3/6–4/3 | 4/3–5/17 | 5/17–5/27 | 9/7–10/4 | 10/4–10/29 |
| | | | 5/27–8/6 | 8/28–9/22 | 9/22–10/16 | |
| **1989** | 3/23–4/16 | 4/16–5/11 | 5/11–6/4 | 6/4–6/29 | 6/29–7/24 | 7/24–8/18 |
| **1990** | 5/4–5/30 | 5/30–6/25 | 6/25–7/20 | 7/20–8/13 | 8/13–9/7 | 9/7–10/1 |
| **1991** | 2/22–3/18 | 3/18–4/13 | 4/13–5/9 | 5/9–6/6 | 6/6–7/11 | 7/11–8/21 |
| | | | | | 8/21–10/6 | 10/6–11/9 |
| **1992** | 4/7–5/1 | 5/1–5/26 | 5/26–6/19 | 6/19–7/13 | 7/13–8/7 | 8/7–8/31 |
| **1993** | 2/2–6/6 | 6/6–7/6 | 7/6–8/1 | 8/1–8/27 | 8/27–9/21 | 9/21–10/16 |
| **1994** | 3/8–4/1 | 4/1–4/26 | 4/26–5/21 | 5/21–6/15 | 6/15–7/11 | 7/11–8/7 |
| **1995** | 4/22–5/16 | 5/16–6/10 | 6/10–7/5 | 7/5–7/29 | 7/29–8/23 | 8/23–9/16 |
| **1996** | 2/9–3/6 | 3/6–4/3 | 4/3–8/7 | 8/7–9/7 | 9/7–10/4 | 10/4–10/29 |
| **1997** | 3/23–4/16 | 4/16–5/10 | 5/10–6/4 | 6/4–6/28 | 6/28–7/23 | 7/23–8/17 |
| **1998** | 5/3–5/29 | 5/29–6/24 | 6/24–7/19 | 7/19–8/13 | 8/13–9/6 | 9/6–9/30 |
| **1999** | 2/21–3/18 | 3/18–4/12 | 4/12–5/8 | 5/8–6/5 | 6/5–7/12 | 7/12–8/15 |
| | | | | | 8/15–10/7 | 10/7–11/9 |
| **2000** | 4/6–5/1 | 5/1–5/25 | 5/25–6/13 | 6/13–7/13 | 7/13–8/6 | 8/6–8/31 |
| **2001** | 2/2–6/6 | 6/6–7/5 | 7/5–8/1 | 8/1–8/26 | 8/26–9/20 | 9/20–10/15 |
| **2002** | 3/7–4/1 | 4/1–4/25 | 4/25–5/20 | 5/20–6/14 | 6/14–7/10 | 7/10–8/7 |
| **2003** | 4/21–5/16 | 5/16–6/9 | 6/9–7/4 | 7/4–7/29 | 7/29–8/22 | 8/22–9/15 |
| **2004** | 2/8–3/5 | 3/5–4/3 | 4/3–8/7 | 8/7–9/6 | 9/6–10/3 | 10/3–10/28 |
| **2005** | 3/22–4/15 | 4/15–5/10 | 5/10–6/3 | 6/3–6/28 | 6/28–7/23 | 7/23–8/17 |
| **2006** | 5/3–5/29 | 5/29–6/24 | 6/24–7/19 | 7/19–8/12 | 8/12–9/6 | 9/6–9/30 |
| **2007** | 2/21–3/16 | 3/17–4/10 | 4/11–5/7 | 5/8–6/4 | 6/5–7/13 | 7/14–8/7 |
| | | | | | 8/8–10/6 | 10/7–11/7 |
| **2008** | 4/6–4/30 | 5/1–5/24 | 5/25–6/17 | 6/18–7/11 | 7/12–8/4 | 8/5–8/29 |
| **2009** | 2/2–4/11 | 6/6–7/5 | 7/5–7/31 | 731/–8/26 | 8/26–9/20 | 9/20–10/14 |
| | 4/24–6/6 | | | | | |

| Libra | Scorpio | Sagittarius | Capricorn | Aquarius | Pisces |
|---|---|---|---|---|---|
| 10/30–11/24 | 11/24–12/18 | 12/18–1/11/81 | | | 1/16–2/9 |
| 8/18–9/12 | 9/12–10/9 | 10/9–11/5 | 1/11–2/4<br>11/5–12/8 | 2/4–2/28<br>12/8–1/23/82 | 2/28–3/24 |
| 10/2–10/26 | 10/26–11/18 | 11/18–12/12 | 1/23–3/2<br>12/12–1/5/83 | 3/2–4/6 | 4/6–5/4 |
| 11/9–12/6 | 12/6–1/1/84 | | | 1/5–1/29 | 1/29–2/22 |
| 9/1–9/25 | 9/25–10/20 | 1/1–1/25<br>10/20–11/13 | 1/25–2/19<br>11/13–12/9 | 2/19–3/14<br>12/10–1/4 | 3/14–4/7 |
| 10/16–11/9 | 11/9–12/3 | 12/3–12/27 | 12/28–1/19 | | 1/4–2/2 |
| 8/7–9/7 | 9/7–1/7 | | | 1/20–2/13 | 2/13–3/9 |
| 9/16–10/10 | 10/10–11/3 | 1/7–2/5<br>11/3–11/28 | 2/5–3/3<br>11/28–12/22 | 3/3–3/28<br>12/22–1/15 | 3/28–4/22 |
| 10/29–11/23 | 11/23–12/17 | 12/17–1/10 | | | 1/15–2/9 |
| 8/18–9/12 | 9/12–10/8 | 10/8–11/5 | 1/10–2/3<br>11/5–12/10 | 2/3–2/27<br>12/10–1/16/90 | 2/27–3/23 |
| 10/1–10/25 | 10/25–11/18 | 11/18–12/12 | 1/16–3/3<br>12/12–1/5 | 3/3–4/6 | 4/6–5/4 |
| 11/9–12/6 | 12/6–12/31 | 12/31–1/25/92 | | 1/5–1/29 | 1/29–2/22 |
| 8/31–9/25 | 9/25–10/19 | 10/19–11/13 | 1/25–2/18<br>11/13–12/8 | 2/18–3/13<br>12/8–1/3/93 | 3/13–4/7 |
| 10/16–11/9 | 11/9–12/2 | 12/2–12/26 | 12/26–1/19 | | 1/3–2/2 |
| 8/7–9/7 | 9/7–1/7 | | | 1/19–2/12 | 2/12–3/8 |
| 9/16–10/10 | 10/10–11/13 | 1/7–2/4<br>11/3–11/27 | 2/4–3/2<br>11/27–12/21 | 3/2–3/28<br>12/21–1/15 | 3/28–4/22 |
| 10/29–11/23 | 11/23–12/17 | 12/17–1/10/97 | | | 1/15–2/9 |
| 8/17–9/12 | 9/12–10/8 | 10/8–11/5 | 1/10–2/3<br>11/5–12/12 | 2/3–2/27<br>12/12–1/9 | 2/27–3/23 |
| 9/30–10/24 | 10/24–11/17 | 11/17–12/11 | 1/9–3/4 | 3/4–4/6 | 4/6–5/3 |
| 11/9–12/5 | 12/5–12/31 | 12/31–1/24 | | 1/4–1/28 | 1/28–2/21 |
| 8/31–9/24 | 9/24–10/19 | 10/19–11/13 | 1/24–2/18<br>11/13–12/8 | 2/18–3/12<br>12/8 | 3/13–4/6 |
| 10/15–11/8 | 11/8–12/2 | 12/2–12/26 | 12/26/01–<br>1/18/02 | 12/8/00–1/3/01 | 1/3–2/2 |
| 8/7–9/7 | 9/7–1/7/03 | | 12/26/01–1/18 | 1/18–2/11 | 2/11–3/7 |
| 9/15–10/9 | 10/9–11/2 | 1/7–2/4<br>11/2–11/26 | 2/4–3/2<br>11/26–12/21 | 3/2–3/27<br>12/21–1/14/04 | 3/27–4/21 |
| 10/28–11/22 | 11/22–12/16 | 12/16–1/9/05 | | 1/1–1/14 | 1/14–2/8 |
| 8/17–9/11 | 9/11–10/8 | 10/8–11/15 | 1/9–2/2<br>11/5–12/15 | 2/2–2/26<br>12/15–1/1/06 | 2/26–3/22 |
| 9/30–10/24 | 10/24–11/17 | 11/17–12/11 | 1/1–3/5 | 3/5–4/6 | 4/6–5/3 |
| 11/8–12/4 | 12/5–12/29 | 12/30–1/24/08 | | 1/3–1/26 | 1/27–2/20 |
| 8/6–9/7 | 9/7–1/7 | | | 1/20–2/13 | 2/13–3/9 |
| 8/30–9/22 | 9/23–10/17 | 10/18–11/11 | 1/24–2/16<br>11/12–12/6 | 2/17–3/11<br>12/7–1/2/09 | 3/12–4/5 |
| 10/14–11/7 | 11/7–12/1 | 12/1–12/25 | 12/25–1/19/10 | 12/7/08–<br>1/31/09 | 1/3–2/2<br>4/11–4/24 |

# How to Use the Mars, Jupiter, and Saturn Tables

Find the year of your birth on the left side of each column. The dates when the planet entered each sign are listed on the right side of each column. (Signs are abbreviated to three letters.) Your birthday should fall on or between each date listed, and your planetary placement should correspond to the earlier sign of that period.

All planet changes are calculated for the Greenwich Mean Time zone.

## MARS SIGNS 1901–2009

| | | | | | | | |
|------|-----|----|-----|------|-----|----|-----|
| 1901 | MAR | 1  | Leo |      | OCT | 1  | Vir |
|      | MAY | 11 | Vir |      | NOV | 20 | Lib |
|      | JUL | 13 | Lib | 1905 | JAN | 13 | Scp |
|      | AUG | 31 | Scp |      | AUG | 21 | Sag |
|      | OCT | 14 | Sag |      | OCT | 8  | Cap |
|      | NOV | 24 | Cap |      | NOV | 18 | Aqu |
| 1902 | JAN | 1  | Aqu |      | DEC | 27 | Pic |
|      | FEB | 8  | Pic | 1906 | FEB | 4  | Ari |
|      | MAR | 19 | Ari |      | MAR | 17 | Tau |
|      | APR | 27 | Tau |      | APR | 28 | Gem |
|      | JUN | 7  | Gem |      | JUN | 11 | Can |
|      | JUL | 20 | Can |      | JUL | 27 | Leo |
|      | SEP | 4  | Leo |      | SEP | 12 | Vir |
|      | OCT | 23 | Vir |      | OCT | 30 | Lib |
|      | DEC | 20 | Lib |      | DEC | 17 | Scp |
| 1903 | APR | 19 | Vir | 1907 | FEB | 5  | Sag |
|      | MAY | 30 | Lib |      | APR | 1  | Cap |
|      | AUG | 6  | Scp |      | OCT | 13 | Aqu |
|      | SEP | 22 | Sag |      | NOV | 29 | Pic |
|      | NOV | 3  | Cap | 1908 | JAN | 11 | Ari |
|      | DEC | 12 | Aqu |      | FEB | 23 | Tau |
| 1904 | JAN | 19 | Pic |      | APR | 7  | Gem |
|      | FEB | 27 | Ari |      | MAY | 22 | Can |
|      | APR | 6  | Tau |      | JUL | 8  | Leo |
|      | MAY | 18 | Gem |      | AUG | 24 | Vir |
|      | JUN | 30 | Can |      | OCT | 10 | Lib |
|      | AUG | 15 | Leo |      | NOV | 25 | Scp |

| | | | | | | | |
|---|---|---|---|---|---|---|---|
| 1909 | JAN | 10 | Sag | | MAR | 9 | Pic |
| | FEB | 24 | Cap | | APR | 16 | Ari |
| | APR | 9 | Aqu | | MAY | 26 | Tau |
| | MAY | 25 | Pic | | JUL | 6 | Gem |
| | JUL | 21 | Ari | | AUG | 19 | Can |
| | SEP | 26 | Pic | | OCT | 7 | Leo |
| | NOV | 20 | Ari | 1916 | MAY | 28 | Vir |
| 1910 | JAN | 23 | Tau | | JUL | 23 | Lib |
| | MAR | 14 | Gem | | SEP | 8 | Scp |
| | MAY | 1 | Can | | OCT | 22 | Sag |
| | JUN | 19 | Leo | | DEC | 1 | Cap |
| | AUG | 6 | Vir | 1917 | JAN | 9 | Aqu |
| | SEP | 22 | Lib | | FEB | 16 | Pic |
| | NOV | 6 | Scp | | MAR | 26 | Ari |
| | DEC | 20 | Sag | | MAY | 4 | Tau |
| 1911 | JAN | 31 | Cap | | JUN | 14 | Gem |
| | MAR | 14 | Aqu | | JUL | 28 | Can |
| | APR | 23 | Pic | | SEP | 12 | Leo |
| | JUN | 2 | Ari | | NOV | 2 | Vir |
| | JUL | 15 | Tau | 1918 | JAN | 11 | Lib |
| | SEP | 5 | Gem | | FEB | 25 | Vir |
| | NOV | 30 | Tau | | JUN | 23 | Lib |
| 1912 | JAN | 30 | Gem | | AUG | 17 | Scp |
| | APR | 5 | Can | | OCT | 1 | Sag |
| | MAY | 28 | Leo | | NOV | 11 | Cap |
| | JUL | 17 | Vir | | DEC | 20 | Aqu |
| | SEP | 2 | Lib | 1919 | JAN | 27 | Pic |
| | OCT | 18 | Scp | | MAR | 6 | Ari |
| | NOV | 30 | Sag | | APR | 15 | Tau |
| 1913 | JAN | 10 | Cap | | MAY | 26 | Gem |
| | FEB | 19 | Aqu | | JUL | 8 | Can |
| | MAR | 30 | Pic | | AUG | 23 | Leo |
| | MAY | 8 | Ari | | OCT | 10 | Vir |
| | JUN | 17 | Tau | | NOV | 30 | Lib |
| | JUL | 29 | Gem | 1920 | JAN | 31 | Scp |
| | SEP | 15 | Can | | APR | 23 | Lib |
| 1914 | MAY | 1 | Leo | | JUL | 10 | Scp |
| | JUN | 26 | Vir | | SEP | 4 | Sag |
| | AUG | 14 | Lib | | OCT | 18 | Cap |
| | SEP | 29 | Scp | | NOV | 27 | Aqu |
| | NOV | 11 | Sag | 1921 | JAN | 5 | Pic |
| | DEC | 22 | Cap | | FEB | 13 | Ari |
| 1915 | JAN | 30 | Aqu | | MAR | 25 | Tau |

| | | | | | | | |
|---|---|---|---|---|---|---|---|
| | MAY | 6 | Gem | | OCT | 26 | Scp |
| | JUN | 18 | Can | | DEC | 8 | Sag |
| | AUG | 3 | Leo | 1928 | JAN | 19 | Cap |
| | SEP | 19 | Vir | | FEB | 28 | Aqu |
| | NOV | 6 | Lib | | APR | 7 | Pic |
| | DEC | 26 | Scp | | MAY | 16 | Ari |
| 1922 | FEB | 18 | Sag | | JUN | 26 | Tau |
| | SEP | 13 | Cap | | AUG | 9 | Gem |
| | OCT | 30 | Aqu | | OCT | 3 | Can |
| | DEC | 11 | Pic | | DEC | 20 | Gem |
| 1923 | JAN | 21 | Ari | 1929 | MAR | 10 | Can |
| | MAR | 4 | Tau | | MAY | 13 | Leo |
| | APR | 16 | Gem | | JUL | 4 | Vir |
| | MAY | 30 | Can | | AUG | 21 | Lib |
| | JUL | 16 | Leo | | OCT | 6 | Scp |
| | SEP | 1 | Vir | | NOV | 18 | Sag |
| | OCT | 18 | Lib | | DEC | 29 | Cap |
| | DEC | 4 | Scp | 1930 | FEB | 6 | Aqu |
| 1924 | JAN | 19 | Sag | | MAR | 17 | Pic |
| | MAR | 6 | Cap | | APR | 24 | Ari |
| | APR | 24 | Aqu | | JUN | 3 | Tau |
| | JUN | 24 | Pic | | JUL | 14 | Gem |
| | AUG | 24 | Aqu | | AUG | 28 | Can |
| | OCT | 19 | Pic | | OCT | 20 | Leo |
| | DEC | 19 | Ari | 1931 | FEB | 16 | Can |
| 1925 | FEB | 5 | Tau | | MAR | 30 | Leo |
| | MAR | 24 | Gem | | JUN | 10 | Vir |
| | MAY | 9 | Can | | AUG | 1 | Lib |
| | JUN | 26 | Leo | | SEP | 17 | Scp |
| | AUG | 12 | Vir | | OCT | 30 | Sag |
| | SEP | 28 | Lib | | DEC | 10 | Cap |
| | NOV | 13 | Scp | 1932 | JAN | 18 | Aqu |
| | DEC | 28 | Sag | | FEB | 25 | Pic |
| 1926 | FEB | 9 | Cap | | APR | 3 | Ari |
| | MAR | 23 | Aqu | | MAY | 12 | Tau |
| | MAY | 3 | Pic | | JUN | 22 | Gem |
| | JUN | 15 | Ari | | AUG | 4 | Can |
| | AUG | 1 | Tau | | SEP | 20 | Leo |
| 1927 | FEB | 22 | Gem | | NOV | 13 | Vir |
| | APR | 17 | Can | 1933 | JUL | 6 | Lib |
| | JUN | 6 | Leo | | AUG | 26 | Scp |
| | JUL | 25 | Vir | | OCT | 9 | Sag |
| | SEP | 10 | Lib | | NOV | 19 | Cap |

| | | | | | | | |
|------|-----|----|-----|------|-----|----|-----|
| | DEC | 28 | Aqu | | FEB | 17 | Tau |
| 1934 | FEB | 4 | Pic | | APR | 1 | Gem |
| | MAR | 14 | Ari | | MAY | 17 | Can |
| | APR | 22 | Tau | | JUL | 3 | Leo |
| | JUN | 2 | Gem | | AUG | 19 | Vir |
| | JUL | 15 | Can | | OCT | 5 | Lib |
| | AUG | 30 | Leo | | NOV | 20 | Scp |
| | OCT | 18 | Vir | 1941 | JAN | 4 | Sag |
| | DEC | 11 | Lib | | FEB | 17 | Cap |
| 1935 | JUL | 29 | Scp | | APR | 2 | Aqu |
| | SEP | 16 | Sag | | MAY | 16 | Pic |
| | OCT | 28 | Cap | | JUL | 2 | Ari |
| | DEC | 7 | Aqu | 1942 | JAN | 11 | Tau |
| 1936 | JAN | 14 | Pic | | MAR | 7 | Gem |
| | FEB | 22 | Ari | | APR | 26 | Can |
| | APR | 1 | Tau | | JUN | 14 | Leo |
| | MAY | 13 | Gem | | AUG | 1 | Vir |
| | JUN | 25 | Can | | SEP | 17 | Lib |
| | AUG | 10 | Leo | | NOV | 1 | Scp |
| | SEP | 26 | Vir | | DEC | 15 | Sag |
| | NOV | 14 | Lib | 1943 | JAN | 26 | Cap |
| 1937 | JAN | 5 | Scp | | MAR | 8 | Aqu |
| | MAR | 13 | Sag | | APR | 17 | Pic |
| | MAY | 14 | Scp | | MAY | 27 | Ari |
| | AUG | 8 | Sag | | JUL | 7 | Tau |
| | SEP | 30 | Cap | | AUG | 23 | Gem |
| | NOV | 11 | Aqu | 1944 | MAR | 28 | Can |
| | DEC | 21 | Pic | | MAY | 22 | Leo |
| 1938 | JAN | 30 | Ari | | JUL | 12 | Vir |
| | MAR | 12 | Tau | | AUG | 29 | Lib |
| | APR | 23 | Gem | | OCT | 13 | Scp |
| | JUN | 7 | Can | | NOV | 25 | Sag |
| | JUL | 22 | Leo | 1945 | JAN | 5 | Cap |
| | SEP | 7 | Vir | | FEB | 14 | Aqu |
| | OCT | 25 | Lib | | MAR | 25 | Pic |
| | DEC | 11 | Scp | | MAY | 2 | Ari |
| 1939 | JAN | 29 | Sag | | JUN | 11 | Tau |
| | MAR | 21 | Cap | | JUL | 23 | Gem |
| | MAY | 25 | Aqu | | SEP | 7 | Can |
| | JUL | 21 | Cap | | NOV | 11 | Leo |
| | SEP | 24 | Aqu | | DEC | 26 | Can |
| | NOV | 19 | Pic | 1946 | APR | 22 | Leo |
| 1940 | JAN | 4 | Ari | | JUN | 20 | Vir |

|      |     |    |     |      |     |    |     |
|------|-----|----|-----|------|-----|----|-----|
|      | AUG | 9  | Lib |      | OCT | 12 | Cap |
|      | SEP | 24 | Scp |      | NOV | 21 | Aqu |
|      | NOV | 6  | Sag |      | DEC | 30 | Pic |
|      | DEC | 17 | Cap | 1953 | FEB | 8  | Ari |
| 1947 | JAN | 25 | Aqu |      | MAR | 20 | Tau |
|      | MAR | 4  | Pic |      | MAY | 1  | Gem |
|      | APR | 11 | Ari |      | JUN | 14 | Can |
|      | MAY | 21 | Tau |      | JUL | 29 | Leo |
|      | JUL | 1  | Gem |      | SEP | 14 | Vir |
|      | AUG | 13 | Can |      | NOV | 1  | Lib |
|      | OCT | 1  | Leo |      | DEC | 20 | Scp |
|      | DEC | 1  | Vir | 1954 | FEB | 9  | Sag |
| 1948 | FEB | 12 | Leo |      | APR | 12 | Cap |
|      | MAY | 18 | Vir |      | JUL | 3  | Sag |
|      | JUL | 17 | Lib |      | AUG | 24 | Cap |
|      | SEP | 3  | Scp |      | OCT | 21 | Aqu |
|      | OCT | 17 | Sag |      | DEC | 4  | Pic |
|      | NOV | 26 | Cap | 1955 | JAN | 15 | Ari |
| 1949 | JAN | 4  | Aqu |      | FEB | 26 | Tau |
|      | FEB | 11 | Pic |      | APR | 10 | Gem |
|      | MAR | 21 | Ari |      | MAY | 26 | Can |
|      | APR | 30 | Tau |      | JUL | 11 | Leo |
|      | JUN | 10 | Gem |      | AUG | 27 | Vir |
|      | JUL | 23 | Can |      | OCT | 13 | Lib |
|      | SEP | 7  | Leo |      | NOV | 29 | Scp |
|      | OCT | 27 | Vir | 1956 | JAN | 14 | Sag |
|      | DEC | 26 | Lib |      | FEB | 28 | Cap |
| 1950 | MAR | 28 | Vir |      | APR | 14 | Aqu |
|      | JUN | 11 | Lib |      | JUN | 3  | Pic |
|      | AUG | 10 | Scp |      | DEC | 6  | Ari |
|      | SEP | 25 | Sag | 1957 | JAN | 28 | Tau |
|      | NOV | 6  | Cap |      | MAR | 17 | Gem |
|      | DEC | 15 | Aqu |      | MAY | 4  | Can |
| 1951 | JAN | 22 | Pic |      | JUN | 21 | Leo |
|      | MAR | 1  | Ari |      | AUG | 8  | Vir |
|      | APR | 10 | Tau |      | SEP | 24 | Lib |
|      | MAY | 21 | Gem |      | NOV | 8  | Scp |
|      | JUL | 3  | Can |      | DEC | 23 | Sag |
|      | AUG | 18 | Leo | 1958 | FEB | 3  | Cap |
|      | OCT | 5  | Vir |      | MAR | 17 | Aqu |
|      | NOV | 24 | Lib |      | APR | 27 | Pic |
| 1952 | JAN | 20 | Scp |      | JUN | 7  | Ari |
|      | AUG | 27 | Sag |      | JUL | 21 | Tau |

|      | SEP | 21 | Gem |      | NOV | 6  | Vir |
|------|-----|----|-----|------|-----|----|-----|
|      | OCT | 29 | Tau | 1965 | JUN | 29 | Lib |
| 1959 | FEB | 10 | Gem |      | AUG | 20 | Scp |
|      | APR | 10 | Can |      | OCT | 4  | Sag |
|      | JUN | 1  | Leo |      | NOV | 14 | Cap |
|      | JUL | 20 | Vir |      | DEC | 23 | Aqu |
|      | SEP | 5  | Lib | 1966 | JAN | 30 | Pic |
|      | OCT | 21 | Scp |      | MAR | 9  | Ari |
|      | DEC | 3  | Sag |      | APR | 17 | Tau |
| 1960 | JAN | 14 | Cap |      | MAY | 28 | Gem |
|      | FEB | 23 | Aqu |      | JUL | 11 | Can |
|      | APR | 2  | Pic |      | AUG | 25 | Leo |
|      | MAY | 11 | Ari |      | OCT | 12 | Vir |
|      | JUN | 20 | Tau |      | DEC | 4  | Lib |
|      | AUG | 2  | Gem | 1967 | FEB | 12 | Scp |
|      | SEP | 21 | Can |      | MAR | 31 | Lib |
| 1961 | FEB | 5  | Gem |      | JUL | 19 | Scp |
|      | FEB | 7  | Can |      | SEP | 10 | Sag |
|      | MAY | 6  | Leo |      | OCT | 23 | Cap |
|      | JUN | 28 | Vir |      | DEC | 1  | Aqu |
|      | AUG | 17 | Lib | 1968 | JAN | 9  | Pic |
|      | OCT | 1  | Scp |      | FEB | 17 | Ari |
|      | NOV | 13 | Sag |      | MAR | 27 | Tau |
|      | DEC | 24 | Cap |      | MAY | 8  | Gem |
| 1962 | FEB | 1  | Aqu |      | JUN | 21 | Can |
|      | MAR | 12 | Pic |      | AUG | 5  | Leo |
|      | APR | 19 | Ari |      | SEP | 21 | Vir |
|      | MAY | 28 | Tau |      | NOV | 9  | Lib |
|      | JUL | 9  | Gem |      | DEC | 29 | Scp |
|      | AUG | 22 | Can | 1969 | FEB | 25 | Sag |
|      | OCT | 11 | Leo |      | SEP | 21 | Cap |
| 1963 | JUN | 3  | Vir |      | NOV | 4  | Aqu |
|      | JUL | 27 | Lib |      | DEC | 15 | Pic |
|      | SEP | 12 | Scp | 1970 | JAN | 24 | Ari |
|      | OCT | 25 | Sag |      | MAR | 7  | Tau |
|      | DEC | 5  | Cap |      | APR | 18 | Gem |
| 1964 | JAN | 13 | Aqu |      | JUN | 2  | Can |
|      | FEB | 20 | Pic |      | JUL | 18 | Leo |
|      | MAR | 29 | Ari |      | SEP | 3  | Vir |
|      | MAY | 7  | Tau |      | OCT | 20 | Lib |
|      | JUN | 17 | Gem |      | DEC | 6  | Scp |
|      | JUL | 30 | Can | 1971 | JAN | 23 | Sag |
|      | SEP | 15 | Leo |      | MAR | 12 | Cap |

| Year | Month | Day | Sign | | Year | Month | Day | Sign |
|---|---|---|---|---|---|---|---|---|
| | MAY | 3 | Aqu | | | JUN | 6 | Tau |
| | NOV | 6 | Pic | | | JUL | 17 | Gem |
| | DEC | 26 | Ari | | | SEP | 1 | Can |
| 1972 | FEB | 10 | Tau | | | OCT | 26 | Leo |
| | MAR | 27 | Gem | | 1978 | JAN | 26 | Can |
| | MAY | 12 | Can | | | APR | 10 | Leo |
| | JUN | 28 | Leo | | | JUN | 14 | Vir |
| | AUG | 15 | Vir | | | AUG | 4 | Lib |
| | SEP | 30 | Lib | | | SEP | 19 | Scp |
| | NOV | 15 | Scp | | | NOV | 2 | Sag |
| | DEC | 30 | Sag | | | DEC | 12 | Cap |
| 1973 | FEB | 12 | Cap | | 1979 | JAN | 20 | Aqu |
| | MAR | 26 | Aqu | | | FEB | 27 | Pic |
| | MAY | 8 | Pic | | | APR | 7 | Ari |
| | JUN | 20 | Ari | | | MAY | 16 | Tau |
| | AUG | 12 | Tau | | | JUN | 26 | Gem |
| | OCT | 29 | Ari | | | AUG | 8 | Can |
| | DEC | 24 | Tau | | | SEP | 24 | Leo |
| 1974 | FEB | 27 | Gem | | | NOV | 19 | Vir |
| | APR | 20 | Can | | 1980 | MAR | 11 | Leo |
| | JUN | 9 | Leo | | | MAY | 4 | Vir |
| | JUL | 27 | Vir | | | JUL | 10 | Lib |
| | SEP | 12 | Lib | | | AUG | 29 | Scp |
| | OCT | 28 | Scp | | | OCT | 12 | Sag |
| | DEC | 10 | Sag | | | NOV | 22 | Cap |
| 1975 | JAN | 21 | Cap | | | DEC | 30 | Aqu |
| | MAR | 3 | Aqu | | 1981 | FEB | 6 | Pic |
| | APR | 11 | Pic | | | MAR | 17 | Ari |
| | MAY | 21 | Ari | | | APR | 25 | Tau |
| | JUL | 1 | Tau | | | JUN | 5 | Gem |
| | AUG | 14 | Gem | | | JUL | 18 | Can |
| | OCT | 17 | Can | | | SEP | 2 | Leo |
| | NOV | 25 | Gem | | | OCT | 21 | Vir |
| 1976 | MAR | 18 | Can | | | DEC | 16 | Lib |
| | MAY | 16 | Leo | | 1982 | AUG | 3 | Scp |
| | JUL | 6 | Vir | | | SEP | 20 | Sag |
| | AUG | 24 | Lib | | | OCT | 31 | Cap |
| | OCT | 8 | Scp | | | DEC | 10 | Aqu |
| | NOV | 20 | Sag | | 1983 | JAN | 17 | Pic |
| 1977 | JAN | 1 | Cap | | | FEB | 25 | Ari |
| | FEB | 9 | Aqu | | | APR | 5 | Tau |
| | MAR | 20 | Pic | | | MAY | 16 | Gem |
| | APR | 27 | Ari | | | JUN | 29 | Can |

| | | | | | | |
|---|---|---|---|---|---|---|
| | AUG | 13 | Leo | 1990 | JAN | 29 | Cap |
| | SEP | 30 | Vir | | MAR | 11 | Aqu |
| | NOV | 18 | Lib | | APR | 20 | Pic |
| 1984 | JAN | 11 | Scp | | MAY | 31 | Ari |
| | AUG | 17 | Sag | | JUL | 12 | Tau |
| | OCT | 5 | Cap | | AUG | 31 | Gem |
| | NOV | 15 | Aqu | | DEC | 14 | Tau |
| | DEC | 25 | Pic | 1991 | JAN | 21 | Gem |
| 1985 | FEB | 2 | Ari | | APR | 3 | Can |
| | MAR | 15 | Tau | | MAY | 26 | Leo |
| | APR | 26 | Gem | | JUL | 15 | Vir |
| | JUN | 9 | Can | | SEP | 1 | Lib |
| | JUL | 25 | Leo | | OCT | 16 | Scp |
| | SEP | 10 | Vir | | NOV | 29 | Sag |
| | OCT | 27 | Lib | 1992 | JAN | 9 | Cap |
| | DEC | 14 | Scp | | FEB | 18 | Aqu |
| 1986 | FEB | 2 | Sag | | MAR | 28 | Pic |
| | MAR | 28 | Cap | | MAY | 5 | Ari |
| | OCT | 9 | Aqu | | JUN | 14 | Tau |
| | NOV | 26 | Pic | | JUL | 26 | Gem |
| 1987 | JAN | 8 | Ari | | SEP | 12 | Can |
| | FEB | 20 | Tau | 1993 | APR | 27 | Leo |
| | APR | 5 | Gem | | JUN | 23 | Vir |
| | MAY | 21 | Can | | AUG | 12 | Lib |
| | JUL | 6 | Leo | | SEP | 27 | Scp |
| | AUG | 22 | Vir | | NOV | 9 | Sag |
| | OCT | 8 | Lib | | DEC | 20 | Cap |
| | NOV | 24 | Scp | 1994 | JAN | 28 | Aqu |
| 1988 | JAN | 8 | Sag | | MAR | 7 | Pic |
| | FEB | 22 | Cap | | APR | 14 | Ari |
| | APR | 6 | Aqu | | MAY | 23 | Tau |
| | MAY | 22 | Pic | | JUL | 3 | Gem |
| | JUL | 13 | Ari | | AUG | 16 | Can |
| | OCT | 23 | Pic | | OCT | 4 | Leo |
| | NOV | 1 | Ari | | DEC | 12 | Vir |
| 1989 | JAN | 19 | Tau | 1995 | JAN | 22 | Leo |
| | MAR | 11 | Gem | | MAY | 25 | Vir |
| | APR | 29 | Can | | JUL | 21 | Lib |
| | JUN | 16 | Leo | | SEP | 7 | Scp |
| | AUG | 3 | Vir | | OCT | 20 | Sag |
| | SEP | 19 | Lib | | NOV | 30 | Cap |
| | NOV | 4 | Scp | 1996 | JAN | 8 | Aqu |
| | DEC | 18 | Sag | | FEB | 15 | Pic |

| | | | |
|---|---|---|---|
| | MAR | 24 | Ari |
| | MAY | 2 | Tau |
| | JUN | 12 | Gem |
| | JUL | 25 | Can |
| | SEP | 9 | Leo |
| | OCT | 30 | Vir |
| 1997 | JAN | 3 | Lib |
| | MAR | 8 | Vir |
| | JUN | 19 | Lib |
| | AUG | 14 | Scp |
| | SEP | 28 | Sag |
| | NOV | 9 | Cap |
| | DEC | 18 | Aqu |
| 1998 | JAN | 25 | Pic |
| | MAR | 4 | Ari |
| | APR | 13 | Tau |
| | MAY | 24 | Gem |
| | JUL | 6 | Can |
| | AUG | 20 | Leo |
| | OCT | 7 | Vir |
| | NOV | 27 | Lib |
| 1999 | JAN | 26 | Scp |
| | MAY | 5 | Lib |
| | JUL | 5 | Scp |
| | SEP | 2 | Sag |
| | OCT | 17 | Cap |
| | NOV | 26 | Aqu |
| 2000 | JAN | 4 | Pic |
| | FEB | 12 | Ari |
| | MAR | 23 | Tau |
| | MAY | 3 | Gem |
| | JUN | 16 | Can |
| | AUG | 1 | Leo |
| | SEP | 17 | Vir |
| | NOV | 4 | Lib |
| | DEC | 23 | Scp |
| 2001 | FEB | 14 | Sag |
| | SEP | 8 | Cap |
| | OCT | 27 | Aqu |
| | DEC | 8 | Pic |
| 2002 | JAN | 18 | Ari |

| | | | |
|---|---|---|---|
| | MAR | 1 | Tau |
| | APR | 13 | Gem |
| | MAY | 28 | Can |
| | JUL | 13 | Leo |
| | AUG | 29 | Vir |
| | OCT | 15 | Lib |
| | DEC | 1 | Scp |
| 2003 | JAN | 17 | Sag |
| | MAR | 4 | Cap |
| | APR | 21 | Aqu |
| | JUN | 17 | Pic |
| | DEC | 16 | Ari |
| 2004 | FEB | 3 | Tau |
| | MAR | 21 | Gem |
| | MAY | 7 | Can |
| | JUN | 23 | Leo |
| | AUG | 10 | Vir |
| | SEP | 26 | Lib |
| | NOV | 11 | Sep |
| | DEC | 25 | Sag |
| 2005 | FEB | 6 | Cap |
| | MAR | 20 | Aqu |
| | MAY | 1 | Pic |
| | JUN | 12 | Ari |
| | JUL | 28 | Tau |
| 2006 | FEB | 17 | Gem |
| | APR | 14 | Can |
| | JUN | 3 | Leo |
| | JUL | 22 | Vir |
| | SEP | 8 | Lib |
| | OCT | 23 | Scp |
| | DEC | 6 | Sag |
| 2007 | JAN | 16 | Cap |
| | FEB | 25 | Aqu |
| | APR | 6 | Pic |
| | MAY | 15 | Ari |
| | JUNE | 24 | Tau |
| | AUG | 7 | Gem |
| | SEP | 28 | Can |
| | DEC | 31 | Gem* |

*Repeat means planet is retrograde.

| 2008 | MAR | 4 | Can | | 2009 | FEB | 4 | Aqu |
|------|-----|-----|-----|---|------|-----|-----|-----|
|      | MAY | 9 | Leo | |      | MAR | 14 | Pic |
|      | JUL | 1 | Vir | |      | APR | 22 | Ari |
|      | AUG | 19 | Lib | |      | MAY | 31 | Tau |
|      | OCT | 3 | Scp | |      | JUL | 11 | Gem |
|      | NOV | 16 | Sag | |      | AUG | 25 | Can |
|      | DEC | 27 | Cap | |      | OCT | 16 | Leo |

## JUPITER SIGNS 1901–2009

| 1901 | JAN | 19 | Cap | | 1924 | DEC | 18 | Cap |
|------|-----|-----|-----|---|------|-----|-----|-----|
| 1902 | FEB | 6 | Aqu | | 1926 | JAN | 6 | Aqu |
| 1903 | FEB | 20 | Pic | | 1927 | JAN | 18 | Pic |
| 1904 | MAR | 1 | Ari | |      | JUN | 6 | Ari |
|      | AUG | 8 | Tau | |      | SEP | 11 | Pic |
|      | AUG | 31 | Ari | | 1928 | JAN | 23 | Ari |
| 1905 | MAR | 7 | Tau | |      | JUN | 4 | Tau |
|      | JUL | 21 | Gem | | 1929 | JUN | 12 | Gem |
|      | DEC | 4 | Tau | | 1930 | JUN | 26 | Can |
| 1906 | MAR | 9 | Gem | | 1931 | JUL | 17 | Leo |
|      | JUL | 30 | Can | | 1932 | AUG | 11 | Vir |
| 1907 | AUG | 18 | Leo | | 1933 | SEP | 10 | Lib |
| 1908 | SEP | 12 | Vir | | 1934 | OCT | 11 | Scp |
| 1909 | OCT | 11 | Lib | | 1935 | NOV | 9 | Sag |
| 1910 | NOV | 11 | Scp | | 1936 | DEC | 2 | Cap |
| 1911 | DEC | 10 | Sag | | 1937 | DEC | 20 | Aqu |
| 1913 | JAN | 2 | Cap | | 1938 | MAY | 14 | Pic |
| 1914 | JAN | 21 | Aqu | |      | JUL | 30 | Aqu |
| 1915 | FEB | 4 | Pic | |      | DEC | 29 | Pic |
| 1916 | FEB | 12 | Ari | | 1939 | MAY | 11 | Ari |
|      | JUN | 26 | Tau | |      | OCT | 30 | Pic |
|      | OCT | 26 | Ari | |      | DEC | 20 | Ari |
| 1917 | FEB | 12 | Tau | | 1940 | MAY | 16 | Tau |
|      | JUN | 29 | Gem | | 1941 | MAY | 26 | Gem |
| 1918 | JUL | 13 | Can | | 1942 | JUN | 10 | Can |
| 1919 | AUG | 2 | Leo | | 1943 | JUN | 30 | Leo |
| 1920 | AUG | 27 | Vir | | 1944 | JUL | 26 | Vir |
| 1921 | SEP | 25 | Lib | | 1945 | AUG | 25 | Lib |
| 1922 | OCT | 26 | Scp | | 1946 | SEP | 25 | Scp |
| 1923 | NOV | 24 | Sag | | 1947 | OCT | 24 | Sag |

| | | | | | | | |
|---|---|---|---|---|---|---|---|
| 1948 | NOV | 15 | Cap | | OCT | 19 | Vir |
| 1949 | APR | 12 | Aqu | 1968 | FEB | 27 | Leo |
| | JUN | 27 | Cap | | JUN | 15 | Vir |
| | NOV | 30 | Aqu | | NOV | 15 | Lib |
| 1950 | APR | 15 | Pic | 1969 | MAR | 30 | Vir |
| | SEP | 15 | Aqu | | JUL | 15 | Lib |
| | DEC | 1 | Pic | | DEC | 16 | Scp |
| 1951 | APR | 21 | Ari | 1970 | APR | 30 | Lib |
| 1952 | APR | 28 | Tau | | AUG | 15 | Scp |
| 1953 | MAY | 9 | Gem | 1971 | JAN | 14 | Sag |
| 1954 | MAY | 24 | Can | | JUN | 5 | Scp |
| 1955 | JUN | 13 | Leo | | SEP | 11 | Sag |
| | NOV | 17 | Vir | 1972 | FEB | 6 | Cap |
| 1956 | JAN | 18 | Leo | | JUL | 24 | Sag |
| | JUL | 7 | Vir | | SEP | 25 | Cap |
| | DEC | 13 | Lib | 1973 | FEB | 23 | Aqu |
| 1957 | FEB | 19 | Vir | 1974 | MAR | 8 | Pic |
| | AUG | 7 | Lib | 1975 | MAR | 18 | Ari |
| 1958 | JAN | 13 | Scp | 1976 | MAR | 26 | Tau |
| | MAR | 20 | Lib | | AUG | 23 | Gem |
| | SEP | 7 | Scp | | OCT | 16 | Tau |
| 1959 | FEB | 10 | Sag | 1977 | APR | 3 | Gem |
| | APR | 24 | Scp | | AUG | 20 | Can |
| | OCT | 5 | Sag | | DEC | 30 | Gem |
| 1960 | MAR | 1 | Cap | 1978 | APR | 12 | Can |
| | JUN | 10 | Sag | | SEP | 5 | Leo |
| | OCT | 26 | Cap | 1979 | FEB | 28 | Can |
| 1961 | MAR | 15 | Aqu | | APR | 20 | Leo |
| | AUG | 12 | Cap | | SEP | 29 | Vir |
| | NOV | 4 | Aqu | 1980 | OCT | 27 | Lib |
| 1962 | MAR | 25 | Pic | 1981 | NOV | 27 | Scp |
| 1963 | APR | 4 | Ari | 1982 | DEC | 26 | Sag |
| 1964 | APR | 12 | Tau | 1984 | JAN | 19 | Cap |
| 1965 | APR | 22 | Gem | 1985 | FEB | 6 | Aqu |
| | SEP | 21 | Can | 1986 | FEB | 20 | Pic |
| | NOV | 17 | Gem | 1987 | MAR | 2 | Ari |
| 1966 | MAY | 5 | Can | 1988 | MAR | 8 | Tau |
| | SEP | 27 | Leo | | JUL | 22 | Gem |
| 1967 | JAN | 16 | Can | | NOV | 30 | Tau |
| | MAY | 23 | Leo | 1989 | MAR | 11 | Gem |
| | | | | | JUL | 30 | Can |

| 1990 | AUG | 18 | Leo |  |  | 2000 | FEB | 14 | Tau |
| 1991 | SEP | 12 | Vir |  |  |  | JUN | 30 | Gem |
| 1992 | OCT | 10 | Lib |  |  | 2001 | JUL | 14 | Can |
| 1993 | NOV | 10 | Scp |  |  | 2002 | AUG | 1 | Leo |
| 1994 | DEC | 9 | Sag |  |  | 2003 | AUG | 27 | Vir |
| 1996 | JAN | 3 | Cap |  |  | 2004 | SEP | 24 | Lib |
| 1997 | JAN | 21 | Aqu |  |  | 2005 | OCT | 26 | Scp |
| 1998 | FEB | 4 | Pic |  |  | 2006 | NOV | 24 | Sag |
| 1999 | FEB | 13 | Ari |  |  | 2007 | DEC | 17 | Cap |
|  | JUN | 28 | Tau |  |  | 2009 | JAN | 5 | Aqu |
|  | OCT | 23 | Ari |  |  |  |  |  |  |

## SATURN SIGNS 1903–2009

| 1903 | JAN | 19 | Aqu |  |  |  | AUG | 13 | Cap |
| 1905 | APR | 13 | Pic |  |  |  | NOV | 20 | Aqu |
|  | AUG | 17 | Aqu |  |  | 1935 | FEB | 14 | Pic |
| 1906 | JAN | 8 | Pic |  |  | 1937 | APR | 25 | Ari |
| 1908 | MAR | 19 | Ari |  |  |  | OCT | 18 | Pic |
| 1910 | MAY | 17 | Tau |  |  | 1938 | JAN | 14 | Ari |
|  | DEC | 14 | Ari |  |  | 1939 | JUL | 6 | Tau |
| 1911 | JAN | 20 | Tau |  |  |  | SEP | 22 | Ari |
| 1912 | JUL | 7 | Gem |  |  | 1940 | MAR | 20 | Tau |
|  | NOV | 30 | Tau |  |  | 1942 | MAY | 8 | Gem |
| 1913 | MAR | 26 | Gem |  |  | 1944 | JUN | 20 | Can |
| 1914 | AUG | 24 | Can |  |  | 1946 | AUG | 2 | Leo |
|  | DEC | 7 | Gem |  |  | 1948 | SEP | 19 | Vir |
| 1915 | MAY | 11 | Can |  |  | 1949 | APR | 3 | Leo |
| 1916 | OCT | 17 | Leo |  |  |  | MAY | 29 | Vir |
|  | DEC | 7 | Can |  |  | 1950 | NOV | 20 | Lib |
| 1917 | JUN | 24 | Leo |  |  | 1951 | MAR | 7 | Vir |
| 1919 | AUG | 12 | Vir |  |  |  | AUG | 13 | Lib |
| 1921 | OCT | 7 | Lib |  |  | 1953 | OCT | 22 | Scp |
| 1923 | DEC | 20 | Scp |  |  | 1956 | JAN | 12 | Sag |
| 1924 | APR | 6 | Lib |  |  |  | MAY | 14 | Scp |
|  | SEP | 13 | Scp |  |  |  | OCT | 10 | Sag |
| 1926 | DEC | 2 | Sag |  |  | 1959 | JAN | 5 | Cap |
| 1929 | MAR | 15 | Cap |  |  | 1962 | JAN | 3 | Aqu |
|  | MAY | 5 | Sag |  |  | 1964 | MAR | 24 | Pic |
|  | NOV | 30 | Cap |  |  |  | SEP | 16 | Aqu |
| 1932 | FEB | 24 | Aqu |  |  |  | DEC | 16 | Pic |

| | | | | | | | | |
|------|-----|----|-----|------|-----|----|-----|
| 1967 | MAR | 3  | Ari | 1988 | FEB | 13 | Cap |
| 1969 | APR | 29 | Tau |      | JUN | 10 | Sag |
| 1971 | JUN | 18 | Gem |      | NOV | 12 | Cap |
| 1972 | JAN | 10 | Tau | 1991 | FEB | 6  | Aqu |
|      | FEB | 21 | Gem | 1993 | MAY | 21 | Pic |
| 1973 | AUG | 1  | Can |      | JUN | 30 | Aqu |
| 1974 | JAN | 7  | Gem | 1994 | JAN | 28 | Pic |
|      | APR | 18 | Can | 1996 | APR | 7  | Ari |
| 1975 | SEP | 17 | Leo | 1998 | JUN | 9  | Tau |
| 1976 | JAN | 14 | Can |      | OCT | 25 | Ari |
|      | JUN | 5  | Leo | 1999 | MAR | 1  | Tau |
| 1977 | NOV | 17 | Vir | 2000 | AUG | 10 | Gem |
| 1978 | JAN | 5  | Leo |      | OCT | 16 | Tau |
|      | JUL | 26 | Vir | 2001 | APR | 21 | Gem |
| 1980 | SEP | 21 | Lib | 2003 | JUN | 3  | Can |
| 1982 | NOV | 29 | Scp | 2005 | JUL | 16 | Leo |
| 1983 | MAY | 6  | Lib | 2007 | SEP | 2  | Vir |
|      | AUG | 24 | Scp | 2009 | OCT | 29 | Lib |
| 1985 | NOV | 17 | Sag |      |     |    |     |

# CHAPTER 4

# Moods and the Moon

How many love songs have been written about the moon? We'll bet the moon easily wins over the sun for mentions in romantic song and poetry, for dreamy representations in painting and photography. The most fascinating aspect of the moon is its connection with our emotions, its ability to evoke strong feelings by the mere sight of its glowing light in the night sky. With the moon, we're moody, romantic, caring, or concerned with our inner self. On the other hand, we associate the sun with radiance, confidence, or an outgoing emotional atmosphere.

Astrologers often refer to the sun and moon as the lights. This is an appropriate description, since the sun and moon are not really planets, but a star and a satellite. But it is also true that these two bodies shed the most light on a horoscope reading.

The sign the moon was transiting at the time of your birth reveals secrets like what you really care about and what makes you feel comfortable and secure. It represents the receptive, reflective, female, and nurturing self. It also reflects who nurtured you, the mother or mother figure in your chart. In a man's chart, the moon position describes his receptive, emotional, and yin side, as well as the woman in his life who will have the deepest effect, usually his mother. (Venus reveals the kind of woman who will attract him physically.)

The moon is more at home in some signs than in others. It rules maternal Cancer and is exalted in Taurus—both comforting, home-loving signs where the natural emotional energies of the moon are easily and productively expressed. But when the moon is in the opposite signs—Capricorn and Scorpio—it leaves the comfortable nest and deals with emotional issues of power and achievement in the outside world. If you were born with the moon in one of these signs, you may find your emotional role in life more challenging.

To determine your moon sign, it is worthwhile to have an accurate horoscope cast, either by an astrologer, a computer program, or one of the online astrology sites that offer free charts. Since detailed moon tables are too extensive for this book, check through the following listing to find the moon sign that feels most familiar.

## Moon in Aries

This placement makes you both independent and ardent. You are an idealist, and you tend to fall in and out of love easily. You love a challenge but could cool once your quarry is captured. Your emotional reactions are fast and fiery, quickly expressed and quickly forgotten. You may not think before expressing your feelings. It's not easy to hide how you feel. Channeling all your emotional energy could be one of your big challenges.

## Moon in Taurus

You are a sentimental soul who is very fond of the good life and gravitates toward solid, secure relationships. You like displays of affection and creature comforts—all the tangible trappings of a cozy, safe, calm atmosphere. You are sensual and steady emotionally, but very stubborn, possessive, and determined. You can't be pushed and tend to dislike changes. You should make an effort to broaden your horizons and to take a risk sometimes. You may become very attached to your home turf, your garden, and your possessions. You may also be a collector of objects that are meaningful to you.

## Moon in Gemini

You crave mental stimulation and variety in life, which you usually get via a varied social life, the excitement of flirtation, or multiple professional involvements. You may marry more than once and have a rather chaotic emotional life due to your difficulty with commitment and settling down, as well as your need to be constantly on the go. (Be sure to find a partner who is as outgoing as you are.) You will have to learn at some point to focus your energies because you tend to be somewhat fragmented—to do two things at once, to have two homes, or even to have two lovers. If you can find a creative way to express your many-faceted nature, you'll be ahead of the game.

## Moon in Cancer

This is the most powerful lunar position, which is sure to make a deep imprint on your character. Your needs are very much associated with your reaction to the needs of others. You are very sensitive, caring, and self-protective, though some of you may mask this with a hard shell, like the moon-sensitive crab. This placement also gives an excellent memory, keen intuition, and an uncanny ability to perceive the needs of others. All of the lunar phases will affect you, especially full moons and eclipses, so you would do well to mark them on your calendar. Because you're happiest at home, you may work at home or turn your office into a second home, where you can nurture and comfort people. (You may tend to mother the world.) With natural psychic, intuitive ability, you might be drawn to occult work in some way. Or you may get professionally involved with providing food and shelter to others.

## Moon in Leo

This warm, passionate moon takes everything to heart. You are attracted to all that is noble, generous, and aristocratic in life (and you may be a bit of a snob). You have an innate ability to take command emotionally, but you do need strong support, loyalty, and loud applause from those you love. You are possessive of your loved ones and your turf and will roar if anyone threatens to take over territory.

## Moon in Virgo

You are rather cool until you decide if others measure up. But once someone or something meets your high standards, you hold up your end of the arrangement perfectly. You may, in fact, drive yourself too hard to attain some notion of perfection. Try to be a bit easier on yourself and others. Don't always act the censor! You love to be the teacher; you are drawn to situations where you can change others for the better, but sometimes you must learn to accept others for what they are—enjoy what you have!

## Moon in Libra

Like other air-sign moons, you think before you feel. Therefore, you may not immediately recognize the emotional needs of others. However, you are relationship-oriented and may find it difficult to be alone or to do things alone. After you have learned emotional balance by leaning on yourself first, you can have excellent partnerships. It is best for you to avoid extremes, which set your scales swinging and can make your love life precarious. You thrive in a rather conservative, traditional, romantic relationship, where you receive attention and flattery—but not possessiveness—from your partner. You'll be your most charming in an elegant, harmonious atmosphere.

## Moon in Scorpio

This is a moon that enjoys and responds to intense, passionate feelings. You may go to extremes and have a very dramatic emotional life, full of ardor, suspicion, jealousy, and obsession. It would be much healthier to channel your need for power and control into meaningful work. This is a good position for anyone in the fields of medicine, police work, research, the occult, psychoanalysis, or intuitive work, because life-and-death situations don't faze you. However, you do take personal disappointments very hard.

## Moon in Sagittarius

You take life's ups and downs with good humor and the proverbial grain of salt. You'll love 'em and leave 'em or take off on a great adventure at a moment's notice. "Born free" could be your slogan. Attracted by the exotic, you have mental and physical wanderlust. You may be too much in search of new mental and spiritual stimulation to ever settle down.

## Moon in Capricorn

Are you ever accused of being too cool and calculating? You have an earthy side, but you take prestige and position very seriously. Your strong drive to succeed extends to your romantic life, where you will be devoted to improving your lifestyle and rising to the top. A structured situation where you can advance methodically makes you feel wonderfully secure. You may be attracted to someone older or very much younger or from a different social world. It may be difficult to look at the lighter side of emotional relationships. Though this moon is placed in the sign of its detriment, the good news is that you tend to be very dutiful and responsible to those you care for.

## Moon in Aquarius

You are a people collector with many friends of all backgrounds. You are happiest surrounded by people, and you may feel uneasy when left alone. Though you usually stay friends with lovers, intense emotions and demanding one-on-one relationships turn you off. You don't like anything to be too rigid or scheduled. Though tolerant and understanding, you can be emotionally unpredictable; you may opt for an unconventional love life. With plenty of space, you will be able to sustain relationships with liberal, freedom-loving types.

## Moon in Pisces

You are very responsive and empathetic to others, especially if they have problems or are the underdog. (Be on guard against attracting too many people with sob stories.) You'll be happiest if you can express your creative imagination in the arts or in the spiritual or healing professions. Because you may tend to escape in fantasies or overreact to the moods of others, you need an emotional anchor to help you keep a firm foothold in reality. Steer clear of too much escapism (especially in alcohol) or reclusiveness. Places near water soothe your moods. Working in a field that gives you emotional variety will also help you be productive.

# CHAPTER 5

# Timing Tips from the Stars

One of the differences between people who achieve their goals and those who never seem to hit the mark is that the achievers usually have more control over the way they use their time. Astrology offers many ways to take control of your time, which could give you the competitive edge. It can show you when to be proactive and make your moves or when to kick back and relax. There are times when your careful plans could be derailed, when sudden changes from out of the blue could upset your schedule or delay your projects. On the other hand, there are days when everything is more likely to go smoothly and effortlessly, people will respond to you favorably, and perhaps you have some extra sex appeal.

For instance, when mischievous Mercury creates havoc with communications, it's time to back up your vital computer files, read between the lines of contracts, and be very patient with coworkers. When Venus passes through your sign, you're more alluring, so it's time to try out a new outfit or hairstyle, and then ask someone you'd like to know better to dinner. Venus timing can also help you charm clients with a stunning sales pitch or make an offer they won't refuse.

In this chapter you will find the tricks of astrological time management. You can find your red-letter days as well as which times to avoid. You will also learn how to make the magic of the moon work for you. Use the information in this chapter and the planet tables in this book and also the moon sign listings in your daily forecasts.

Here are the happenings to note on your agenda:

- Dates of your sun sign (high-energy period)

- The month previous to your sun sign (low-energy time)
- Dates of planets in your sign this year
- Full and new moons (Pay special attention when these fall in your sun sign!)
- Eclipses
- Moon in your sun sign every month, as well as moon in the opposite sign (listed in daily forecast)
- Mercury retrogrades
- Other retrograde periods

# Your Most Proactive Time

Every birthday starts off a new cycle of solar energy for you. You should feel a new surge of vitality as the powerful sun enters your sign. This is the time when predominant energies are most favorable to you. So go for it! Start new projects, and make your big moves (especially when the new moon is in your sign, doubling your charisma). You'll get the recognition you deserve now, when everyone is attuned to your sun sign. Look in the tables in this book to see if other planets will also be passing through your sun sign at this time. Venus (love, beauty), Mars (energy, drive), and Mercury (communication, mental sharpness) reinforce the sun and give an extra boost to your life in the areas they affect. Venus will rev up your social and love life, making you seem especially attractive. Mars amplifies your energy and drive. Mercury fuels your brainpower and helps you communicate. Jupiter signals an especially lucky period of expansion.

There are two downtimes related to the sun. During the month before your birthday period, when you are winding up your annual cycle, you could be feeling especially vulnerable and depleted. So at that time get extra rest, watch your diet, and take it easy. Don't overstress yourself. Use this time to gear up for a big push when the sun enters your sign.

Another downtime is when the sun is in the sign opposite your sun sign (six months from your birthday). This is a reactive time, when the prevailing energies are very different from yours. You may feel at odds with the world. You'll have to work harder for recognition because people are not on your wavelength. However, this could be a good time to work on a team, in cooperation with others, or behind the scenes.

# Be a Moon Watcher

The moon is a powerful tool to divine the mood of the moment. You can work with the moon in two ways. Plan by the sign the moon is in; plan by the phase of the moon. The sign will tell you the kind of activities that suit the moon's mood. The phase will tell you the best time to start or finish a certain activity.

Working with the phases of the moon is as easy as looking up at the night sky. During the new moon, when both the sun and moon are in the same sign, begin new ventures—especially activities that are favored by that sign. Then you'll utilize the powerful energies pulling you in the same direction. You'll be focused outward, toward action, and in a doing mode. Postpone breaking off, terminating, deliberating, or reflecting—activities that require introspection and passive work. These are better suited to a later moon phase.

Get your project under way during the first quarter. Then go public at the full moon, a time of high intensity, when feelings come out into the open. This is your time to shine—to express yourself. Be aware, however, that because pressures are being released, other people will also be letting off steam. Since confrontations are possible, take advantage of this time either to air grievances or to avoid arguments.

About three days after the full moon comes the disseminating phase, a time when the energy of the cycle begins to wind down. From the last quarter of the moon to the next new moon, it's a time to cut off unproductive relationships, do serious thinking, and focus on inward-directed activities.

You'll feel some new and full moons more strongly than others, especially those new moons that fall in your sun sign and full moons in your opposite sign. Because that full moon happens at your low-energy time of year, it is likely to be an especially stressful time in a relationship, when any hidden problems or unexpressed emotions could surface.

# Full and New Moons in 2009

All dates are calculated for eastern standard time and eastern daylight time.

Full Moon—January 10 in Cancer
New Moon—January 26 in Aquarius (solar eclipse)

Full Moon—February 9 in Leo (lunar eclipse)
New Moon—February 24 in Pisces

Full Moon—March 10 in Virgo
New Moon—March 26 in Aries

Full Moon—April 9 in Libra
New Moon—April 24 in Taurus

Full Moon—May 9 in Scorpio
New Moon—May 24 in Gemini

Full Moon—June 7 in Sagittarius
New Moon—June 22 in Cancer

Full Moon—July 7 in Capricorn (lunar eclipse)
New Moon—July 21 in Cancer (second new moon in Cancer, solar eclipse)

Full Moon—August 5 in Aquarius (lunar eclipse)
New Moon—August 20 in Leo

Full Moon—September 4 in Pisces
New Moon—September 18 in Virgo

Full Moon—October 4 in Aries
New Moon—October 18 in Libra

Full Moon—November 2 in Taurus
New Moon—November 16 in Scorpio

Full Moon—December 2 in Gemini
New Moon—December 16 in Sagittarius
Full Moon—December 31 in Cancer (lunar eclipse)


# Timing by the Moon's Sign

To forecast the daily emotional "weather," to determine your monthly high and low days, or to synchronize your activities with the cycles of the moon, take note of the moon's sign under your daily forecast at the end of the book. Here are some of the activities favored and the moods you are likely to encounter under each moon sign.


## Moon in Aries: Get Moving

The new moon in Aries is an ideal time to start new projects. Everyone is pushy, raring to go, rather impatient, and short-tempered. Leave details and follow-up for later. Competitive sports or martial arts are great ways to let off steam. Quiet types could use some assertiveness, but it's a great day for dynamos. Be careful not to step on too many toes.


## Moon in Taurus: Lay the Foundations for Success

Do solid, methodical tasks like follow-through or backup work. Make investments, buy real estate, do appraisals, or do some hard bargaining. Attend to your property. Get out in the country or spend some time in your garden. Enjoy creature comforts, music, a good dinner, or sensual love-making. Forget starting a diet—this is a day when you'll feel self-indulgent.

## Moon in Gemini: Communicate

Talk means action today. Telephone, write letters, and fax! Make new contacts; stay in touch with steady customers. You can juggle lots of tasks today. It's a great time for mental activity of any kind. Don't try to pin people down—they too are feeling restless. Keep it light. Flirtations and socializing are good. Watch gossip—and don't give away secrets.

## Moon in Cancer: Pay Attention to Loved Ones

This is a moody, sensitive, emotional time. People respond to personal attention and mothering. Stay at home, have a family dinner, or call your mother. Nostalgia, memories, and psychic powers are heightened. You'll want to hang on to people and things (don't clean out your closets now). You could have shrewd insights into what others really need and want. Pay attention to dreams, intuition, and gut reactions.

## Moon in Leo: Be Confident

Everybody is in a much more confident, warm, generous mood. It's a good day to ask for a raise, show what you can do, or dress like a star. People will respond to flattery and enjoy a bit of drama and theater. You may be extravagant, treat yourself royally, and show off a bit—but don't break the bank! Be careful not to promise more than you can deliver.

## Moon in Virgo: Be Practical

Do practical, down-to-earth chores. Review your budget, make repairs, or be an efficiency expert. Not a day to ask for a raise. Tend to personal care and maintenance. Have a health checkup, go on a diet, or buy vitamins or health food. Make your home spotless. Take care of details and piled-up chores. Reorganize your work and life so they run more smoothly and efficiently. Save money. Be prepared for others to be in critical, faultfinding moods.

## Moon in Libra: Be Diplomatic

Attend to legal matters. Negotiate contracts. Arbitrate. Do things with your favorite partner. Socialize. Be romantic. Buy a special gift or a beautiful object. Decorate yourself or your surroundings. Buy new clothes. Throw a party. Have an elegant, romantic evening. Smooth over any ruffled feathers. Avoid confrontations. Stick to civilized discussions.

## Moon in Scorpio: Solve Problems

This is a day to do things with passion. You'll have excellent concentration and focus. Try not to get too intense emotionally. Avoid sharp exchanges with loved ones. Others may tend to go to extremes, get jealous, or overreact. Great for troubleshooting, problem solving, research, scientific work—and making love. Pay attention to those psychic vibes.

## Moon in Sagittarius: Sell and Motivate

A great time for travel, philosophical discussions, or setting long-range career goals. Work out, do sports, or buy athletic equipment. Others will be feeling upbeat, exuberant, and adventurous. Taking risks is favored. You may feel like gambling, betting on the horses, visiting a local casino, or buying a lottery ticket. Teaching, writing, and spiritual activities also get the green light. Relax outdoors. Take care of animals.

# Moon in Capricorn: Get Organized

You can accomplish a lot now, so get on the ball! Attend to business. Issues concerning your basic responsibilities, duties, family, and elderly parents could crop up. You'll be expected to deliver on promises. Weed out the deadwood from your life. Get a dental checkup. Not a good day for gambling or taking risks.

## Moon in Aquarius: Join the Group

A great day for doing things with groups—clubs, meetings, outings, politics, or parties. Campaign for your candidate. Work for a worthy cause. Deal with larger issues that affect humanity—the environment and metaphysical questions. Buy a computer or electronic gadget. Watch TV. Wear something outrageous. Try something you've never done before. Present an original idea. Don't stick to a rigid schedule; go with the flow. Take a class in meditation, mind control, or yoga.

## Moon in Pisces: Be Creative

This can be a very creative day, so let your imagination work overtime. Film, theater, music, and ballet could inspire you. Spend some time resting and reflecting, reading, or writing poetry. Daydreams can also be profitable. Help those less fortunate. Lend a listening ear to someone who may be feeling blue. Don't overindulge in self-pity or escapism. People are especially vulnerable to substance abuse. Turn your thoughts to romance and someone special.

# Eclipses Clear the Air

This is a year with six eclipses, an unusually high number. Eclipses can bring on milestones in your life, if they aspect a key point in your horoscope. In general, they shake up the status quo, bringing hidden areas out into the open. During this time, problems you've been avoiding or have brushed aside can surface to demand your attention. A good coping strategy is to accept whatever comes up as a challenge that could make a positive difference in your life. And don't forget the power of your sense of humor. If you can laugh at something, you'll never be afraid of it.

When the natural rhythms of the sun and moon are disturbed, it's best to postpone important activities. Be sure to mark eclipse days on your calendar, especially if the eclipse falls in your birth sign. This year, those born under Cancer, Leo, Aquarius, and Capricorn should take special note of the feelings that arise. If your moon is in one of these signs, you may be especially affected. With lunar eclipses, some possibilities could be a break from attachments, or the healing of an illness or substance abuse that was triggered by the subconscious. The temporary event could be a healing time, when you gain perspective. During solar eclipses, when you might be in a highly subjective state, pay attention to the hidden subconscious patterns that surface, the emotional truth that is revealed at this time.

The effect of the eclipse can reverberate for some time, often months after the event. But it is especially important to stay cool and make no major moves during the period known as the shadow of the eclipse, which begins about a week before and lasts until at least three days after the eclipse. After three days, the daily rhythms should return to normal, and you can proceed with business as usual.

## This Year's Eclipse Dates

January 26: Solar Eclipse in Aquarius
February 9: Lunar Eclipse in Leo
July 7: Lunar Eclipse in Capricorn
July 22: Solar Eclipse in Cancer
August 5: Lunar eclipse in Aquarius
December 31: Lunar Eclipse in Cancer

# Retrogrades: When the Planets Seem to Backstep

All the planets, except for the sun and moon, have times when they appear to move backward—or retrograde—as it seems from our point of view on Earth. At these times, planets do not work as they normally do. So it's best to "take a break" from that planet's energies in our life and to do some work on an inner level.

## Mercury Retrograde: The Key Is in "Re"

Mercury goes into retrograde most often, and its effects can be especially irritating. When it reaches a short distance ahead of the sun several times a year, it seems to move backward from our point of view. Astrologers often compare retrograde motion to the optical illusion that occurs when we ride on a train that passes another train traveling at a different speed—the second train appears to be moving in reverse.

What this means to you is that the Mercury-ruled areas of your life—analytical thought processes, communications, scheduling—are subject to all kinds of confusion. Be prepared. Communications equipment can break down. Schedules may be changed on short notice. People are late for appointments or don't show up at all. Traffic is terrible. Major purchases malfunction, don't work out, or get delivered in the wrong color. Letters don't arrive or are delivered to the wrong address. Employees will make errors that have to be corrected later. Contracts don't work out or must be renegotiated.

Since most of us can't put our lives on "hold" during Mercury retrogrades, we should learn to tame the trickster and make it work for us. The key is in the prefix re-. This is the time to go back over things in your life, reflect on what you've done during the previous months. Now you can get deeper insights, and spot errors you've missed. So take time to review and reevaluate what has happened. Rest and reward yourself—it's a good time to take a vacation, especially if you revisit a favorite place. Reorganize your work and finish up projects that are backed up. Clean out your desk and closets. Throw away what you can't recycle. If you must sign contracts or agreements, do so with a contingency clause that lets you reevaluate the terms later.

Postpone major purchases or commitments for the time being. Don't get married (unless you're remarrying the same person). Try not to rely on other people keeping appointments, contracts, or agreements to the letter; have several alternatives. Double-check and read between the lines. Don't buy anything connected with communications or transportation (if you must, be sure to cover yourself).

Mercury retrograding through your sun sign will intensify its effect on your life.

If Mercury was retrograde when you were born, you may be one of the lucky people who don't suffer the frustrations of this period. If so, your mind probably works in a very intuitive, insightful way.

The sign in which Mercury is retrograding can give you an idea of what's in store—as well as the sun signs that will be especially challenged.

## Mercury Retrogrades in 2009

Mercury has three major retrograde periods this year, then turns retrograde in late December, in time for New Year's Eve, when there is also a lunar eclipse and retrograding Mars. This means it will be especially important to watch all activities which involve mental processes and communication.

January 11 to February 1 from Aquarius to Capricorn
May 6 to May 30 in Taurus to Gemini
September 6 to September 29 from Libra to Virgo
December 26 in Capricorn until January 15, 2010

## Venus Retrograde: Relationships Are Affected

Retrograding Venus can cause your relationships to take a backward step, or you may feel that a key relationship is on hold. Singles may be especially lonely, yet find it difficult to connect with someone special. If you wish to make amends in an already troubled relationship, make peaceful overtures at this time. You may feel more extravagant or overindulge in shopping or sweet treats. Shopping till you drop and buying what you cannot afford are bad at this time. It's *not* a good time to redecorate—you'll hate the color of the walls later. Postpone getting a new hairstyle. It only lasts for a relatively short time this year; however, Aries should take special note.

## Venus Retrogrades in 2009

Venus retrogrades from March 6 to April 17, from Pisces to Aries.

## Use the Power of Mars

Mars shows how and when to get where you want to go. Timing your moves with Mars on your side can give you a big push. On the other hand, pushing Mars the wrong way can guarantee that you'll run into frustrations around every corner. Your best times to forge ahead are during the weeks when Mars is traveling through your sun sign or your Mars sign (look these up in the planet tables in this book). Also consider times when Mars is in a compatible sign (fire signs with air signs, or earth signs with water signs). You'll be sure to have planetary power on your side.

## Holiday Happenings

It should be a lively holiday season this year. Mars will start a lengthy retrograde in extravagant Leo beginning December 20, in the midst of the holiday season, followed by Mercury turning retrograde on December 26 and a lunar eclipse in Cancer on December 31. Your patience may be tested more than usual during this year's festivities, so plan ahead and perhaps do your shopping early. Be flexible with travel plans, if you are vacationing, especially if you are a Leo or Cancer. Be especially cautious during the New Year's lunar eclipse. Resolve to practice anger management and self-control, even when those around you are on a short fuse. The Mars retrograde in Leo will last until March of 2010, during which there are sure to be repercussions on the international level.

# Mars Retrogrades in 2009

Mars turns retrograde in Leo on December 20 until March 10, 2010.

## When Other Planets Retrograde

The slower-moving planets stay retrograde for many months at a time (Jupiter, Saturn, Neptune, Uranus, and Pluto).

When Saturn is retrograde, it's an uphill battle with self-discipline. You may not be in the mood for work. You may feel more like hanging out at the beach than getting things done.

Neptune retrograde promotes a dreamy escapism from reality, when you may feel you're in a fog (Pisces will feel this, especially).

Uranus retrograde may mean setbacks in areas where there have been sudden changes, when you may be forced to regroup or reevaluate the situation.

Pluto retrograde is a time to work on establishing proportion and balance in areas where there have been recent dramatic transformations.

When the planets move forward again, there's a shift in the atmosphere. Activities connected with each planet start moving ahead; plans that were stalled get rolling. Make a special note of those days on your calendar and proceed accordingly.

## Other Retrogrades in 2009

The five slower-moving planets all go retrograde in 2009.

Jupiter retrogrades from June 15 to October 12 in Aquarius.

Saturn is retrograde as the year begins and turns direct on May 16 in Virgo.

Uranus retrogrades from July 1 to December 1 in Pisces.

Neptune retrogrades from May 28 to November 4 in Aquarius.

Pluto turns retrograde April 4 to September 11 in Capricorn.

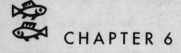

## CHAPTER 6

# Your Sign's Bottom Line in 2009: Is Success in Your Stars?

Though no sign wins the financial lottery—all have their share of billionaires and paupers—the signs of success are those who make the most of their particular financial talents. But every year, Jupiter, the planet of luck, gives an extra boost to a different sign. This year, it's the air signs (Gemini, Libra, and especially Aquarius) who should profit most from the lucky rays of Jupiter in Aquarius. Of all the signs, Aquarius is best suited for analyzing and coping with the unpredictable nature of the stock market and able to detach emotionally from investments. Most of us could benefit from using some Aquarius-inspired intuition, socially conscious investment philosophy, and experimental nature, especially in the area of our horoscope where Jupiter will be giving us growth opportunities.

## Aries

You've got a taste for fast money, quick turnover, and edgy investments, with no patience for gradual, long-term gains. You're an impulse buyer with the nerve for risky tactics that could backfire. On the other hand, you're a pioneer who can see into the future, who dares to take a gamble on a new idea or product that could change the world . . . like Sam Walton of the Wal-Mart stores, who changed the way we shop. You need a backup plan in case one of your big ideas burns out. To protect your money, get a backup plan you can follow without thinking about it. Have a percentage of your income automatically put into a savings or retirement account. Then give yourself some extra funds to play with. Your weak point is your impatience; so you're not one to wait out a slow market or watch savings slowly accumulate. You're inspired by Aquarius this year, so it's time to support your long-range goals and ideals, by exploring socially conscious investments, especially in the clean-energy field.

## Taurus

You're a saver who loves to see your cash, as well as your possessions, accumulate. You have no qualms about steadily increasing your fortune. You're a savvy trader and a shrewd investor, in there for long-term gains. You have low toleration for risk; you hate to lose anything. But you do enjoy luxuries, and may need to reward yourself frequently. You might pass up an opportunity because it seems too risky, but you should take a chance once in a while. Lucky Jupiter accents your career this year, which means new opportunities. So don't hesitate to explore job offers. You're especially lucky in real estate or any occupation that requires appraising and trading, as well as earth-centered businesses like farming and conservation.

## Gemini

With Gemini, the cash can flow in and then out just as quickly. You naturally multi-task, and you are sure to have several projects going at once, as well as several credit cards, which can easily get out of hand. Saving is not one of your strong points—too boring. You fall in and out of love with different ideas; you have probably tried a round of savings techniques. Diversification is your best strategy. Have several different kinds of investments—at least one should be a long-term plan. Set savings goals and then regularly deposit small amounts into your accounts. Follow the lead of Gemini financial adviser Suze Orman and get a good relationship going with your money! With lucky Jupiter accenting travel this year, investigate foreign investment opportunities and jobs connected with travel and tourism.

# Cancer

You can be a natural moneymaker with your peerless intuition. You can spot a winner that everyone else misses. Consider Cancer success stories like those of cosmetics queen Estee Lauder and Roxanne Quimby, of Burt's Bees, who turned her friend's stash of beeswax into a thriving cosmetics business. Who knew? So trust your intuition. You are a saver who always has a backup plan, just in case. Remember to treat and nurture yourself as well as others. Investments in the food industry, restaurants, hotels, shipping, and water-related industries are Cancer territory.

# Leo

You love the first-class lifestyle, but may not always have the resources to support it. Finding a way to fund your extravagant tastes is the Leo challenge. Some courses in money management or an expert financial coach could set you on the right track. However, you're also a terrific salesperson, and you're fabulous in high-profile jobs that pay a lot. You're the community tastemaker; you satisfy your appetite for "the best" by working for a quality company that sells luxury goods, splendid real estate, dream vacations, and first-class travel—that way you'll have access to the lifestyle without having to pay for it. With Jupiter in Aquarius accenting partnerships, you might want to team up for investing purposes this year.

# Virgo

Your sign is a stickler for details, which includes your money management. You like to follow your spending and saving closely; you enjoy planning, budgeting, and price comparison. Your sign usually has no problem sticking to a savings or investment plan. You have a critical eye for quality, and you like to bargain and to shop to get the best value. In fact, Warren Buffet, a Virgo billionaire, is known for value investing. You buy cheap and sell at a profit. Investing in health care, organic products, and food could be profitable for you, especially this year, when Jupiter accents the care and maintenance part of your life.

# Libra

Oh, do you ever love to shop! And you often have an irresistible urge to acquire an exquisite object or a designer dress you can't really afford or to splurge on the perfect antique armoire. You don't like to settle for second-rate or bargain buys. Learning to prioritize your spending is especially difficult for your sign, so try to find a good money manager to do it for you. Following a strictly balanced budget is your key to financial success. With Libra's keen eye for quality and good taste, you are a savvy picker at auctions and antiques fairs, so you might be able to turn around your purchase for a profit. Jupiter in Aquarius will bless creativity and self-expression.

# Scorpio

Scorpios prefer to stay in control of their finances at all times. You're sure to have a financial-tracking program on your computer. You're not an impulse buyer, unless you see something that immediately turns you on. Rely on your instincts! Scorpio is the sign of credit cards, taxes, and loans, so you are able to use these tools cleverly. Investing for Scorpio is rarely casual. You'll do extensive research and track your investments by reading the financial pages, annual reports, and profit-loss statements.

# Sagittarius

Sagittarius is a natural gambler, with a high tolerance for risk. It's important for you to learn when to hold 'em, and when to fold 'em, as the song goes, by setting limits on your risk taking and covering your assets. You enjoy the thrill of playing the stock market, where you could win big and lose big. Money itself is rarely the object for Sagittarius—it's the game that counts. Since your sign rarely saves for a rainy day, your best strategy might be a savings plan that transfers a certain amount into a savings account. Regular bill-paying plans are another strategy to keep you on track. You could benefit from an inspirational money manager who gets you fired up about an investment plan. Go where the action is and circulate. Your ruling planet, Jupiter, blesses social contacts this year. Why not join an investment club?

# Capricorn

You're one of the strongest money managers in the zodiac, which should serve you well this year when Jupiter, the planet of luck and expansion, is blessing your house of finance. You're a born bargain hunter and clever negotiator—a saver rather than a spender. You are the sign of self-discipline, which works well when it comes to sticking with a budget and living frugally while waiting for resources to accumulate. You are likely to plan carefully for your elder years, profiting from long-term investments. You have a keen sense of value, and you will pick up a bargain and then turn it around at a nice profit.

# Aquarius

Luck is with you this year, with Jupiter blessing your sign. There should be many chances to speculate on forward-looking ventures. The Aquarius trait of unpredictability extends to your financial life, where you surprise us all with your ability to turn something totally unique into a money spinner. Consider your wealthy sign mate Oprah Winfrey, who has been able to intuit what the public will buy at a given moment. Some of your ideas might sound far-out, but they turn out to be right on the money. Investing in high-tech companies that are on the cutting edge of their field is good for Aquarius. You'll probably intuit which ones will stay the course. You'll feel good about investing in companies that improve the environment, such as new types of fuel, or ones that are related to your favorite cause.

# Pisces

The typical Pisces is probably the sign least interested in money management. However, there are many billionaires born under your sign, such as Michael Dell, David Geffen, and Steve Jobs. Generally they have made money from innovative ideas and left the details to others. That might work for you. Find a Scorpio, Capricorn, or Virgo to help you set a profitable course and systematically save (which is not in your nature). Sign up for automatic bill paying so you won't have to think about it. If you keep in mind how much less stressful life will be and how much more you can do when you're not worried about paying bills, you might be motivated enough to stick to a sensible budget. Investment-wise, consider anything to do with water—off-shore drilling, water conservation and purifying, shipping, and seafood. Petroleum is also ruled by your sign, as are institutions related to hospitals.

## CHAPTER 7

# Sun-Sign Seduction Secrets

Haven't found the one yet? Maybe you haven't been using astrology. If you want to charm a Capricorn, hook a Pisces, or corral a Taurus, here are sun-sign seduction tips guaranteed to keep your lover begging for more.

## Aries: Play Hard to Get

This highly physical sign is walking dynamite with a brief attention span. Don't be too easy to get, ladies. A little challenge, a lively debate, and a merry chase only heat them up. They want to see what you're made of. Once you've lured them into your lair, be a challenge and a bit of a daredevil. Pull out your X-rated tricks. Don't give your all—let them know there's more where that came from. Make it exciting; show you're up for adventure. Wear bright red somewhere interesting. Since Aries rules the head and face, be sure to focus on these areas in your lovemaking. Use your lips, tongue, breath, and even your eyelashes to the max. Practice scalp massages and deep kissing techniques. Aries won't wait, so when you make your move, be sure you're ready to follow through. No head games or teasing!

To keep you happy, you've got to voice your *own* needs, because this lover will be focused on *his*. Teach him how to please, or this could be a one-sided adventure.

## Taurus: Appeal to All Their Senses

Taurus wins as the most sensual sign, with the most sexual stamina. This man is earthy and lusty in bed; he can go on all night. This is not a sign to tease. Like a bull, he'll see red, not bed. So make him comfortable, and then bombard all his senses. Good food gets Taurus in the mood. So do the right music, fragrance, revealing clothes, and luxurious bedlinens. Give him a massage with delicious-smelling and -tasting oils; focus on the neck area.

Don't forget to turn off the phone! Taurus hates interruptions. Since they can be very vocal lovers, choose a setting where you won't be disturbed. And don't ever rush; enjoy a long, slow, delicious encounter.

## Gemini: Be a Playmate

Playful Gemini loves games, so make your seduction fun. Be their lost twin soul or confidante. Good communication is essential, so share deep secrets and live out fantasies. This sign adores variety. Nothing bores Gemini more than making love the same way all the time, or bringing on the heavy emotions. So trot out all the roles you've been longing to play. Here's the perfect partner. But remember to keep it light and fun. Gemini's turn-on zone is the hands, and this sign gives the best massages. Gadgets that can be activated with a touch amuse Gemini. This sign is great at doing two things at once, like making love while watching an erotic film. Turn the cell phone off unless you want company. On the other hand, Gemini is your sign for superhot phone sex.

Gemini loves a change of scene. So experiment on the floor, in the shower, or on the kitchen table. Borrow a friend's apartment or rent a hotel room for variety.

## Cancer: Use the Moon

The key to Cancer is to get this moon child in the mood. Consult the moon—a full moon is best. Wining, dining, old-fashioned courtship, and breakfast in bed are turn-ons. Whatever makes your Cancer feel secure will promote shedding inhibitions in the sack. (Don't try any of your

Aries daredevil techniques here!) Cancer prefers familiar, comfortable, homey surroundings. Cancer's turn-on zone is the breasts. Cancer women often have naturally inflated chests. Cancer men may fantasize about a well-endowed playmate. If your breasts are enhanced, show them off. Cancer will want to know all your deepest secrets, so invent a few good ones. But lots of luck delving into *their* innermost thoughts!

Take your Cancer near water. The sight and sound of the sea can be their aphrodisiac. A moonlit beach, a deserted swimming pool, a Jacuzzi, or a bubble bath are good seduction spots. Listen to the rain patter on the roof in a mountain cabin.

# Leo: Offer the Royal Treatment

Leo must be the best and hear it from you often. In return, they'll perform for you, telling you just what you want to hear (true or not). They like a lover with style and endurance, and to be swept off their feet and into bed. Leos like to go first-class all the way, so build them up with lots of attention, wining and dining, and special gifts.

Never mention other lovers or make them feel second-best. A sure signal for Leo to look elsewhere is a competitive spouse. Leos take great pride in their bodies, so you should pour on the admiration. A few well-placed mirrors could inspire them. So would a striptease with beautiful lingerie, expensive fragrance on the sheets, and, if female, an occasional luxury hotel room, with champagne and caviar delivered by room service. Leo's erogenous zone is the lower back, so a massage with expensive oils would make your lion purr with pleasure.

# Virgo: Let Them Be the Teacher

Virgo's standards are so sky-high that you may feel intimidated at first. The key to pleasing fussy Virgo lovers is to look for the hot fantasy beneath their cool surface. They're really looking for someone to make over. So let Virgo play teacher, and you play the willing student; the doctor-patient routine works as well. Be Eliza Doolittle to his Henry Higgins.

Let Virgo help you improve your life, quit smoking, learn French, and diet. Read an erotic book together, and then practice the techniques. Or study esoteric, erotic exercises from the Far East.

The Virgo erogenous zone is the tummy area, which should be your base of operations. Virgo likes things pristine and clean. Fall onto crisp, immaculate white sheets. Wear a sheer virginal white nightie. Smell shower-fresh with no heavy perfume. Be sure your surroundings pass the hospital test. A shower together afterward (with great-smelling soap) could get the ball rolling again.

## Libra: Look Your Best

Libra must be turned on aesthetically. Make sure you look as beautiful as possible, and wear something stylishly seductive but never vulgar. Have a mental affair first, as you flirt and flatter this sign. Then proceed to the physical. Approach Libra like a dance partner, ready to waltz or tango.

Libra must be in the mood for love; otherwise, forget it. Any kind of ugliness is a turnoff. Provide an elegant and harmonious atmosphere, with no loud noise, clashing colors, or uncomfortable beds. Libra is not an especially spontaneous lover, so it is best to spend time warming them up. Libra's back is his erogenous zone, your cue to provide back rubs with scented potions. Once in bed, you can be a bit aggressive sexually. Libra loves strong, decisive moves. Set the scene, know what you want, and let Libra be happy to provide it.

## Scorpio: Be an All-or-Nothing Lover

Scorpio is legendary in bed, often called the sex sign of the zodiac. But seducing them is often a power game. Scorpio likes to be in control, even the quiet, unassuming ones. Scorpio loves a mystery, so don't tell all. Keep them guessing about you, offering tantalizing hints along the way. The hint of danger often turns Scorpio on, so you'll find members of this sign experimenting with the exotic and highly erotic forms of sex. Sadomasochism, bondage, or anything that tests the limits of power could be a turn-on for Scorpio.

Invest in some sexy black leather and some powerful music. Clothes that lace, buckle, or zip tempt Scorpio to untie you. Present yourself as a mysterious package just waiting to be unwrapped.

Once in bed, there are no holds barred with Scorpio. They'll find your most pleasurable pressure points, and touch you as you've never been touched before. They are quickly aroused (the genital area belongs to this sign) and are willing to try anything. But they can be possessive. Don't expect your Scorpio to share you with anyone. It's all or nothing for them.

# Sagittarius: Be a Happy Wanderer

Sagittarius men are the Don Juans of the zodiac—love-'em-and-leave-'em types who are difficult to pin down. Your seduction strategy is to join them in their many pursuits, and then hook them with love on the road. Sagittarius enjoys sex in venues that suggest movement; planes, SUVs, or boats. But a favorite turn-on place is outdoors, in nature. A deserted hiking path, a field of tall grass, or a remote woodland glade—all give the centaur sexy ideas. Athletic Sagittarius might go for some personal training in an empty gym. Join your Sagittarius for amorous aerobics, meditate together, and explore the tantric forms of sex. Lovemaking after hiking and skiing would be healthy fun.

Sagittarius enjoys lovers from exotic ethnic backgrounds, or lovers met in spiritual pursuits or on college campuses. Sagittarius are great cheerleaders and motivators, and will enjoy feeling that they have inspired you to be all that you can be.

There may be a canine or feline companion sharing your

Sagittarius lover's bed with you, so check your allergies. And bring Fido or Felix a toy to keep them occupied.

# Capricorn: Take Their Mind off Business

The great news about Capricorn lovers is that they improve with age. They are probably the sexiest seniors. So stick around, if you have a young one. They're lusty in bed (it's not the sign of the goat for nothing), and can be quite raunchy and turned on by X-rated words and deeds. If this is not your thing, let them know. The Capricorn erogenous zone is the knees. Some discreet fondling in public places could be your opener. Capricorn tends to think of sex as part of a game plan for the future. They are well-organized, and might regard lovemaking as relaxation after a long day's work. This sign often combines business with pleasure. So look for a Capricorn where there's a convention, trade show, or work-related conference.

Getting Capricorn's mind off his agenda and onto yours could take some doing. Separate him from his buddies by whispering sexy secrets in his ear. Then convince him you're an asset to his image and a boon to his health. Though he may seem uptight at first, you'll soon discover he's a love animal who makes a wonderful and permanent pet.

# Aquarius: Give Them Enough Space

This sign really does not want an all-consuming passion or an all-or-nothing relationship. Aquarius needs space. But once they feel free to experiment with a spontaneous and exciting partner, Aquarius can give you a far-out sexual adventure.

Passion begins in the mind, so a good mental buildup is key. Aquarius is an inventive sign who believes love is a playground without rules. Plan surprise, unpredictable encounters in unusual places. Find ways to make love transcendental, an extraordinary and unique experience. Be ready to try anything Aquarius suggests, if only once. Calves and ankles are the special Aquarius erogenous zone, so perfect your legwork.

Be careful not to be too possessive. Your Aquarius needs lots of space and tolerance for friends (including old lovers) and their many outside interests.

## Pisces: Live Their Fantasies

Pisces is the sign of fantasy and imagination. This sign has great theatrical talent. Pisces looks for lovers who will take care of them. Pisces will return the favor! Here is someone who can psych out your deepest desires without mentioning them. Pisces falls for sob stories and is always ready to empathize. It wouldn't hurt to have a small problem for Pisces to help you overcome. It might help if you cry on his shoulder, for this sign needs to be needed. Use your imagination when setting the scene for love. A dramatic setting brings out Pisces theatrical talents. Or creatively use the element of water. Rain on the roof, waterfalls, showers, beach houses, water beds, and Jacuzzis could turn up the heat. Experiment with pulsating jets of water. Take midnight skinny-dips in deserted pools.

The Pisces erogenous zone is the feet. This is your cue to give a sensuous foot massage using scented lotions. Let him paint your toes. Beautiful toenails in sexy sandals are a special turn-on.

## Your Hottest Love Match

Here's a tip for finding your hottest love match. If your lover's Mars sign makes favorable aspects to your Venus, is in the same element (earth, air, fire, water), or is in the same sign, your lover will do what you want done! Mars influences how we act when we make love, while Venus shows what we like done to us. Sometimes fighting and making up is the sexiest fun of all. If you're the type who needs a spark to keep lust alive (you know who you are!), then look for Mars and Venus in different signs of the same quality (fixed or cardinal or mutable). For instance, a fixed sign (Taurus, Leo, Scorpio, Aquarius) paired with another fixed sign can have a sexy tug-of-war before you finally surrender. Two cardinal signs (Aries, Cancer, Libra, Capricorn) set off passionate fireworks when they clash. Mutable signs (Gemini, Virgo, Sagittarius, Pisces) play a fascinating game of cat and mouse, never quite catching each other.

## Your Most Seductive Time

The best time for love is when Venus is in your sign, making you the most desirable sign in the zodiac. This only lasts about three weeks (unless Venus is retrograde) so don't waste time! And find out the time this year when Venus is in your sign by consulting the Venus chart at the end of chapter three.

## What's the Sexiest Sign?

It depends on what sign you are. Astrology has traditionally given this honor to Scorpio, the sign associated with the sex organs. However, we are all a combination of different signs (and turn-ons). Gemini's communicating ability and manual dexterity could deliver the magic touch. Cancer's tenderness and understanding could bring out your passion more than regal Leo.

## Which Is the Most Faithful Sign?

The earth signs of Capricorn, Taurus, and Virgo are usually the most faithful. They tend to be more home- and family-oriented, and they are usually choosy about their mates. It's impractical, inconvenient, and probably expensive to play around, or so they think.

# Who'll Play Around?

The mutable signs of Gemini, Pisces, and Sagittarius win the playboy or playgirl sweepstakes. These signs tend to be changeable, fickle, and easily bored. But they're so much fun!

# CHAPTER 8

# Children of 2009, Born in Changing Times

Parents of several children may see a marked difference between children born in 2009 and their older siblings, because the cosmic atmosphere is changing, which should imprint the personalities of this year's children. Astrologers look to the slow-moving outer planets—Uranus, Neptune, and Pluto—to describe a generation.

This year, Uranus and Neptune are still passing through Pisces and Aquarius, both visionary and spiritual signs. However, there is also much more earth-sign emphasis than in previous years due to the earthly pull of Pluto in Capricorn, plus the closer planets. Saturn also in an earth sign, will counterbalance this spirituality with extreme practicality and pragmatism. This generation will be focused on getting the job done, on fixing up the planet, and on making things work.

Astrology can be an especially helpful tool when used to design an environment that enhances and encourages each child's positive qualities. Some parents start before conception, planning the birth of their child as far as possible to harmonize with the signs of other family members. However, each baby has its own schedule, so if yours arrives a week early or late, or elects a different sign than you'd planned, recognize that the new sign may be more in line with the mission your child is here to accomplish. In other words, if you were hoping for a Libra child and he arrives during Virgo, that Virgo energy may be just what is needed to stimulate or complement your family. Remember that there are many astrological elements besides the sun sign that indicate strong family ties. Usually each child will share a particular planetary placement, an emphasis on a particular sign or house, or a certain chart configuration with his parents and other family members. Often there is a significant planetary angle that will define the parent-child relationship, such as family sun signs that form a T-square or a triangle.

One important thing you can do is to be sure the exact moment of birth is recorded. This will be essential in calculating an accurate astrological chart. The following descriptions can be applied to the sun or moon sign (if known) of a child—the sun sign will describe basic personality and the moon sign indicates the child's emotional needs.

# The Aries Child

Baby Aries is quite a handful. This energetic child will walk—and run—as soon as possible, and perform daring feats of exploration. Caregivers should be vigilant. Little Aries seems to know no fear (and is especially vulnerable to head injuries). Many Aries children, in their rush to get on with life, seem hyperactive, and they are easily frustrated when they can't get their own way. Violent temper tantrums and dramatic physical displays are par for the course with this child, requiring a time-out mat or naughty chair.

The very young Aries should be monitored carefully, since he is prone to take risks and may injure himself. Aries love to take things apart and may break toys easily, but with encouragement, the child will develop formidable coordination. Aries's bossy tendencies should be molded into leadership qualities, rather than bullying, which should be easy to do with this year's babies. Encourage these children to take out aggressions and frustrations in active, competitive sports, where they usually excel. When young Aries learns to focus energies long enough to master a subject and learns consideration for others, the indomitable Aries spirit will rise to the head of the class.

Aries born in 2009 will be a more subdued version of this sign, but still loaded with energy. The Capricorn effect should make little Aries easier to discipline and more focused on achievement. A natural leader!

# The Taurus Child

This is a cuddly, affectionate child who eagerly explores the world of the senses, especially the senses of taste and touch. The Taurus child can be a big eater and will put on weight easily if not encouraged to exercise. Since this child likes comfort and gravitates to beauty, try coaxing little Taurus to exercise to music, or take him or her out of doors, with hikes or long walks. Though Taurus may be a slow learner, this sign has an excellent retentive memory and generally masters a subject thoroughly. Taurus is interested in results and will see each project patiently through to completion, continuing long after others have given up. This year's earth sign planets will give him a wonderful sense of support and accomplishment.

Choose Taurus toys carefully to help develop innate talents. Construction toys, such as blocks or erector sets, appeal to their love of building. Paints or crayons develop their sense of color. Many Taurus have musical talent and love to sing, which is apparent at a young age.

This year's Taurus will want a pet or two, and a few plants of his own. Give little Taurus a small garden, and watch the natural green thumb develop. This child has a strong sense of acquisition and an early grasp of material value. After filling a piggy bank, Taurus graduates to a savings account, before other children have started to learn the value of money.

This year's Taurus gets a bonanza of good luck and support from Jupiter, Pluto, and Saturn, all in compatible earth signs. These should give little Taurus an especially easygoing disposition and provide many opportunities to live up to his sign's potential.

# The Gemini Child

Little Gemini will talk as soon as possible, filling the air with questions and chatter. This is a friendly child who enjoys social contact, seems to require company, and adapts quickly to different surroundings. Geminis have quick minds that easily grasp the use of words, books, and telephones, and will probably learn to talk and read at an earlier age than most. Though they are fast learners, Gemini may have a short attention span, darting from subject to subject. Projects and games that help focus the mind could be used to help them concentrate. Musical instruments, typewriters, and computers help older Gemini children combine mental with manual dexterity. Geminis should be encouraged to finish what they start before they go on to another project. Otherwise, they can become jack-of-all-trade types who have trouble completing anything they do. Their disposition is usually cheerful and witty, making these children popular with their peers and delightful company at home.

This year's Gemini baby should go to the head of the class. Uranus in Pisces could inspire Gemini to make an unusual career choice, perhaps in a financial field. When he grows up, this year's Gemini may change jobs several times before he finds a position that satisfies his need for stimulation and variety.

# The Cancer Child

This emotional, sensitive child is especially influenced by patterns set in early life. Young Cancers cling to their first memories as well as their childhood possessions. They thrive in calm emotional waters, with a loving, protective mother, and usually remain close to her (even if their relationship with her was difficult) throughout their lives. Divorce and death—anything that disturbs the safe family unit—are devastating to Cancers, who may need extra support and reassurance during a family crisis.

They sometimes need a firm hand to push the positive, creative side of their personality and discourage them from getting swept away by emotional moods or resorting to emotional manipulation to get their way. If this child is praised and encouraged to find creative expression, Cancers will be able to express their positive side consistently, on a firm, secure foundation.

This year's Cancer baby should be a social, cooperative child, oriented toward others, thanks to Jupiter and Pluto blessing relationships.

# The Leo Child

Leo children love the limelight and will plot to get the lion's share of attention. These children assert themselves with flair and drama, and can behave like tiny tyrants to get their way. But in general, they have a sunny, positive disposition and are rarely subject to blue moods.

At school, they're the types voted most popular, head cheerleader, or homecoming queen. Leo is sure to be noticed for personality, if not for stunning looks or academic work; the homely Leo will be a class clown, and the unhappy Leo can be the class bully.

Above all, a Leo child cannot tolerate being ignored for long. Drama or performing-arts classes, sports, and school politics are healthy ways for Leo to be a star. But Leos must learn to take lesser roles occasionally, or they will have some painful putdowns in store. Usually, their popularity is well earned; they are hard workers who try to measure up to their own high standards—and usually succeed.

This year's Leo should be a less flamboyant, more down-to-earth version of his sign, as the earthy planets exert their influence. This should add more financial and practical talents to the expressive Leo personality.

# The Virgo Child

The young Virgo can be a quiet, rather serious child, with a quick, intelligent mind. Early on, little Virgo shows far more attention to detail and concern with small things than other children. Little Virgo has a built-in sense of order and a fascination with how things work. It is important for these children to have a place of their own, which they can order as they wish and where they can read or busy themselves with crafts and hobbies. This child's personality can be very sensitive. Little Virgo may get hyper and overreact to seemingly small irritations, which can take the form of stomach upsets or delicate digestive systems. But this child will flourish where there is mental stimulation and a sense of order. Virgos thrive in school, especially in writing or language skills, and they seem truly happy when buried in books. Chances are, young Virgo will learn to read ahead of classmates. Hobbies that involve detail work or that develop fine craftsmanship are especially suited to young Virgos.

Baby Virgo of 2009 is likely to be an especially high achiever with Saturn, also in Virgo, adding focus and discipline, while Jupiter transiting the house of self-expression endows extra creativity.

# The Libra Child

The Libra child learns early about the power of charm and appearance. This is often a very physically appealing child with an enchanting dimpled smile, who is naturally sociable and enjoys the company of both children and adults. It is a rare Libra child who is a discipline problem, but when their behavior is unacceptable, they respond better to calm discussion than displays of emotion, especially if the discussion revolves around fairness. Because young Libras without a strong direction tend to drift with the mood of the group, these children should be encouraged to develop their unique talents and powers of discrimination, so they can later stand on their own.

In school, this child is usually popular and will often have to choose between social invitations and studies. In the teen years, social pressures mount as the young Libra begins to look for a partner. This is the sign of best friends, so Libra's choice of companions can have a strong effect on his future direction. Beautiful Libra girls may be tempted to go steady or have an unwise early marriage. Chances are, both sexes will fall in and out of love several times in their search for the ideal partner.

Little Libra of 2009 is an especially social, talkative child, who gets along well with siblings as Jupiter in Capricorn enhances family life. This child is endowed with much imagination and creativity, as well as communication skills.

# The Scorpio Child

The Scorpio child may seem quiet and shy, but will surprise others with intense feelings and formidable willpower. Scorpio children are single-minded when they want something and intensely passionate about whatever they do. One of a caregiver's tasks is to teach this child to balance activities and emotions, yet at the same time to make the most of his great concentration and intense commitment.

Since young Scorpios do not show their depth of feelings easily, parents will have to learn to read almost imperceptible signs that troubles are brewing beneath the surface. Both Scorpio boys and girls enjoy games of power and control on or off the playground. Scorpio girls may take an early interest in the opposite sex, masquerading as tomboys, while Scorpio boys may be intensely competitive and loners. When her powerful energies are directed into work, sports, or challenging studies, Scorpio is a superachiever, focused on a goal. With trusted friends, young Scorpio is devoted and caring—the proverbial friend through thick and thin, loyal for life.

Scorpio 2009 has a strong financial emphasis, which could make these children big money earners in adulthood. Uranus in Pisces in their house of creativity should put them on the cutting edge of whichever field they choose.

# The Sagittarius Child

This restless, athletic child will be out of the playpen and off on explorative adventures as soon as possible. Little Sagittarius is remarkably well-coordinated, attempting daredevil feats on any wheeled vehicle from scooters to skateboards. These natural athletes need little encouragement to channel their energies into sports. Their cheerful friendly dispositions earn them popularity in school, and once they have found a subject where their talent and imagination can soar, they will do well academically. They love animals, especially horses, and will be sure to have a pet or two, if not a home zoo. When they are old enough to take care of themselves, they'll clamor to be off on adventures of their own, away from home, if possible.

This is a child who loves to travel, who will not get homesick at summer camp, and who may sign up to be a foreign-exchange student or spend summers abroad. Outdoor adventure appeals to little Sagittarius, especially if it involves an active sport, such as skiing, cycling or mountain climbing. Give them enough space and encouragement, and their fiery spirit will propel them to achieve high goals.

Baby Sagittarius of 2009 has a natural generosity of spirit and an optimistic, expansive nature. They will also demand a great deal of freedom. They may need reality checks from time to time, since they may be risk takers, especially in the financial area. They should learn early in life how to handle money.

# The Capricorn Child

These purposeful, goal-oriented children will work to capacity if they feel this will bring results. They're not ones who enjoy work for its own sake—there must be a goal in sight. Authority figures can do much to motivate these children, but once set on an upward path, young Capricorn will mobilize his energy and talent and work harder, and with more perseverance, than any other sign. Capricorn has built-in self-discipline that can achieve remarkable results, even if lacking the flashy personality, quick brainpower, or penetrating insight of others. Once involved, young Capricorn will stick to a task until it is mastered. This child also knows how to use others to his advantage and may well become the team captain or class president.

A wise parent will set realistic goals for the Capricorn child, paving the way for the early thrill of achievement. Youngsters should be encouraged to express their caring, feeling side to others, as well as their natural aptitude for leadership. Capricorn children may be especially fond of grandparents and older relatives, and will enjoy spending time with them and learning from them. It is not uncommon for young Capricorns to have an older mentor or teacher who guides them. With their great respect for authority, Capricorn children will take this influence very much to heart.

The Capricorn born in 2009 will have an upbeat cheerful personality. This child should have a generous, expansive nature, and be more outgoing than the usual member of this sign.

## The Aquarius Child

The Aquarius child has a well-focused, innovative mind that often streaks so far ahead of peers that this child seems like an oddball. Routine studies never hold the restless youngster for long; he or she will look for another, more experimental place to try out his ideas and develop his inventions. Life is a laboratory to the inquiring Aquarius mind. School politics, sports, science, and the arts offer scope for their talents. But if there is no room for expression within approved social limits, Aquarius is sure to rebel. Questioning institutions and religions comes naturally, so these children may find an outlet elsewhere, becoming rebels with a cause. It is better not to force these children to conform, but rather to channel forward-thinking young minds into constructive group activities.

This year's Aquarius will have far-out glamour as well as charisma, thanks to his ruler, Uranus, in a friendly bond with Neptune. This could be a rock star, a statesman, or a scientist.

## The Pisces Child

Give young Pisces praise, applause, and a gentle, but firm, push in the right direction. Lovable Pisces children may be abundantly talented, but may be hesitant to express themselves, because they are quite sensitive and easily hurt. It is a parent's challenge to help them gain self-esteem and self-confidence. However, this same sensitivity makes them trusted friends who'll have many confidants as they develop socially. It also endows many Pisces with spectacular creative talent.

Pisces adores drama and theatrics of all sorts; therefore, encourage them to channel their creativity into art forms rather than indulging in emotional dramas. Understand that they may need more solitude than other children may as they develop their creative ideas. But though daydreaming can be creative, it is important that these natural dreamers not dwell too long in the world of fantasy. Teach them practical coping skills for the real world.

Since Pisces are sensitive physically, parents should help them build strong bodies with proper diet and regular exercise. Young Pisces may gravitate to more individual sports, such as swimming, sailing, and skiing, rather than to team sports. Or they may prefer more artistic physical activities, like dance or ice-skating.

Born givers, these children are often drawn to the underdog (they quickly fall for sob stories) and attract those who might take advantage of their empathic nature. Teach them to choose friends wisely, to set boundaries in relationships, and to protect their emotional vulnerability—invaluable lessons in later life.

With the planet Uranus now in Pisces, the 2009 baby belongs to a generation of Pisces movers and shakers. This child may have a rebellious streak that rattles the status quo. But this generation also has a visionary nature, which will be much concerned with the welfare of the world at large.

# CHAPTER 9

# Dive Deeper into Astrology with a Personal Reading

Ever wondered what a professional astrologer would have to say about the issues in your personal life? Then it might be worth your while to have a personal reading. A customized reading can deal with what matters most to you. It can help you sort out a problem, find and use the strengths in your horoscope, set you on a more fulfilling career path, or help you decide where to relocate. Many people consult astrologers to find the optimum time to schedule an important event such as a wedding or business meeting.

Another good reason for a reading is to refine your knowledge of astrology by consulting with someone who has years of experience analyzing charts. You might choose an astrologer with a specialty that intrigues you. Armed with the knowledge of your chart that you have acquired so far, you can then learn to interpret subtle nuances or gain insight into your talents and abilities.

How do you choose when there are so many different kinds of readings available, especially since the Internet has brought astrology into the mainstream? Besides individual one-on-one readings with a professional astrologer, there are personal readings by mail, telephone, Internet, and tape. Well-advertised computer-generated reports and celebrity-sponsored readings are sure to attract your attention on commercial Web sites and in magazines. You can even purchase a reading that is incorporated into an expensive handmade fine art book. Then there are astrologers who specialize in specific areas such as finance or medical astrology. And unfortunately, there are many questionable practitioners who range from streetwise Gypsy fortune-tellers to unscrupulous scam artists.

The following basic guidelines can help you sort out your options to find the reading that's right for you.

# One-on-One Consultations with a Professional Astrologer

Nothing compares to a one-on-one consultation with a professional astrologer who has analyzed thousands of charts and can pinpoint the potential in yours. During your reading, you can get your specific questions answered and discuss possible paths you might take. There are many astrologers who now combine their skills with training in psychology and are well-suited to help you examine your alternatives.

To give you an accurate reading, an astrologer needs certain information from you: the date, time, and place where you were born. (A horoscope can be cast about anyone or anything that has a specific time and place.) Most astrologers will then enter this information into a computer, which will calculate a chart in seconds, and interpret the resulting chart.

If you don't know your exact birth time, you can usually locate it at the Bureau of Vital Statistics at the city hall of the town or the county seat in the state where you were born. If you still have no success in getting your time of birth, some astrologers can estimate an approximate birth time by using past events in your life to determine the chart. This technique is called rectification.

# How to Find an Astrologer

Choose your astrologer with the same care as you would any trusted adviser, such as a doctor, lawyer, or banker. Unfortunately, anyone can claim to be an astrologer—to date, there is no licensing of astrologers or universally established professional criteria. However, there are nation-wide organizations of serious, committed astrologers that can help you in your search.

Good places to start your investigation are organizations such as the American Federation of Astrologers (AFA) or the National Council for Geocosmic Research (NCGR), which offer a program of study and certification. If you live near a major city, there is sure to be an active NCGR chapter or astrology club in your area; many are listed in astrology magazines available at your local newsstand. In response to many requests for referrals, both the AFA and the NCGR have directories of professional astrologers listed on their Web sites; these directories include a glossary of terms and an explanation of specialties within the astrological field. Contact the NCGR and AFA headquarters for information. (See also Chapter 13.)

# What Happens in a Reading

As a potentially lucrative freelance business, astrology has always attracted self-styled experts who may not have the knowledge or the counseling experience to give a helpful reading. These astrologers can range from the well-meaning amateur to the charlatan or street-corner Gypsy who has for many years given astrology a bad name. Be very wary of astrologers who claim to have occult powers or who make pretentious claims of celebrated clients or miraculous achievements. You can often tell from the initial phone conversation if the astrologer is legitimate. He or she should ask for your birthday time and place and then conduct the conversation in a professional manner. Any astrologer who gives a reading based only on your sun sign is highly suspect.

When you arrive at the reading, the astrologer should be prepared. The consultation should be conducted in a private, quiet place. The astrologer should be interested in your problems of the moment. A good reading is interactive and involves feedback on your part, so if the reading is not relating to your concerns, you should let the astrologer know. You should feel free to ask questions and get clarifications of any technical terms. The more you actively participate, rather than expecting the astrologer to carry the reading or come forth with oracular predictions, the more meaningful your experience will be. An astrologer should help you validate your current experience and be frank about possible negative happenings, but also suggest a positive course of action.

In their approach to a reading, some astrologers may be more literal and others more intuitive. Those who have had counseling training may take a more psychological approach. Though some astrologers may seem to have an almost psychic ability, extrasensory perception or any other parapsychological talent is not essential. A very accurate picture can be drawn from the data in your horoscope chart.

An astrologer may do several charts for each client, including one for the time of birth and a progressed chart, showing the evolution from birth to the present time. According to your individual needs, there are many other possibilities, such as a chart for a different location if you are contemplating a change of place. Relationships between any two people, things, or events can be interpreted with a chart that compares one partner's horoscope with the other's. A composite chart, which uses the midpoint between planets in two individual charts to describe the relationship, is another commonly used device.

An astrologer will be particularly interested in transits, those times when cycling planets activate the planets or sensitive points in your birth chart. These indicate important events in your life.

Many astrologers offer readings recorded on tape or CD, which is another option to consider, especially if the astrologer you choose lives at a distance from you. In this case, you'll be mailed a recorded reading based on your birth chart. This type of reading is more personal than a computer printout and can give you valuable insights, though it is not equivalent to a live dialogue with the astrologer when you can discuss your specific interest and issues of the moment.

# The Telephone Reading

Telephone readings come in two varieties: a dial-in taped reading, usually recorded in advance by an astrologer, or a live consultation with an "astrologer" on the other end of the line. The taped readings are general daily or weekly forecasts, applied to all members of your sign and charged by the minute. The quality depends on the astrologer. Be aware that these readings can run up quite a telephone bill, especially if you get into the habit of calling every day. Be sure that you are aware of the per-minute cost of each call beforehand.

Live telephone readings also vary with the expertise of the astrologer. Ideally, the astrologer at the other end of the line enters your birth data into a computer, which then quickly calculates your chart. This chart will be referred to during the consultation. The advantage of a live telephone reading is that your individual chart is used and you can ask about a specific problem. However, before you invest in any reading, be sure that your astrologer is qualified and that you fully understand in advance how much you will be charged. There should be no unpleasant financial surprises later. The best astrologer is one who is recommended to you by a friend or family member.

# Computer-Generated Reports

Companies that offer computer programs (such as ACS, Matrix, and Astrolabe) also offer a variety of computer-generated horoscope readings. These can be quite comprehensive, offering a beautiful printout of the chart plus many pages of detailed information about each planet and aspect of the chart. You can then study it at your convenience. Of course, the interpretations will be general, since there is no personal input from you, and might not cover your immediate concerns. Since computer-generated horoscopes are much lower in cost than live consultations, you might consider them as either a supplement or a preparation for an eventual live reading You'll then be more familiar with your chart and able to plan specific questions in advance. They also make a terrific gift for astrology fans. In chapter 12, there are listed several companies that offer computerized readings prepared by reputable astrologers.

Whichever option you decide to pursue, may your reading be an empowering one!

# CHAPTER 10

# The Key Role of Your Rising Sign

In order to interpret a chart accurately, an astrologer must know where in a person's life an activity will take place. That is determined by the rising sign, which is the degree of the zodiac ascending over the eastern horizon at the time you were born. (That's why it's often called the ascendant.) It marks the first point in the horoscope, the beginning of the first house. This house is one of twelve divisions of the horoscope, each of which represents a different area of life. After the rising sign, the other houses parade around the chart in sequence, with the following sign on the next house cusp.

Though you can learn much about a person by the signs and interactions of the sun, moon, and planets in the horoscope, without a valid rising sign, the collection of planets have no "homes." One would have no idea which area of life could be influenced by a particular planet. For example, you might know that a person has Mars in Aries, which will describe that person's dynamic fiery energy. But if you also know that the person has a Capricorn rising sign, this Mars will fall in the fourth house of home and family, so you know where that energy will operate.

Due to the earth's rotation, the rising sign changes every two hours, which means that babies born later or earlier on the same day in the same hospital will have most planets in the same signs, but may not have the same rising sign. Therefore, their planets may fall in different houses in the chart. For instance, if Mars is in Gemini and your rising sign is Taurus, Mars will most likely be active in the second or financial house of your chart. Someone born later in the same day when the rising sign is Virgo would have Mars positioned at the top of the chart, energizing the tenth house of career.

Most astrologers insist on knowing the exact time of a client's birth before they analyze a chart. The more accurate your birth time, the more accurately an astrologer can position the planets in your chart by determining the correct rising sign.

## How Your Rising Sign Can Influence Your Sun Sign

Your rising sign has an important relationship with your sun sign. Some will complement the sun sign; others hide it under a totally different mask, as if playing an entirely different role, making it difficult to guess the person's sun sign from outer appearances. This may be the reason why you might not look or act like your sun sign's archetype. For example, a Leo with a conservative Capricorn ascendant would come across as much more serious than a Leo with a fiery Aries or Sagittarius ascendant.

Though the rising sign usually creates the first impression you make, there are exceptions. When the sun sign is reinforced by other planets in the same sign, this might overpower the impression of the rising sign. For instance, a Leo sun plus a Leo Venus and Leo Jupiter would counteract the more conservative image that would otherwise be conveyed by the person's Capricorn ascendant.

Those born early in the morning when the sun was on the horizon will be most likely to project the image of their sun sign. These people are often called a "double Aries" or a "double Virgo" because the same sun sign and ascendant reinforce each other.

## Find Your Rising Sign

Look up your rising sign on the chart at the end of this chapter. Since rising signs change every two hours, it is important to know your birth time as close to the minute as possible. Even a few minutes' difference could change the rising sign and therefore the setup of your chart. If you are unsure about the exact time, but know within a few hours, check the following descriptions to see which is most like the personality you project.

## Aries Rising: Alpha Energy

You are the most aggressive version of your sun sign, with boundless energy that can be used productively if it's channeled in the right direction. Watch a tendency to overreact emotionally and blow your top. You come across as openly competitive, a positive asset in business or sports. Be on guard against impatience, which could lead to head injuries. Your walk and bearing could have the telltale head-forward Aries posture. You may wear more bright colors, especially red, than others of your sign, or be a redhead. You may also have a tendency to drive your car faster.

Can you see the alpha Aries tendency in Barbra Streisand (a sun sign Taurus) and Bette Midler (a sun sign Sagittarius)?

## Taurus Rising: Down-to-Earth

You're slow-moving, with a beautiful (or distinctive) speaking or singing voice. You probably surround yourself with comfort, good food, luxurious surroundings, and other sensual pleasures. You prefer welcoming others into your home to gadding about. You may have a talent for business,especially in trading, appraising, and real estate. A Taurus ascendant gives a well-padded physique that gains weight easily, like Liza Minnelli. This ascendant can also endow females with a curvaceous beauty.

## Gemini Rising: A Way with Words

You're naturally sociable, with lighter, more ethereal mannerisms than others of your sign, especially if you're female. You love to communicate with people, and express your ideas easily, like former British prime minister Tony Blair. You may have a talent for writing or public speaking. You thrive on variety, a constantly changing scene, and a lively social life. However, you may relate to others at a deeper level than might be suspected. And you will be far more sympathetic and caring than you project. You will probably travel widely, changing partners and jobs several times (or juggle two at once). Physically, your nerves are quite sensitive. Occasionally, you would benefit from a calm, tranquil atmosphere away from your usual social scene.

## Cancer Rising: Nurturing Instincts

You are naturally acquisitive, possessive, private, a moneymaker like Bill Gates or Michael Bloomberg. You easily pick up others' needs and feelings—a great gift in business, the arts, and personal relationships. But you must guard against overreacting or taking things too personally, especially during full-moon periods. Find creative outlets for your natural nurturing gifts, such as helping the less fortunate, particularly children. Your insights would be helpful in psychology. Your desire to feed and care for others would be useful in the restaurant, hotel, or child-care industries. You may be especially fond of wearing romantic old clothes, collecting antiques, and dining on exquisite food. Since your body may retain fluids, pay attention to your diet. To relax, escape to places near water.

## Leo Rising: Diva Dazzle

You may come across as more poised than you really feel. However, you play it to the hilt, projecting a proud royal presence. A Leo ascendant gives you a natural flair for drama, like Marilyn Monroe, and you might be accused of stealing the spotlight. You'll also project a much more outgoing, optimistic, and sunny personality than others of your sign. You take care to please your public by always projecting star quality, probably tossing a luxuriant mane of hair, sporting a striking hairstyle, or dressing to impress. Females often dazzle with colorful clothing or spectacular jewelry. Since you may have a strong parental nature, you could well become a family matriarch or patriarch, like George H. W. Bush.

## Virgo Rising: Hiqh Standards

Virgo rising endows you with a practical, analytical outer image. You seem neat, orderly, and more particular than others of your sign. Others in your life may feel they must live up to your high standards. Though at times you may be openly critical, this masks a well-meaning desire to have only the best for loved ones. Your sharp eye for details could be used in the financial world, or your literary skills could draw you to teaching or publishing. The healing arts, health care, and service-oriented professions attract many with a Virgo ascendant. You're likely to take good care of yourself, with great attention to health, diet, and exercise, like Madonna. You might even show some hypochondriac tendencies, like Woody Allen. Physically, you may have a very sensitive digestive system.

## Libra Rising: The Charmer

Libra rising gives you a charming, social, and public persona, like John F. Kennedy and Bill Clinton. You tend to avoid confrontations in relationships, preferring to smooth the way or negotiate diplomatically rather than give in to an emotional reaction. Because you are interested in all aspects of a situation, you may be slow to reach decisions. Physically, you'll have good proportions and physical symmetry. You will move with natural grace and balance. You're likely to have pleasing, if not beautiful, facial features, with a winning smile, like Cary Grant. You'll show natural good taste and harmony in your clothes and home decor. Legal, diplomatic, or public relations professions could draw your interest.

## Scorpio Rising: Air of Mystery

You project an intriguing air of mystery with this ascendant, as the Scorpio secretiveness and sense of underlying power combine with your sun sign. Like Jacqueline Kennedy Onassis, you convey that there's more to you than meets the eye. You seem like someone who is always in control and who can move comfortably in the world of power. Your physical look comes across as intense. Many of you have remarkable eyes, with a direct, penetrating gaze. But you'll never reveal your private agenda, and you tend to keep your true feelings under wraps (watch a tendency toward paranoia). You may have an interesting romantic history with secret love affairs, like Grace Kelly. Many of you heighten your air of mystery by wearing black. You're happiest near water; you should provide yourself with a seaside retreat.

## Sagittarius Rising: The Explorer

You travel with this ascendant. You may also be a more outdoor, sportive type, with an athletic, casual, and outgoing air. Your moods are camouflaged with cheerful optimism or a philosophical attitude. Though you don't hesitate to speak your mind—like Ted Turner, who was called the Mouth of the South—you can also laugh at your troubles or crack a joke more easily than others of your sign. A Sagittarius ascendant can also draw you to the field of higher education or to spiritual life. You'll seem to have less attachment to things and people, and you may explore the globe. Your strong, fast legs are a physical bonus.

## Capricorn Rising: Serious Business

This rising sign makes you come across as serious, goal-oriented, disciplined, and careful with cash. You are not one of the zodiac's big spenders, though you might splurge occasionally on items with good investment value. You're the conservative type in dress and environment, and you might come across as quite formal and businesslike, like Rupert Murdoch. You'll function well in a structured or corporate environment where you can climb to the top. (You are always aware of who's the boss.) In your personal life, you could be a loner or a single parent who is father and mother to your children.

# Aquarius Rising: One of a Kind

You come across as less concerned about what others think and could even be a bit eccentric. Your appearance is sure to be unique and memorable. You're more at ease with groups of people than others in your sign, and you may be attracted to public life, like Jay Leno. Your appearance may be unique, either unconventional or unimportant to you. Those of you whose sun is in a water sign (Cancer, Scorpio, or Pisces) may exercise your nurturing qualities with a large group, an extended family, or a day-care or community center.

# Pisces Rising: Romantic Roles

Your creative, nurturing talents are heightened and so is your ability to project emotional drama. And, like Antonio Banderas, your dreamy eyes and poetic air bring out the protective instinct in others. You could be attracted to the arts, especially theater, dance, film, and photography, or to psychology, spiritual practice, and charity work. You are happiest when you are using your creative ability to help others. Since you are vulnerable to mood swings, it is important for you to find interesting, creative work where you can express your talents and heighten your self-esteem. Accentuate the positive. Be wary of escapist tendencies, particularly involving alcohol or drugs to which you are supersensitive, like Whitney Houston.

# RISING SIGNS—A.M. BIRTHS

|         | 1 AM | 2 AM | 3 AM | 4 AM | 5 AM | 6 AM | 7 AM | 8 AM | 9 AM | 10 AM | 11 AM | 12 NOON |
|---------|------|------|------|------|------|------|------|------|------|-------|-------|---------|
| Jan 1   | Lib  | Sc   | Sc   | Sc   | Sag  | Sag  | Cap  | Cap  | Aq   | Aq    | Pis   | Ar      |
| Jan 9   | Lib  | Sc   | Sc   | Sag  | Sag  | Sag  | Cap  | Cap  | Aq   | Pis   | Ar    | Tau     |
| Jan 17  | Sc   | Sc   | Sc   | Sag  | Sag  | Cap  | Cap  | Aq   | Aq   | Pis   | Ar    | Tau     |
| Jan 25  | Sc   | Sc   | Sag  | Sag  | Sag  | Cap  | Cap  | Aq   | Pis  | Ar    | Tau   | Tau     |
| Feb 2   | Sc   | Sc   | Sag  | Sag  | Cap  | Cap  | Aq   | Pis  | Pis  | Ar    | Tau   | Gem     |
| Feb 10  | Sc   | Sag  | Sag  | Sag  | Cap  | Cap  | Aq   | Pis  | Ar   | Tau   | Tau   | Gem     |
| Feb 18  | Sc   | Sag  | Sag  | Cap  | Cap  | Aq   | Pis  | Pis  | Ar   | Tau   | Gem   | Gem     |
| Feb 26  | Sag  | Sag  | Sag  | Cap  | Aq   | Aq   | Pis  | Ar   | Tau  | Tau   | Gem   | Gem     |
| Mar 6   | Sag  | Sag  | Cap  | Cap  | Aq   | Pis  | Pis  | Ar   | Tau  | Gem   | Gem   | Can     |
| Mar 14  | Sag  | Cap  | Cap  | Aq   | Aq   | Pis  | Ar   | Tau  | Tau  | Gem   | Gem   | Can     |
| Mar 22  | Sag  | Cap  | Cap  | Aq   | Pis  | Ar   | Ar   | Tau  | Gem  | Gem   | Can   | Can     |
| Mar 30  | Cap  | Cap  | Aq   | Pis  | Pis  | Ar   | Tau  | Tau  | Gem  | Can   | Can   | Can     |
| Apr 7   | Cap  | Cap  | Aq   | Pis  | Ar   | Ar   | Tau  | Gem  | Gem  | Can   | Can   | Leo     |
| Apr 14  | Cap  | Aq   | Aq   | Pis  | Ar   | Tau  | Tau  | Gem  | Gem  | Can   | Can   | Leo     |
| Apr 22  | Cap  | Aq   | Pis  | Ar   | Ar   | Tau  | Gem  | Gem  | Gem  | Can   | Leo   | Leo     |
| Apr 30  | Aq   | Aq   | Pis  | Ar   | Tau  | Tau  | Gem  | Can  | Can  | Can   | Leo   | Leo     |
| May 8   | Aq   | Pis  | Ar   | Ar   | Tau  | Gem  | Gem  | Can  | Can  | Leo   | Leo   | Leo     |
| May 16  | Aq   | Pis  | Ar   | Tau  | Gem  | Gem  | Can  | Can  | Can  | Leo   | Leo   | Vir     |
| May 24  | Pis  | Ar   | Ar   | Tau  | Gem  | Gem  | Can  | Can  | Leo  | Leo   | Leo   | Vir     |
| June 1  | Pis  | Ar   | Tau  | Gem  | Gem  | Can  | Can  | Can  | Leo  | Leo   | Vir   | Vir     |
| June 9  | Ar   | Ar   | Tau  | Gem  | Gem  | Can  | Can  | Leo  | Leo  | Leo   | Vir   | Vir     |
| June 17 | Ar   | Tau  | Gem  | Gem  | Can  | Can  | Can  | Leo  | Leo  | Vir   | Vir   | Vir     |
| June 25 | Tau  | Tau  | Gem  | Gem  | Can  | Can  | Leo  | Leo  | Leo  | Vir   | Vir   | Lib     |
| July 3  | Tau  | Gem  | Gem  | Can  | Can  | Can  | Leo  | Leo  | Vir  | Vir   | Vir   | Lib     |
| July 11 | Tau  | Gem  | Gem  | Can  | Can  | Leo  | Leo  | Leo  | Vir  | Vir   | Lib   | Lib     |
| July 18 | Gem  | Gem  | Can  | Can  | Can  | Leo  | Leo  | Vir  | Vir  | Vir   | Lib   | Lib     |
| July 26 | Gem  | Gem  | Can  | Can  | Can  | Leo  | Leo  | Vir  | Vir  | Lib   | Lib   | Lib     |
| Aug 3   | Gem  | Can  | Can  | Can  | Leo  | Leo  | Vir  | Vir  | Vir  | Lib   | Lib   | Sc      |
| Aug 11  | Gem  | Can  | Can  | Leo  | Leo  | Leo  | Vir  | Vir  | Lib  | Lib   | Lib   | Sc      |
| Aug 18  | Can  | Can  | Can  | Leo  | Leo  | Vir  | Vir  | Vir  | Lib  | Lib   | Sc    | Sc      |
| Aug 27  | Can  | Can  | Leo  | Leo  | Leo  | Vir  | Vir  | Lib  | Lib  | Lib   | Sc    | Sc      |
| Sept 4  | Can  | Can  | Leo  | Leo  | Leo  | Vir  | Vir  | Vir  | Lib  | Lib   | Sc    | Sc      |
| Sept 12 | Can  | Leo  | Leo  | Leo  | Vir  | Vir  | Lib  | Lib  | Lib  | Sc    | Sc    | Sag     |
| Sept 20 | Leo  | Leo  | Leo  | Vir  | Vir  | Vir  | Lib  | Lib  | Lib  | Sc    | Sc    | Sag     |
| Sept 28 | Leo  | Leo  | Leo  | Vir  | Vir  | Lib  | Lib  | Lib  | Sc   | Sc    | Sag   | Sag     |
| Oct 6   | Leo  | Leo  | Vir  | Vir  | Vir  | Lib  | Lib  | Sc   | Sc   | Sc    | Sag   | Sag     |
| Oct 14  | Leo  | Vir  | Vir  | Vir  | Lib  | Lib  | Lib  | Sc   | Sc   | Sag   | Sag   | Cap     |
| Oct 22  | Leo  | Vir  | Vir  | Lib  | Lib  | Lib  | Sc   | Sc   | Sc   | Sag   | Sag   | Cap     |
| Oct 30  | Vir  | Vir  | Vir  | Lib  | Lib  | Sc   | Sc   | Sc   | Sag  | Sag   | Cap   | Cap     |
| Nov 7   | Vir  | Vir  | Lib  | Lib  | Lib  | Sc   | Sc   | Sc   | Sag  | Sag   | Cap   | Cap     |
| Nov 15  | Vir  | Vir  | Lib  | Lib  | Lib  | Sc   | Sc   | Sag  | Sag  | Cap   | Cap   | Aq      |
| Nov 23  | Vir  | Lib  | Lib  | Lib  | Sc   | Sc   | Sag  | Sag  | Cap  | Cap   | Aq    | Aq      |
| Dec 1   | Vir  | Lib  | Lib  | Sc   | Sc   | Sc   | Sag  | Sag  | Cap  | Cap   | Aq    | Aq      |
| Dec 9   | Lib  | Lib  | Lib  | Sc   | Sc   | Sag  | Sag  | Sag  | Cap  | Cap   | Aq    | Pis     |
| Dec 18  | Lib  | Lib  | Sc   | Sc   | Sc   | Sag  | Sag  | Cap  | Cap  | Aq    | Aq    | Pis     |
| Dec 28  | Lib  | Lib  | Sc   | Sc   | Sag  | Sag  | Sag  | Cap  | Aq   | Aq    | Pis   | Ar      |

# RISING SIGNS—P.M. BIRTHS

| | 1 PM | 2 PM | 3 PM | 4 PM | 5 PM | 6 PM | 7 PM | 8 PM | 9 PM | 10 PM | 11 PM | 12 MID-NIGHT |
|---|---|---|---|---|---|---|---|---|---|---|---|---|
| Jan 1 | Tau | Gem | Gem | Can | Can | Can | Leo | Leo | Vir | Vir | Vir | Lib |
| Jan 9 | Tau | Gem | Gem | Can | Can | Leo | Leo | Leo | Vir | Vir | Vir | Lib |
| Jan 17 | Gem | Gem | Can | Can | Can | Leo | Leo | Leo | Vir | Vir | Lib | Lib |
| Jan 25 | Gem | Gem | Can | Can | Leo | Leo | Leo | Vir | Vir | Lib | Lib | Lib |
| Feb 2 | Gem | Can | Can | Can | Leo | Leo | Vir | Vir | Vir | Lib | Lib | Sc |
| Feb 10 | Gem | Can | Can | Leo | Leo | Leo | Vir | Vir | Lib | Lib | Lib | Sc |
| Feb 18 | Can | Can | Can | Leo | Leo | Vir | Vir | Vir | Lib | Lib | Sc | Sc |
| Feb 26 | Can | Can | Leo | Leo | Leo | Vir | Vir | Lib | Lib | Lib | Sc | Sc |
| Mar 6 | Can | Leo | Leo | Leo | Vir | Vir | Vir | Lib | Lib | Sc | Sc | Sc |
| Mar 14 | Can | Leo | Leo | Vir | Vir | Vir | Lib | Lib | Lib | Sc | Sc | Sag |
| Mar 22 | Leo | Leo | Leo | Vir | Vir | Lib | Lib | Lib | Sc | Sc | Sc | Sag |
| Mar 30 | Leo | Leo | Vir | Vir | Vir | Lib | Lib | Sc | Sc | Sc | Sag | Sag |
| Apr 7 | Leo | Leo | Vir | Vir | Lib | Lib | Lib | Sc | Sc | Sc | Sag | Sag |
| Apr 14 | Leo | Vir | Vir | Vir | Lib | Lib | Sc | Sc | Sc | Sag | Sag | Cap |
| Apr 22 | Leo | Vir | Vir | Lib | Lib | Lib | Sc | Sc | Sc | Sag | Sag | Cap |
| Apr 30 | Vir | Vir | Vir | Lib | Lib | Sc | Sc | Sc | Sag | Sag | Cap | Cap |
| May 8 | Vir | Vir | Lib | Lib | Lib | Sc | Sc | Sag | Sag | Sag | Cap | Cap |
| May 16 | Vir | Vir | Lib | Lib | Sc | Sc | Sc | Sag | Sag | Cap | Cap | Aq |
| May 24 | Vir | Lib | Lib | Lib | Sc | Sc | Sag | Sag | Sag | Cap | Cap | Aq |
| June 1 | Vir | Lib | Lib | Sc | Sc | Sc | Sag | Sag | Cap | Cap | Aq | Aq |
| June 9 | Lib | Lib | Lib | Sc | Sc | Sag | Sag | Sag | Cap | Cap | Aq | Pis |
| June 17 | Lib | Lib | Sc | Sc | Sc | Sag | Sag | Cap | Cap | Aq | Aq | Pis |
| June 25 | Lib | Lib | Sc | Sc | Sag | Sag | Sag | Cap | Cap | Aq | Pis | Ar |
| July 3 | Lib | Sc | Sc | Sc | Sag | Sag | Cap | Cap | Aq | Aq | Pis | Ar |
| July 11 | Lib | Sc | Sc | Sag | Sag | Sag | Cap | Cap | Aq | Pis | Ar | Tau |
| July 18 | Sc | Sc | Sc | Sag | Sag | Cap | Cap | Aq | Aq | Pis | Ar | Tau |
| July 26 | Sc | Sc | Sag | Sag | Sag | Cap | Cap | Aq | Pis | Ar | Tau | Tau |
| Aug 3 | Sc | Sc | Sag | Sag | Cap | Cap | Aq | Aq | Pis | Ar | Tau | Gem |
| Aug 11 | Sc | Sag | Sag | Sag | Cap | Cap | Aq | Pis | Ar | Tau | Tau | Gem |
| Aug 18 | Sc | Sag | Sag | Cap | Cap | Aq | Pis | Pis | Ar | Tau | Gem | Gem |
| Aug 27 | Sag | Sag | Sag | Cap | Cap | Aq | Pis | Ar | Tau | Tau | Gem | Gem |
| Sept 4 | Sag | Sag | Cap | Cap | Aq | Pis | Pis | Ar | Tau | Gem | Gem | Can |
| Sept 12 | Sag | Sag | Cap | Aq | Aq | Pis | Ar | Tau | Tau | Gem | Gem | Can |
| Sept 20 | Sag | Cap | Cap | Aq | Pis | Pis | Ar | Tau | Gem | Gem | Can | Can |
| Sept 28 | Cap | Cap | Aq | Aq | Pis | Ar | Tau | Tau | Gem | Gem | Can | Can |
| Oct 6 | Cap | Cap | Aq | Pis | Ar | Ar | Tau | Gem | Gem | Can | Can | Leo |
| Oct 14 | Cap | Aq | Aq | Pis | Ar | Tau | Tau | Gem | Gem | Can | Can | Leo |
| Oct 22 | Cap | Aq | Pis | Ar | Ar | Tau | Gem | Gem | Can | Can | Leo | Leo |
| Oct 30 | Aq | Aq | Pis | Ar | Tau | Tau | Gem | Can | Can | Can | Leo | Leo |
| Nov 7 | Aq | Aq | Pis | Ar | Tau | Tau | Gem | Can | Can | Can | Leo | Leo |
| Nov 15 | Aq | Pis | Ar | Tau | Gem | Gem | Can | Can | Can | Leo | Leo | Vir |
| Nov 23 | Pis | Ar | Ar | Tau | Gem | Gem | Can | Can | Leo | Leo | Leo | Vir |
| Dec 1 | Pis | Ar | Tau | Gem | Gem | Can | Can | Can | Leo | Leo | Vir | Vir |
| Dec 9 | Ar | Tau | Tau | Gem | Gem | Can | Can | Leo | Leo | Leo | Vir | Vir |
| Dec 18 | Ar | Tau | Gem | Gem | Can | Can | Can | Leo | Leo | Vir | Vir | Vir |
| Dec 28 | Tau | Tau | Gem | Gem | Can | Can | Leo | Leo | Vir | Vir | Vir | Lib |

# CHAPTER 11

# The Secret Language of Astrology: What the Glyphs Reveal About the Signs and Planets

At last, you've got your very first horoscope chart. Perhaps you've downloaded it from one of the many Internet sites that offer free charts, or you're trying out new astrology software. But then you find that the chart is covered with strange symbols that look like an exotic language, indecipherable by a neophyte astrology fan. Reading a horoscope chart can be a daunting task if you don't understand the meaning of the mysterious symbols, called glyphs, used as a kind of universal shorthand on the horoscope chart. There's no avoiding it—if you want to read an astrology chart, you've got to learn the glyphs!

The glyphs are more than just pictographs. They contain a kind of code, with built-in clues that will tell you not only which sign or planet each represents, but what the symbol means in a deeper, more esoteric sense. Actually the physical act of writing the symbol is a mystical experience in itself, a way to invoke the deeper meaning of the sign or planet through age-old visual elements that have been with us since time began.

Since there are only twelve signs and ten planets (not counting a few asteroids and other space objects some astrologers use), it's a lot easier than learning to read a foreign language. Here's a code cracker for the glyphs, beginning with the glyphs for the planets. To those who already know their glyphs, don't just skim over the chapter.

These familiar graphics have hidden meanings you will discover!

# The Glyphs for the Planets

The glyphs for the planets are easy to learn. They're simple combinations of the most basic visual elements: the circle, the semicircle or arc, and the cross. However, each component of a glyph has a special meaning in relation to the other parts of the symbol.

The circle, which has no beginning or end, is one of the oldest symbols of spirit or spiritual forces. Early diagrams of the heavens—spiritual territory—are shown in circular form. The never-ending line of the circle is the perfect symbol for eternity. The semicircle or arc is an incomplete circle, symbolizing the receptive, finite soul, which contains spiritual potential in the curving line.

The vertical line of the cross symbolizes movement from heaven to earth. The horizontal line describes temporal movement, here and now, in time and space. Combined in a cross, the vertical and horizontal planes symbolize manifestation in the material world.

## The Sun Glyph ☉

The sun is always shown by this powerful solar symbol, a circle with a point in the center. The center point is you, your spiritual center, and the symbol represents your infinite personality incarnating (the point) into the finite cycles of birth and death.

The sun has been represented by a circle or disk since ancient Egyptian times when the solar disk represented the sun god, Ra. Some archaeologists believe the great stone circles found in England were centers of sun worship. This particular version of the symbol was brought into common use in the sixteenth century after German occultist and scholar Cornelius Agrippa (1486–1535) wrote a book called *Die Occulta Philosophia,* which became accepted as the authority in the field. Agrippa collected many of the medieval astrological and magical symbols in this book, which have been used by astrologers since then.

## The Moon Glyph ☽

The moon glyph is the most recognizable symbol on a chart, a left-facing arc stylized into the crescent moon. As part of a circle, the arc symbolizes the potential fulfillment of the entire circle, the life force that is still incomplete. Therefore, it is the ideal representation of the reactive, receptive, emotional nature of the moon.

## The Mercury Glyph ☿

Mercury contains all three elemental symbols: the crescent, the circle, and the cross in vertical order. This is the "Venus with a hat" glyph (compare with the symbol of Venus). With another stretch of the imagination, can't you see the winged cap of Mercury the messenger? Think of the up-turned crescent as antennae that tune in and transmit messages from the sun, reminding you that Mercury is the way you communicate, the way your mind works. The upturned arc is receiving energy into the spirit or solar circle, which will later be translated into action on the material plane, symbolized by the cross. All the elements are equally sized because Mercury is neutral; it doesn't play favorites! This planet symbolizes objective, detached, unemotional thinking.

## The Venus Glyph ♀

Here the relationship is between two components: the circle of spirit and the cross of matter. Spirit is elevated over matter, pulling it upward. Venus asks, "What is beautiful? What do you like best? What do you love to have done to you?" Consequently, Venus determines both your ideal of beauty and what feels good sensually. It governs your own allure and power to attract, as well as what attracts and pleases you.

# The Mars Glyph ♂

In this glyph, the cross of matter is stylized into an arrow-head pointed up and outward, propelled by the circle of spirit. With a little imagination, you can visualize it as the shield and spear of Mars, the ancient god of war. You can deduce that Mars embodies your spiritual energy projected into the outer world. It's your assertiveness, your initiative, your aggressive drive, what you like to do to others, your temper. If you know someone's Mars, you know whether they'll blow up when angry or do a slow burn. Your task is to use your outgoing Mars energy wisely and well.

# The Jupiter Glyph ♃

Jupiter is the basic cross of matter, with a large stylized crescent perched on the left side of the horizontal, temporal plane. You might think of the crescent as an open hand, because one meaning of Jupiter is "luck," what's handed to you. You don't have to work for what you get from Jupiter; it comes to you, if you're open to it.

The Jupiter glyph might also remind you of a jumbo jet plane, with a huge tail fin, about to take off. This is the planet of travel, mental and spiritual, of expanding your horizons via new ideas, new spiritual dimensions, and new places. Jupiter embodies the optimism and enthusiasm of the traveler about to embark on an exciting adventure.

# The Saturn Glyph ♄

Flip Jupiter over, and you've got Saturn. This might not be immediately apparent because Saturn is usually stylized into an "h" form like the one shown here. The principle it expresses is the opposite of Jupiter's expansive tendencies. Saturn pulls you back to earth: the receptive arc is pushed down underneath the cross of matter. Before there are any rewards or expansion, the duties and obligations of the material world must be considered. Saturn says, "Stop, wait, finish your chores before you take off!"

Saturn's glyph also resembles the sickle of old "Father Time." Saturn was first known as Chronos, the Greek god of time, for time brings all matter to an end. When it was the most distant planet (before the discovery of Uranus), Saturn was believed to be the place where time stopped. After the soul departed from earth, it journeyed back to the outer reaches of the universe and finally stopped at Saturn, or at "the end of time."

## The Uranus Glyph ♅

The glyph for Uranus is often stylized to form a capital *H* after Sir William Herschel, who discovered the planet. But the more esoteric version curves the two pillars of the H into crescent antennae, or "ears," like satellite disks receiving signals from space. These are perched on the horizontal material line of the cross of matter and pushed from below by the circle of the spirit. To many sci-fi fans, Uranus looks like an orbiting satellite.

Uranus channels the highest energy of all, the white electrical light of the universal spiritual force that holds the cosmos together. This pure electrical energy is gathered from all over the universe. Because Uranus energy doesn't follow any ordinary celestial drumbeat, it can't be controlled or predicted (which is also true of those who are strongly influenced by this eccentric planet). In the symbol, this energy is manifested through the balance of polarities (the two opposite arms of the glyph) like the two polarized wires of a lightbulb.

## The Neptune Glyph ♆

Neptune's glyph is usually stylized to look like a trident, the weapon of the Roman god Neptune. However, on a more esoteric level, it shows the large upturned crescent of the soul pierced through by the cross of matter. Neptune nails down, or materializes, soul energy, bringing impulses from the soul level into manifestation. That is why Neptune is associated with imagination or "imagining in," making an image of the soul. Neptune works through feelings, sensitivity, and the mystical capacity to bring the divine into the earthly realm.

# The Pluto Glyph ♀

Pluto is written two ways. One is a composite of the letters *PL*, the first two letters of the word Pluto and coincidentally the initials of Percival Lowell, one of the planet's discoverers. The other, more esoteric symbol is a small circle above a large open crescent that surmounts the cross of matter. This depicts Pluto's power to regenerate. Imagine a new little spirit emerging from the sheltering cup of the soul. Pluto rules the forces of life and death. After this planet has passed a sensitive point in your chart, you are transformed, reborn in some way.

Sci-fi fans might visualize this glyph as a small satellite (the circle) being launched. It was shortly after Pluto's discovery that we learned how to harness the nuclear forces that made space exploration possible. Pluto rules the transformative power of atomic energy, which totally changed our lives and from which there is no turning back.

# The Glyphs for the Signs

On an astrology chart, the glyph for the sign will appear after that of the planet. For example, when you see the moon glyph followed first by a number and then by another glyph representing the sign, this means that the moon was passing over a certain degree of that astrological sign at the time of the chart. On the dividing lines between the houses on your chart, you'll find the symbol for the sign that rules the house.

Because sun sign symbols do not contain the same basic geometric components of the planetary glyphs, we must look elsewhere for clues to their meanings. Many have been passed down from ancient Egyptian and Chaldean civilizations with few modifications. Others have been adapted over the centuries.

In deciphering many of the glyphs, you'll often find that the symbols reveal a dual nature of the sign, which is not always apparent in the usual sun sign descriptions. For instance, the Gemini glyph is similar to the Roman numeral for two, and reveals this sign's longing to discover a twin soul. The Cancer glyph may be interpreted as resembling either the nurturing breasts or the self-protective claws of a crab, both symbols associated with the contrasting qualities of this sign. Libra's glyph embodies the duality of the spirit balanced with material reality. The Sagittarius glyph shows that the aspirant must also carry along the earthly animal nature in his quest. The Capricorn sea goat is another symbol with dual emphasis. The goat climbs high, yet is always pulled back by the deep waters of the unconscious. Aquarius embodies the double waves of mental detachment, balanced by the desire for connection with others, in a friendly way. Finally, the two fishes of Pisces, which are forever tied together, show the duality of the soul and the spirit that must be reconciled.

## The Aries Glyph ♈

Since the symbol for Aries is the Ram, this glyph is obviously associated with a ram's horns, which characterize one aspect of the Aries personality—an aggressive, me-first, leaping-headfirst attitude. But the symbol can be interpreted in other ways as well. Some astrologers liken it to a fountain of energy, which Aries people also embody. The first sign of the zodiac bursts on the scene eagerly, ready to go. Another analogy is to the eyebrows and nose of the human head, which Aries rules, and the thinking power that is initiated by the brain.

One theory of this symbol links it to the Egyptian god Amun, represented by a ram in ancient times. As Amun-Ra, this god was believed to embody the creator of the universe, the leader of all the other gods. This relates easily to the position of Aries as the leader (or first sign) of the zodiac, which begins at the spring equinox, a time of the year when nature is renewed.

## The Taurus Glyph ♉

This is another easy glyph to draw and identify. It takes little imagination to decipher the bull's head with long curving horns. Like its symbol the Bull, the archetypal Taurus is slow to anger but ferocious when provoked, as well as stubborn, steady, and sensual. Another association is the larynx (and thyroid) of the throat area (ruled by Taurus) and the eustachian tubes running up to the ears, which coincides with the relationship of Taurus to the voice, song, and music. Many famous singers, musicians, and composers have prominent Taurus influences.

Many ancient religions involved a bull as the central figure in fertility rites or initiations, usually symbolizing the victory of man over his animal nature. Another possible origin is in the sacred bull of Egypt, who embodied the incarnate form of Osiris, god of death and resurrection. In early Christian imagery, the Taurus Bull represented St. Luke.

## The Gemini Glyph ♊

The standard glyph immediately calls to mind the Roman numeral for two (II) and the Twins symbol, as it is called, for Gemini. In almost all drawings and images used for this sign, the relationship between two persons is emphasized. Usually one twin will be touching the other, which signifies communication, human contact, the desire to share.

The top line of the Gemini glyph indicates mental communication, while the bottom line indicates shared physical space.

The most famous Gemini legend is that of the twin sons, Castor and Pollux, one of whom had a mortal father while the other was the son of Zeus, king of the gods. When it came time for the mortal twin to die, his grief-stricken brother pleaded with Zeus, who agreed to let them spend half the year on earth in mortal form and half in immortal life, with the gods on Mount Olympus. This reflects a basic duality of humankind, which possesses an immortal soul yet is also subject to the limits of mortality.

## The Cancer Glyph ♋

Two convenient images relate to the Cancer glyph. It is easiest to decode the curving claws of the Cancer symbol, the Crab. Like the crab's, Cancer's element is water. This sensitive sign also has a hard protective shell to protect its tender interior. The crab must be wily to escape predators, scampering sideways and hiding under rocks. The crab also responds to the cycles of the moon, as do all shellfish. The other image is that of two female breasts, which Cancer rules, showing that this is a sign that nurtures and protects others as well as itself.

In ancient Egypt, Cancer was also represented by the scarab beetle, a symbol of regeneration and eternal life.

## The Leo Glyph ♌

Notice that the Leo glyph seems to be an extension of Cancer's glyph, with a significant difference. In the Cancer glyph, the lines curve inward protectively. The Leo glyph expresses energy outwardly. And there is no duality in the symbol, the Lion, or in Leo, the sign.

Lions have belonged to the sign of Leo since earliest times. It is not difficult to imagine the king of beasts with his sweeping mane and curling tail from this glyph. The upward sweep of the glyph easily describes the positive energy of Leo: the flourishing tail, the flamboyant qualities. Anther analogy, perhaps a stretch of the imagination, is that of a heart leaping up with joy and enthusiasm, also very typical of Leo, which also rules the heart. In early Christian imagery, the Leo Lion represented St. Mark.

## The Virgo Glyph ♍

You can read much into this mysterious glyph. For instance, it could represent the initials of "Mary Virgin," or a young woman holding a staff of wheat, or stylized female genitalia, all common interpretations. The M shape might also remind you that Virgo is ruled by Mercury. The cross beneath the symbol reveals the grounded, practical nature of this earth sign.

The earliest zodiacs link Virgo with the Egyptian goddess Isis, who gave birth to the god Horus after her husband Osiris had been killed, in the archetype of a miraculous conception. There are many ancient statues of Isis nursing her baby son, which are reminiscent of medieval Virgin and Child motifs. This sign has also been associated with the image of the Holy Grail, when the Virgo symbol was substituted with a chalice.

## The Libra Glyph ☌

It is not difficult to read the standard image for Libra, the Scales, into this glyph. There is another meaning, however, that is equally relevant: the setting sun as it descends over the horizon. Libra's natural position on the zodiac wheel is the descendant, or sunset position (as the Aries natural position is the ascendant, or rising sign). Both images relate to Libra's personality. Libra is always weighing pros and cons for a balanced decision. In the sunset image, the sun (male) hovers over the horizontal earth (female) before setting. Libra is the space between these lines, harmonizing yin and yang, spiritual and material, male and female, ideal and real worlds. The glyph has also been linked to the kidneys, which are associated with Libra.

## The Scorpio Glyph ♏

With its barbed tail, this glyph is easy to identify as the Scorpion for the sign of Scorpio. It also represents the male sexual parts, over which the sign rules. From the arrowhead, you can draw the conclusion that Mars was once its ruler. Some earlier Egyptian glyphs for Scorpio represent it as an erect serpent, so the Serpent is an alternate symbol.

Another symbol for Scorpio, which is not identifiable in this glyph, is the Eagle. Scorpios can go to extremes, either in soaring like the eagle or self-destructing like the scorpion. In early Christian imagery, which often used zodiacal symbols, the Scorpio Eagle was chosen to symbolize the intense apostle St. John the Evangelist.

## The Sagittarius Glyph ♐

This is one of the easiest to spot and draw: an upward pointing arrow lifting up a cross. The arrow is pointing skyward, while the cross represents the four elements of the material world, which the arrow must convey. Elevating materiality into spirituality is an important Sagittarius quality, which explains why this sign is associated with higher learning, religion, philosophy, travel—the aspiring professions. Sagittarius can also send barbed arrows of frankness in the pursuit of truth, so the Archer symbol for Sagittarius is apt. (Sagittarius is also the sign of the supersalesman.)

Sagittarius is symbolically represented by the centaur, a mythological creature who is half man, half horse, aiming his arrow toward the skies. Though Sagittarius is motivated by spiritual aspiration, it also must balance the powerful appetites of the animal nature. The centaur Chiron, a figure in Greek mythology, became a wise teacher who, after many adventures and world travels, was killed by a poisoned arrow.

## The Capricorn Glyph ♑

One of the most difficult symbols to draw, this glyph may take some practice. It is a representation of the sea goat: a mythical animal that is a goat with a curving fish's tail. The goat part of Capricorn wants to leave the waters of the emotions and climb to the elevated areas of life. But the fish tail is the unconscious, the deep chaotic psychic level that draws the goat back. Capricorn is often trying to escape the deep, feeling part of life by submerging himself in work, steadily ascending to the top. To some people, the glyph represents a seated figure with a bent knee, a reminder that Capricorn governs the knee area of the body.

An interesting aspect of this glyph is the contrast of the sharp pointed horns—which represent the penetrating, shrewd, conscious side of Capricorn—with the swishing tail—which represents its serpentine, unconscious, emotional force. One Capricorn legend, which dates from Roman times, tells of the earthy fertility god, Pan, who tried to save himself from uncontrollable sexual desires by jumping into the Nile. His upper body then turned into a goat, while the lower part became a fish. Later, Jupiter gave him a safe haven as a constellation in the skies.

## The Aquarius Glyph ♒

This ancient water symbol can be traced back to an Egyptian hieroglyph representing streams of life force. Symbolized by the Water Bearer, Aquarius is distributor of the waters of life—the magic liquid of regeneration. The two waves can also be linked to the positive and negative charges of the electrical energy that Aquarius rules, a sort of universal wavelength. Aquarius is tuned in intuitively to higher forces via this electrical force. The duality of the glyph could also refer to the dual nature of Aquarius, a sign that runs hot and cold and that is friendly but also detached in the mental world of air signs.

In Greek legends, Aquarius is represented by Ganymede, who was carried to heaven by an eagle in order to become the cupbearer of Zeus and to supervise the annual flooding of the Nile. The sign later became associated with aviation and notions of flight. Like the other fixed signs (Taurus, Scorpio, and Leo), Aquarius is associated with an apostle, in this case St. Matthew.

## The Pisces Glyph ♓

Here is an abstraction of the familiar image of Pisces, two Fishes swimming in opposite directions yet bound together by a cord. The Fishes represent the spirit—which yearns for the freedom of heaven—and the soul—which remains attached to the desires of the temporal world. During life on earth, the spirit and the soul are bound together. When they complement each other, instead of pulling in opposite directions, they facilitate the Pisces creativity. The ancient version of this glyph, taken from the Egyptians, had no connecting line, which was added in the fourteenth century.

In another interpretation, it is said that the left fish indicates the direction of involution or the beginning of a cycle, while the right fish signifies the direction of evolution, the way to completion of a cycle. It's an appropriate grand finale for Pisces, the last sign of the zodiac.

147

# CHAPTER 12

# The Astrology Software Shop

Once upon a time, casting a horoscope required consulting thick books of tables, poring over atlases, and punching numbers on a calculator. Now a few clicks of the computer mouse can provide an accurate and beautifully drawn chart that's equal to any a professional astrologer could cast. A few more clicks will give you a professional interpretation by a world-famous astrologer. How easy is that?

Astrology technology has advanced to the point where even a computerphobe can put a chart on the screen in seconds. It does help to have some basic knowledge of the signs, houses, planets, and especially, the glyphs for the planets and the signs. Then you can practice reading charts and relating the planets to the lives of friends, relatives, and daily events, the ideal way to get more involved with astrology.

When it comes to choosing your astrology software, there are endless options. How do you make the right choice? First, define your goals. Do you want to do charts of friends and family, study celebrity charts, or check the aspects every day on your Palm Pilot? Do you want to invest in a more comprehensive program that adapts to your changing needs as you learn astrology?

The good news is that there's a program for every level of interest at all price points—starting with free. For the dabbler, there is the affordable Winstar Express, Know, and Time Passages. For the serious student, there's Astrolog (free), Solar Fire, Kepler, Winstar Plus—software that does every technique on the planet and gives you beautiful chart printouts. You can do a chart of someone you've just met on your PDA with Astracadabra. If you're a Mac user, you'll be satisfied with the wonderful IO and Time Passages software.

However, since all the programs use the astrology symbols, or glyphs, for planets and signs, rather than written words, you should learn the glyphs before you purchase your software. Chapter 11 will help you do just that. Here are some software options for you to explore.

# Easy for Beginners

## Time Passages

Designed for either a Macintosh or Windows computer, Time Passages is straightforward and easy to use. It allows you to generate charts and interpretation reports for yourself or friends and loved ones at the touch of a button. If you haven't yet learned the astrology symbols, this might be the program for you. Just roll your mouse over any symbols of the planets, signs, or house cusps, and you'll be shown a description in plain English below the chart. Then click on the planet, sign, or house cusp and up pops a detailed interpretation. Couldn't be easier. A new Basic Edition, under fifty dollars at this writing, is bargain priced and ideal for beginners.

Time Passages
(866) 772-7876 (866-77-ASTRO)
Web site: www.astrograph.com

## The "Know Thru Astrology" Series

This new series is designed especially for the nonastrologer. There are four programs in the series: KNOW Your Self, KNOW your future, KNOW Your Lover, and KNOW Your Child, each priced at an affordable $49.95 (at this writing). Though it is billed as beginner software, the KNOW series offers many sophisticated options, such as a calendar to let you navigate future or past influences, detailed chart interpretations, built-in pop-ups to show you what everything means. You'll need a PC running current

Windows versions starting with Windows 98 SE, with 64 Mb RAM, and a hard drive with 170–300 Mb free space.

Matrix Software
126 South Michigan Avenue
Big Rapids, MI 49307
(800) 416-3924
Web site: www.astrologysoftware.com

# Growth Opportunities

## Astrolabe

Astrolabe is one of the top astrology software resources. Check out the latest version of their powerful Solar Fire software for Windows. It's a breeze to use and will grow with your increasing knowledge of astrology to the most sophisticated levels. This company also markets a variety of programs for all levels of expertise and a wide selection of computer-generated astrology readings. This is a good resource for innovative software as well as applications for older computers.

The Astrolabe Web site is a great place to start your astrology tour of the Internet. Visitors to the site are greeted with a chart of the time you log on. And you can get your chart calculated, also free, with a mini interpretation e-mailed to you.

Astrolabe
Box 1750-R
Brewster, MA 02631
Phone: (800) 843-6682
Web site: www.alabe.com

## Matrix Software

You'll find a wide variety of software at student and advanced levels in all price ranges, demo disks, lots of interesting readings. Check out Winstar Express, a powerful but reasonably priced program suitable for all skill levels. The

Matrix Web site offers lots of fun activities for Web surfers, such as free readings from the I Ching, the runes, and the tarot. There are many free desktop backgrounds with astrology themes. Here's where to connect with news groups and online discussions. Their online almanac helps you schedule the best day to sign on the dotted line, ask for a raise, or plant your tomatoes.

Matrix Software
126 South Michigan Avenue
Big Rapids, MI 49307
Phone: (800) 416-3924
Web site: www.astrologysoftware.com

## Astro Communications Services (ACS)

Books, software, individual charts, and telephone readings are offered by this California company. Their freebies include astrology greeting cards and new moon reports. Find technical astrology materials here such as *The American Ephemeris* and PC atlases. ACS will calculate and send charts to you, a valuable service if you do not have a computer.

ACS Publications
P.O. Box 1646
El Cajon, CA 92022-1646
Phone: (800) 514-5070
Fax: (619) 631-0180
Web site: www.astrocom.com

## Air Software

Here you'll find powerful, creative astrology software, plus current stock market analysis. Financial astrology programs for stock market traders are a specialty. There are some interesting freebees at this site. Check out the maps of eclipse paths for any year and a free astrology clock program.

Air Software
115 Caya Avenue

West Hartford, CT 06110
Phone: (800) 659-1247
Web site: www.alphee.com

## Kepler: State of the Art

Here's a program that's got everything. Gorgeous graphic images, audio-visual effects, and myriad sophisticated chart options are built into this fascinating software. It's even got an astrological encyclopedia, plus diagrams and images to help you understand advanced concepts. This program is pricey, but if you're serious about learning astrology, it's an investment that will grow with you! Check out its features at www.astrologysoftwareshop.com.

## Timecycles Research: For Mac Users

Here's where Mac users can find astrology software that's as sophisticated as it gets. If you have a Mac, you'll love their beautiful graphic IO Series programs.

Time Cycles Research
P.O. Box 797
Waterford, CT 06385
(800) 827-2240
Web site: www.timecycles.com

# Shareware and Freeware: The Price Is Right!

## Halloran Software: A Super Shareware Program

Check out Halloran Software's Web site, which offers several levels of Windows astrology software. Beginners should consider their Astrology for Windows shareware program, which is available in unregistered demo form as a free download and in registered form for a very reasonable price.

Halloran Software
P.O. Box 75713
Los Angeles, CA 90075
(800) 732-4628
Web site: www.halloran.com

## ASTROLOG

If you're computer-savvy, you can't go wrong with Walter Pullen's amazingly complete Astrology program, which is offered absolutely free at the site. The Web address is www.astrolog.org/astrolog.htm.

Astrolog is an ultrasophisticated program with all the features of much more expensive programs. It comes in versions for all formats: DOS, Windows, Mac, and UNIX. It has some cool features, such as a revolving globe and a constellation map. If you are looking for astrology software with all the bells and whistles that doesn't cost big bucks, this program has it all!

## Software for the Pocket PDA and Palm Pilot

Would you like to have astrology at your fingertips everywhere you go? No need to drag along your laptop. You can now check the chart of the moment or of someone you've just met on your Pocket PDA or Palm Pilot. As with most other astrology software, you'll need to know the astrological symbols in order to read the charts.

For the pocket PC that has the Microsoft Windows Mobile operating system, there is the versatile Astracadabra, which can interchange charts with the popular Solar Fire software. It can be ordered at www.leelehman.com or www.astrology softwareshop.com.

For the Palm OSS and compatible handheld devices, there is Astropocket from www.astropocket.com. This is a shareware program that allows you to use all the features free. However, you cannot store more than one chart at a time until you pay a mere 28-dollar registration fee for the complete version.

# Buying a Computer with Astrology in Mind?

The good news is that astrology software is becoming more sophisticated and fun to use. It won't be long before there are programs for the iPhone and BlackBerry. However, if you've inherited an old computer, don't despair. You don't need the fastest processor and all the newest bells and whistles to run perfectly adequate astrology software. It is still possible to find programs for elder systems, including many new exciting programs.

To take full advantage of all the options, however, it is best to have a system that runs versions of Windows starting with Windows 98 SE. If you're buying a new computer, invest in one with as much RAM as possible, at least 1 GB. A CD drive will be necessary to load programs or an Internet connection, if you prefer to download programs online.

Mac fans who want to run Windows astrology software should invest in the new dual boot computers that will operate both the Mac and the Windows XP and Vista platforms.

# CHAPTER 13

# Join the Astrology Community

If you've become hooked on astrology, you'll want to share your enthusiasm with others, and perhaps join an astrology club in your city or go to a conference where you can meet the world's top astrologers. Connecting with astrology fans and learning more about this fascinating subject has never been easier. In fact the many options available with just a click of your computer are mind-boggling.

You need only type the word *astrology* into any Internet search engine and watch hundreds of listing of astrology-related sites pop up. There are local meetings and international conferences where you can meet and study with other astrologers, and books and tapes to help you learn at home. You could even combine your vacation with an astrological workshop in an exotic locale, such as Bali or Mexico.

To help you sort out the variety of options available, here are our top picks of the Internet and the astrological community at large.

## National Council for Geocosmic Research (NCGR)

Whether you'd like to know more about such specialties as financial astrology or techniques for timing events, or if you'd prefer the psychological or mythological approach, you'll meet the top astrologers at conferences sponsored by the National Council for Geocosmic Research. NCGR is dedicated to providing quality education, bringing astrologers and astrology fans together at conferences, and promoting fellowship. Their course structure provides a systematized study of the many facets of astrology. The organization sponsors educational workshops, taped lectures, conferences, and a directory of professional astrologers.

For an annual membership fee, you get their excellent publications and newsletters, plus the opportunity to network with other astrology buffs at local chapter events. At this writing there are chapters in twenty-six states and four countries.

To join NCGR and for the latest information on upcoming events and chapters in your city, consult their Web site: www.geocosmic.org.

## American Federation of Astrologers (AFA)

Established in 1938, this is one of the oldest astrological organizations in the United States. AFA offers conferences, conventions, and a correspondence course. If you are looking for a reading, their interesting Web site will refer you to an accredited AFA astrologer.

6535 South Rural Road
Tempe, AZ 85283
Phone: (888) 301-7630 or (480) 838-1751
Fax: (480) 838-8293
Web site: www.astrologers.com

## Association for Astrological Networking (AFAN)

Did you know that astrologers are still being harassed for practicing astrology? AFAN provides support and legal information, and works toward improving the public image of astrology. AFAN's network of local astrologers links with the international astrological community. Here are the people who will go to bat for astrology when it is attacked in the media. Everyone who cares about astrology should join!

8306 Wilshire Boulevard
PMB 537

Beverly Hills, CA 90211
Phone: (800) 578-2326
E-mail: info@afan.org
Web site: www.afan.org

## International Society for Astrology Research (ISAR)

An international organization of professional astrologers dedicated to encouraging the highest standards of quality in the field of astrology with an emphasis on research. Among ISAR's benefits are quarterly journals, a weekly e-mail newsletter, and a free membership directory.

P.O. Box 38613
Los Angeles, CA 90038
Fax: (800) 933-0301
Web site: www.isarastrology.com

## Astrology Magazines

In addition to articles by top astrologers, most have listings of astrology conferences, events, and local happenings.

*Horoscope Guide*
Kappa Publishing Group
6198 Butler Pike
Suite 200
Blue Bell, PA 19422-2600
Web site: www.kappapublishing.com/astrology

*Dell Horoscope*
Their Web site features a listing of local astrological meetings.

Customer Service
6 Prowitt Street
Norwalk, CT 06855
Phone: (800) 220-7443
Web site: www.dellhoroscope.com

*The Mountain Astrologer*

A favorite magazine of astrology fans, *The Mountain Astrologer* also has an interesting Web site featuring the latest news from an astrological point of view, plus feature articles from the magazine.

P.O. Box 970
Cedar Ridge, CA 95924
Web site: www.mountainastrologer.com

# Astrology College

## Kepler College of Astrological Arts and Sciences

A degree-granting college, which is also a center of astrology, has long been the dream of the astrological community and is a giant step forward in providing credibility to the profession. Therefore, the opening of Kepler College in 2000 was a historical event for astrology. It is the only college in the United States authorized to issue BA and MA degrees in astrological studies. Here is where to study with the best scholars, teachers, and communicators in the field. A long-distance study program is available for those interested.

4630 200th Street SW
Suite P
Lynnwood, WA 98036
Phone: (425) 673-4292
Fax: (425) 673-4983
Web site: www.kepler.edu

# Our Favorite Websites

Of the thousands of astrological Web sites that come and go on the Internet, these have stood the test of time and are likely to still be operating when this book is published.

## Astrodienst (www.astro.com)

Don't miss this fabulous international site, which has long been one of the best astrology resources on the Internet. It's a great place to view your own astrology chart. The world atlas on this site will give you the accurate longitude and latitude of your birthplace for setting up your horoscope. Then you can print out your free chart in a range of easy-to-read formats. Other attractions: a list of famous people born on your birth date, a feature that helps you choose the best vacation spot, and articles by world-famous astrologers.

## AstroDatabank (www.astrodatabank.com)

When the news is breaking, you can bet this site will be the first to get accurate birthdays of the headliners. The late astrologer Lois Rodden was a stickler for factual information and her meticulous research is being continued, much to the benefit of the astrological community. The Web site specializes in charts of current newsmakers, political figures, and international celebrities. You can also participate in discussions and analysis of the charts and see what some of the world's best astrologers have to say about them. Their AstroDatabank program, which you can purchase at the site, provides thousands of birthdays sorted into categories. It's an excellent research tool.

## StarIQ (www.stariq.com)

Find out how top astrologers view the latest headlines at the must-see StarIQ site. Many of the best minds in astrology comment on the latest news, stock market ups and downs, and political contenders. You can sign up to receive e-mail forecasts at the most important times keyed to your individual chart. (This is one of the best of the online forecasts.)

## Astro-Noetics (www.astro-noetics.com)

For those who are ready to explore astrology's interface with politics, popular culture, and current events, here is a sophisticated site with in-depth articles and personality profiles. Lots of depth and content here for the astrology-savvy surfer.

## Astrology Books (www.astroamerica.com)

The Astrology Center of America sells a wide selection of books on all aspects of astrology, from the basics to the most advanced, at this online bookstore. Also available are many hard-to-find and used books.

## Astrology Scholars' Sites:

See what Robert Hand, one of astrology's great teachers, has to offer on his site at www.robhand.com. A leading expert on the history of astrology, he's on the cutting edge of the latest research.

The Project Hindsight group of astrologers is devoted to restoring the astrology of the Hellenistic period, the primary source for all later Western astrology. There are fascinating articles for astrology fans on this site at www.projecthindsight.com.

## Financial Astrology Sites

Financial astrology is a hot specialty, with many tipsters, players, and theorists. There are online columns, newsletters, specialized financial astrology software, and mutual funds run by astrology seers. One of the more respected financial astrologers is Ray Merriman, whose market comments on www.mmacycles.com are a must for those following the bulls and bears.

# How to Zoom Around the Sky

If you haven't already discovered the wonders of Google Earth (www.earth.google.com), then you've been missing close-up aerial views of anyplace on the planet from your old hometown to the beaches of Hawaii. Even more fascinating for astrology buffs is the newest feature called Google Sky, a marvel of computer technology that lets you view the sky overhead from anyplace you choose. Want to see the stars over Paris at the moment? A few clicks of your mouse will take you there. Then you can follow the tracks of the sun, moon, and planets or check astronomical information and beautiful Hubble images. Go to the Google Web site to download this free program. Then get ready to take a cosmic tour around the earth and sky.

## Listen to the Sounds of Your Sign

Astrology Weekly (www.astrologyweekly.com) is a Web site from Romania, with lots to offer astro surfers. Here you can check all the planetary placements for the week, get free charts, join an international discussion group, and check out charts for countries and world leaders. Of special interest is the chart generator, an easy-to-use feature that will create a natal chart. Just click on *new chart* and enter the year, month, day, time, longitude, and latitude of your birth place. Select the Placidus or Koch house system and click on *show it*. Your chart should come right up on the screen. You can then copy the link to your astrology chart, store it, and later share your chart with friends. If you don't have astrology software, this is a good way to view charts instantly. This site also has some fun ways to pass the time, such as listening to music especially chosen for your sun sign.

## Stellar Gifts

If you've ever wondered what to give your astrology buddies, here's the place to find foolproof gifts. How about a mug, mouse pad, or plaque decorated with someone's chart? Would a special person like a pendant personalized with their planets? Check out www.milestonegifts.co.uk for some great ideas for putting those astrology charts to decorative use.

# CHAPTER 14

# Going Green in 2009: How to Help Save the Planet

Living a sustainable life is a high priority in 2009, as ecological concerns continue to dominate the news, and the media devote more resources to educating consumers in how to help the planet. Astrologically, this corresponds to the joining of Jupiter (expansion) and Neptune (creativity) in socially conscious Aquarius, which will influence us to move beyond differences as we share responsibility for the future of the environment.

Whether you're choosing to commit to the green movement, or wondering how you can do something about this critical situation by making lifestyle changes or helping local efforts, astrology can help you decide where to make a difference. Here are some suggestions for each sign.

## Aries: The Eco-Warrior

What could be a more appropriate cause for fire sign Aries than taking up the cause of global warming? Pioneering Aries such as Al Gore and Jane Goodall were among the first to give the world wake-up calls, bringing environmental concerns to the public's attention with great urgency. Now is the time to research the new options in fuel-efficient cars and prod local dealers to offer them to consumers. Be the first in your town to drive a hot new electric sports car. Some of you may opt for low-tech solutions by taking bikes to work or crusading for better public transportation. Energy-saving appliances and lightbulbs should be on your shopping list. For a complete list of green energy utilities across the country, visit the U.S. Department of Energy's Web site, and use a clickable map to find options in your state.

## Taurus: The Nurturer of Nature

Nature-loving Taurus is ideally suited to protecting our parks and wildlife, as well as promoting the humane treatment of animals. Supporting your local farmers by buying organic produce at farmers' markets gives you the pleasure of superior food and drink while you nurture local agriculture. You can participate in creating gardens and beautifying the landscape in your area, or perhaps raise your own organic produce using compost and nontoxic fertilizers. Taurus is a natural fund-raiser for worthy causes, so how about starting a thrift shop or conducting yard sales for your favorite charity?

## Gemini: Media Savvy

There are many ways to use your Gemini communications skills in the service of sustainable living. Beat the drum loudly to bring local environmental problems to the attention of the public. For inspiration, there's Gemini beauty Angelina Jolie, who has crusaded for the underprivileged around the world. Write a newsletter for your favorite cause, contribute to the op-ed page, call in to talk shows. Use your way with words to sway the public. Since you love to socialize, why not throw a fund-raising party for a local charity?

## Cancer: Home Remedies

Green living begins at home, so start by using eco-friendly cleaning products and buy furniture made of nontoxic materials. If you are building a home, use recycled or green materials as much as possible. Volunteer to help food-based charities like Meals on Wheels, which provide food to the elderly, ill, or homeless. Offer help and visits to the elderly in your neighborhood so they can remain in their own homes. A Cancer-ruled area is the hospitality industry—one that should pay special attention to its impact on the environment. Campaign for regulation of cruise boats and hotels, which have been major polluters. Vacation in eco-friendly resorts, like Maho Bay in the Caribbean and Central America, for a beautiful healthy alternative.

## Leo: Change a Child's Life

Child-oriented charities are naturally attuned to Leo's generous nature. Bill Clinton and Arnold Schwarzenegger, both Leos, have collaborated to focus on fighting one of our nation's leading health threats—childhood obesity—and to inspire young people to form lifelong healthy habits. You could join their efforts or sponsor a child in a third-world country. You can make a big difference in a child's life by supporting organizations that provide health care, education, and social services. Publicize your favorite causes by organizing charity events, fashion shows, and fund-raisers with entertainment.

## Virgo: The Activist Educator

Virgo has a special affinity for health and education issues, promoting literacy, raising educational standards, and supporting schools and libraries. Why not volunteer at a local school or hospital, to promote change from within these institutions, such as implementing sustainable energy policies, reducing carbon emissions, and teaching children to recycle? Support local programs that bring health care to the underinsured or international projects such as Doctors Without Borders or the Smile Train, which transforms the lives of children with cleft palates.

# Libra: Fair Trading

Libra's concern for fairness extends to purchasing products made by sustainable methods—ones that also ensure that the farmer or worker is paid a fair wage. Your love of the arts and beautiful objects could inspire you to promote native handicrafts in undeveloped countries and rescue ancient artistic techniques from becoming obsolete. We also need to pay attention to where and how our fashionable clothing is made and to encourage the use of nontoxic materials and finishes, as well as humane working conditions in third-world factories.

# Scorpio: Creating Transformation

As a water sign and the sign of transformation, Scorpio has a special affinity for recycling, waste treatment, and water purification. Support the fight against pollution of the oceans and destruction of coral reefs. Join your local eco-warriors to clean up toxic waste in bays and rivers. With your detective skills, find the local toxic waste dumps and help to bring polluters to justice. Preventing the spread of AIDs and supporting organizations that fight deadly diseases are other special interests of your sign. Locally, you could organize recycling events for used electronics and clothing.

# Sagittarius: The Outdoor Activist

You're a natural motivator, so why not turn this talent to a green cause? Get involved in local activities that encourage young people to live a healthy lifestyle. Coach a local team, take a group of children to a ball game, or help maintain athletic facilities in your area. Animal rescue and welfare is another Sagittarius concern. Volunteering at a local animal shelter, adopting a rescued pet, or fostering local wildlife would be rewarding. Like Bette Midler, you could form an organization to clean up local parks and green areas, creating hiking trails and picnic areas for outdoor family fun.

## Capricorn: Green Business Opportunities

Capricorn is destined to play a transformative role in preserving the environment, especially the endangered forests and jungles around the world, as well as helping to build a green economy. As an investor, insist on corporate responsibility to the environment and employees. Lend your organizing skills to create a healthier workplace, with better air quality and lighting, use of recycled or natural materials, and energy control. Consider business opportunities in underdeveloped countries, such as providing microloans that help local people become self-sufficient. Be a mentor to a young entrepreneur who is starting a green business.

## Aquarius: The Eco-Politician

Aquarius is a visionary thinker, ideally suited to influence politicians in your local area and campaign for causes that promote green enterprises, social welfare, and environmental action. Organize green festivals for a lively exchange of ideas, commerce, and movement building in your local area, with educational workshops, speakers, and networking opportunities for people looking to work together for change at the local, national, and global level. Address air pollution, toxins in the environment, and mold in buildings. Start a Web site devoted to improving your local environment.

## Pisces: The art of Change

Green concerns can combine with the creative arts to make the world a more beautiful and livable place. Pisces is endowed with imaginative gifts that can find new ways to use recycled materials or design products and homes that complement the environment. Support your local arts, especially organizations that bring music, theater, and dance expression to underprivileged children. We live on a water-dependent planet on which access to clean water is denied to many people. You can help the severe water-pollution problem by joining an organization devoted to protecting our oceans, fisheries, and water supply.

CHAPTER 15

# Rock Stars: Empower Yourself with Zodiac Gems

Could a ruby bring you luck on Tuesday, or how about wearing a rainbow moonstone during the full moon? When we think of wearing astrological jewelry, we usually think of birthstones, but did you know that there are planetary fingers and that your hands transmit solar and lunar energy? Jewelry can be much more meaningful, as well as fun to wear, when it is believed to resonate with our personalities or empower us in some way. With the current earthy Capricorn influence in the cosmos, we'll be examing all the value-added ways to wear our favorite gems, so let's take a look in our jewelry box for some astrological benefits.

Since ancient times, gems have been used to empower as well as decorate the wearer. In India, Egypt, and Babylonia, rare and beautiful gemstones were thought to have magical properties. People are said to have consulted astrologers for advice on wearing the appropriate gem for each occasion. Ancient Egyptians carried scarabs and tiny figures of their gods for protection and luck. These were carved in semiprecious stones like lapis lazuli, carnelian, and turquoise. In India, one of the most powerful talismans was the Nava Ratna, an amulet designed with precious stones representing the known planets at the time. This very talisman is still being worn today.

Another astrological connection was the wearing of gems associated with a planet on that planet's special day. Mars-ruled rubies would be worn on the Mars day, Tuesday, or moonstones on Monday. You could cover the bases by wearing *all* the gems in your horoscope at once. There are astrologer jewelers who will make up a special pendant or necklace that displays all your horoscope's special stones in a beautiful design.

To complicate matters when deciding when and how to wear your gems, there is the belief that each finger of the hand corresponds to a certain planet. So wearing that beautiful turquoise ring on your pointer or lucky Jupiter finger would be especially auspicious, according to ancient wisdom. The middle finger invokes the wisdom and discipline of Saturn, so try a garnet there. The Venus or third finger is the finger of love, which is why we wear wedding bands there. A stone associated with Libra or Taurus, the Venus-ruled signs, worn on that digit might help you attract a soul mate. The little finger enhances Mercury, the planet of communication, so pull out your Gemini or Virgo jewels and decorate your pinky when you have something special to say.

Then there's the question of which hand to wear your rings on. The right hand is associated with masculine outgoing energy and the left with female, receptive energy. Perhaps that is one reason why empowered young women are celebrating their career success by purchasing diamonds to wear proudly on the right hand.

In the Judeo-Christian tradition, the astrological association with gemstones dates from the sacred twelve-gem breastplate of Aaron, recorded in Exodus. Each gem symbolized one of the twelve tribes of Israel. Later these gems became connected with the twelve signs of the zodiac. However, it was not until the eighteenth century that people began to wear their special birthstones. For more information on the history and mystery of gemstones, including their astrological use, read *The Curious Lore of Precious Stones* by George Frederick Kunz, written in 1913 and still consulted today.

There is quite a bit of confusion over which stone is best for each sign, because we are often given birthstones according to the month of our birthday rather than our zodiac sign. You may be wondering if the amethyst is more suitable than the aquamarine for a February-born Pisces, or you might prefer the gems associated with your moon sign because they resonate with your emotional nature, or your Venus sign, which appeals to your sense of fashion and good taste. Lovers of precious gems could choose one that reflects the element of their sun sign. Earth signs (Taurus, Virgo, Capricorn) resonate to the bright green emerald, fire signs (Aries, Leo, Sagittarius) belong to the flaming ruby, water signs (Cancer, Scorpio, Pisces) might prefer the deep blue sapphire, and air signs (Gemini, Libra, Aquarius) may gravitate to the clear, brilliant diamond.

If you don't care for your birthstone, you could choose a talisman by color—one that is associated with your sun, moon, or Venus sign. An Aries with a moon in Cancer might prefer a pale lunar jewel like the pearl or moonstone. A Pisces with Venus in Aries might love to wear bright red stones like ruby or spinel.

Here are some suggestions for choosing stones associated with a given zodiac sign. Bear in mind that there are no hard and fast rules; you might find yourself attracted to a certain gem without fully understanding why. That might well be the gem you are supposed to wear, regardless of your sign. The bottom line is, wear whatever you love!

# Aries

Though most sources give the birthstone for April as the diamond, Aries may feel more affinity for Mars-ruled stones with red hues, such as ruby, spinels, fire opals, garnets, coral, and carnelian. Go for the flash and fire!

# Taurus

Emeralds are most associated with Taurus. However, Taurus might gravitate toward some of the earthy agates and green stones such as tourmaline, jade, serpentine (which is believed to draw good fortune), green quartz, or green turquoise. Try a newly available gem, like pale sage prasiolite, subtle glowing prenite, and the lustrous green seraphinite, flickering with white "angel wings," newly available from Russia.

# Gemini

Pearls and agates are associated with Gemini, but you might prefer fascinating gems like alexandrite or tanzanite, which change color according to the angle of light. Or watermelon tourmaline, which has dual colorations. Interesting rutilated quartzes with fine hairlike inclusions are associated with communication and might be perfect for your sign.

# Cancer

July has often been linked with the ruby; however, that fiery stone might be better suited to Leos born in late July than to early-July birthdays. Cancer seems to resonate more with the elegant blue sapphire, moonstone, and chalcedony, and the deep blue flashes of labradorite and rainbow moonstone.

# Leo

The yellow-green peridot and all golden stones belong to sun-ruled Leos. You may also love the ruby, yellow diamonds, amber, and citrine. Go for the golden tones!

# Virgo

Sapphires, which come in many colors, carnelian, onyx, and pink jasper are associated with Virgo. You may also respond to the earthy agates and the green tones of emerald and jade.

# Libra

Opal was once considered exclusive to Libra and comes in many variations. In fact, the opal was deemed unlucky for any other sign. This beautiful stone comes in many color variations, from the deeper Australian opals to the pale Russian opals. You might try the blue or pink Peruvian opal or the mysterious earthy boulder opal. Libra is also associated with the color pink, as in rose quartz, rhodonite, pink sapphires, pink diamonds, and kunzite. Apple green chrysoprase is another beautiful choice.

# Scorpio

This mysterious sign was given the topaz, which comes in blue or golden variations. You might also respond to the deep tones of smoky quartz, tigereye, black onyx, rainbow obsidian, black diamonds, or black South Sea pearls. You could be attracted to the deep multihued Pietersite, a mysterious stone that flickers with color.

# Sagittarius

Visionary Sagittarius respond to turquoise, the mystical stone of Native Americans and Tibetans. No medicine man's outfit was complete without a turquoise. It was treasured by the Persians, who believed that turquoise could protect from evil and bring good fortune. Also consider lapis lazuli, blue topaz, and ruby.

# Capricorn

The burgundy red garnet is the usual stone for Capricorn, but garnets are now available in many other colors, such as the green Tsavorite garnet and the orange hessionite garnet. Also consider the beautifully marked green malachite. Onyx in all its color variations is especially compatible with Capricorn.

# Aquarius

Aquarius is associated with the purple amethyst, a type of quartz that was once thought to prevent drunkenness. This sign might respond to some of the newer stones on the market, such as labradorite, a gray stone that flashes electric blue, or to some of the other purple stones such as sugilite, tanzanite, or purple jade. Choose an unusual stone to highlight your originality, like Russian charoite, a gorgeous purple gem now being used in rings and pendants. Dumortuite, with a subtle glow, is also terrific for lovers of the color purple. The colorful quartzes, which are able to conduct electricity, could be your gem. Diamonds of all kinds also resonate with Aquarius, according to the glamorous Aquarius Gabor sisters and Carol Channing, who sang "Diamonds Are a Girl's Best Friend."

# Pisces

The blue-green aquamarine and the earthy bloodstone are usually associated with Pisces. During the sixteenth century, bloodstone was believed to cure hemorrhages caused by the plague. Jasper is also a Pisces stone, now available in many beautiful colors such as picture jasper and poppy jasper, which look like miniature paintings. Pisces also responds to jewels from the sea: pearls, coral, and ocean blue sapphires. Elizabeth Taylor, a great Pisces jewel collector, owns the famous Peregrina pearl as well as many deep blue sapphires.

# CHAPTER 16

# The Year to Get Organized

With Saturn in Virgo and Pluto in Capricorn, both signs of organization, neatness, and efficiency, there couldn't be a better time to put your life in order. If you haven't conquered clutter, if your to-do list has become overwhelming, and if your schedule is overloaded, why not use your sign's natural inclinations to help you get things done and restore peace of mind?

Here are some strategies tailored to each sun sign to help you get life under control again.

## Aries

Do you have the common Aries trait of wanting to get things done immediately? If a task can't be crossed off the list right away, Aries tends to put it out of sight and out of mind. With your amazing energy, you can forge through a project until it is completed, so make it fast and fun. Think of your task as a military campaign you're sure to win. Divide long, complicated cleanup or fix-up projects into several (or many) small portions, each of which can be completed within a time limit—no lingering or postponing. Then attack each segment until it is done. Afterward, reward yourself! Give yourself a bright, colorful, fashionable place to work, so you'll feel like captain of the ship.

## Taurus

Taurus often needs to take some weight off your shoulders, in terms of too many possessions. But your sign finds it so difficult to part with your treasures. After all, you're one of the zodiac's great collectors, and you value each and every item you've accumulated. However, there are sure to be piles of things you haven't seen or enjoyed for a while. You may also have piled up in the attic or garage boxes of possessions—ones you haven't opened in years. Sharing your possessions with others can bring you great joy, so consider donating some to charity. Out-of-style clothing could be dropped off at your local thrift shop. You could sell some of the clothes you've been saving from former sizes in case you lose weight. Taking a temporary booth in a local flea market could be a fun weekend activity and bring you in extra money, as well as freeing up space in your home.

# Gemini

Busy, multitasking Gemini often forgets to organize their living space. Gemini accumulates paper and books, communications devices, party-giving clutter. You may have half-completed projects piled up in hopes that one day you'll get around to finishing them. A good storage system could help you keep track of your projects, even complete those you've abandoned or put aside. Invest in shelving, bookcases, and file cabinets to keep the clutter at bay and help you find things instead of wasting time searching for them. A cabinet or armoire dedicated to entertainment supplies would be ready for an instant party. To find important papers fast, Gemini financial counselor Suze Orman keeps them in a separate waterproof case, ready for any emergency. There's never any doubt where to find wills, insurance policies, or birth certificates.

# Cancer

Cancer is another sign that has difficulty letting go of possessions, especially if there is some sentimental value attached. Be sure that you are not just hoarding items for a feeling of security. You'll be more serene emotionally and creative in a tranquil, ordered environment. Turn clutter into art by editing your favorites to the most special ones and then arranging them in a beautiful display. Choose your organization items for their decorative value as well as functionality. Antique armoires and chests of drawers or vintage trunks could provide storage while adding character to your room. Consider photographing your possessions for inventory purposes, and invest in one of the many inventory computer applications to keep track of what you own and its value.

# Leo

Leo loves a well-ordered lair where you can proudly entertain friends, but your busy lifestyle can leave clutter in its wake and closets overflowing with fashionable clothing. Do what Leo does best—delegate the organization to someone else. Consult a store with a resident expert who could design a custom closet with colorful hangers to store your wardrobe in style and expand your space. Well-stocked makeup tables and cosmetics cabinets are also Leo musts. You're sure to have a good entertainment system. Invest in special shelving for your DVD and CD collection so your favorite video games, shows, and music are available when the right mood strikes.

# Virgo

Desiring to be of service to others, Virgo can take on too many tasks. Learn to say no, and choose your commitments wisely. That way you'll avoid becoming overwhelmed and be better able to give quality time to the most important projects and people in your life. Virgo is supposed to be one of the most organized signs; however, too many to-do lists could be counterproductive. The task for many Virgos is to simplify your systems. Take advantage of the many computer programs that can help organize your finances and catalog possessions.

# Libra

For beauty-loving Libra, storage solutions should be aesthetically pleasing as well as efficient. Color-coordinated hangers and storage boxes make keeping neat closets a pleasure. Since you often have large wardrobes, invest in a beautiful armoire or mirrored closet. Disguise a rolling garment rack with decorator fabric. Office armoires that can hide your work area are a good solution for Libras who work at home.

# Scorpio

Whether choosing minimal or maximal decorating effects, all-or-nothing Scorpio likes to keep his environment under control. You often have a secret closet or storage room to stash possessions. A well-organized filing system and furniture that does double duty—such as an ottoman that hides a storage bin—are perfect for Scorpio. This sign, not usually a clutterer, has no problem tossing away what is no longer useful. Make digital photographs of your rooms or valuable objects for insurance purposes and also for your will. Hide your file cabinets and storage containers behind a beautiful screen or curtain on a ceiling track.

# Sagittarius

On-the-go Sagittarius usually accumulates luggage, sporting goods, and travel items. You need these items to be easily accessible when you decide to take off on a spur-of-the-moment adventure or pile the family into the car for a road trip. A good backseat organizer is a must for conquering car clutter. A garage storage system could maximize space by getting sports equipment off the floor and onto elevated shelving. Frequent flyers might keep a small bag of necessary items in travel sizes and travel documents packed in a suitcase.

# Capricorn

The most naturally organized of all the signs, Capricorn is quick to latch on to new techniques and shortcuts to utilize every bit of living and working space. And you can be coolly objective when it comes to throwing out what is no longer useful. A good recycling station is a must for Capricorn, who dislikes waste of any kind. Schedule regular times to go through your wardrobe and possessions to weed out what you don't need and donate items to charity. Put your affairs in order with an up-to-date filing system, which can be disguised in an attractive cabinet. Be careful not to overorganize—keep your system simple and easy to remember.

# Aquarius

So many things, so little time could be the complaint of Aquarius, whose active lifestyle is often order-challenged. This sign dislikes anything that infringes on freedom and independence, such as too much structure and a rigid schedule. However, you and everyone around you will function much better in an ordered environment. When things get out of control, call in the troups, enlist help, or hire a professional organizer. Make cleanup time fun by throwing a party. Invite friends to help you with specific tasks, and then reward them with a terrific meal. Or barter one of your many talents for some cleanup skills. Take advantage of computer technology to pay bills and keep records up-to-date.

# Pisces

Most Pisces avoid tackling clutter until it threatens to take over their space. However, taking charge of your environment is not only empowering, but it can free you up for the creative activities you love. Who needs to waste time looking for important papers? Get an attractive container and assemble your passport, credit cards, lease, and tax information where you can easily find them. Scan key documents into your computer so you'll have duplicates handy. Keep things where you'd naturally look for them (keys in a pretty container by the door, clothes you wear most often in the front of the closet). Pay special attention to organization of footwear, perhaps dedicating a closet or small cabinet to your shoe and boot collection. Sentimental Pisces also needs to learn to let go of gifts that will never be used. Don't feel guilty. Remember the good feelings, and then embrace your freed-up space!

# CHAPTER 17

# Your Pisces Close-Up: Introduction to Man, Woman, and Family

Did you know that your Pisces sun sign can enhance all areas of your life? That includes what and whom you like, your family relationships, your strengths on the job, and even the way you furnish your home. The more you understand your Pisces personality and potential, the more you'll benefit from using your special solar power to help you make good decisions. You might use it for something as basic as choosing what to wear or the color to paint a room. Or you could tap into your Pisces power to deal with more important issues, such as getting along with your boss or spicing up your love life.

Let the following chapters empower you with the confidence that you're moving in harmony with your natural Pisces inclinations. As the ancient oracle advised, "Know thyself." To know yourself, as astrology helps you to do, is to gain confidence and strength.

So let's get up close and personal with Pisces. You may wonder how astrologers determine what a Pisces personality is like. To begin with, we use a type of recipe, blending several ingredients. Your Pisces element: water. The way Pisces operates: mutable—a sign of movement, of change. Your sign's polarity: negative, feminine, yin. And your planetary ruler: Neptune, the planet of imagination. Add your sign's place in the zodiac: twelfth and last, in the house of spirituality, of selflessness, of charity. Finally, stir in your symbol, the Fish swimming in opposite directions, indicating duality.

This cosmic mix influences everything we say about Pisces. Could a water sign with a Neptune ruler have any other signature color than aqua blue? No way. Is your personality likely to be creative, a bit dreamy? Very likely. But remember that your total astrological personality contains a blend of may other planets, colored by the signs they occupy, plus factors such as the sign coming over the horizon at the exact moment of your birth. The more planets in Pisces in your horoscope, the more likely you'll follow your sun sign's prototype. Howevewr, if many planets are grouped together in another sign, they will color your horoscope accordingly, sometimes making a low-key, mellow sun sign come on much stronger. So if the Pisces traits mentioned here don't describe you, there could be other factors flavoring your cosmic stew. (Look up your other planets in the tables in this book to find out what they might be!)

# The Pisces Man: Shark or Charming Goldfish

The Pisces man has been characterized too often as a romantic adventurer with no roots in reality. However, in the last decade Pisces men have ridden the highest waves of success. Computer wizards Michael Dell and Steve Jobs, entertainment mogul David Geffen and media's Rupert Murdoch are a few examples of the Pisces man who shows that he can be a shark as well as a charming goldfish, a surfer of life with an uncanny sense of when and how to catch the best wave.

The Pisces man often puzzles more predictable signs with a chameleon-like personality that seems to take on the colorations of each environment. You have an amazing ability to adapt to different situations and people, socializing with the jet set one day and hanging out at a working-class bar the next, reveling in a constantly changing cast of characters.

What makes you so adaptable is your sensitivity, which some Pisces go to great lengths to hide, with good reason.

Your compassion also attracts many who take advantage of your good nature. And, since Pisces picks up moods from your surroundings, negative influences from these people can be disastrous. It is often a Pisces challenge to find a way to help others without being drained and martyred yourself.

Once you find a place where your talents are appreciated, you can be extremely successful. Your intuitive ability to spot trends, your creative imagination, and your ability to second-guess the competition work in your favor. But, before you settle down, you may go through a period of drifting and soul-searching until you determine who you are and where you are going. Sadly, some Pisces men fall under the influence of drugs and alcohol during this time, unless they have strong outside support. With positive, constructive influences, you'll use your varied experiences as grist for creative ideas or find work that gives you the variety you crave, like writer Tom Wolfe or film directors Spike Lee and Robert Altman.

## In a Relationship

The positive Pisces man makes a loving partner who will keep the romance going long after the wedding. You are very susceptible to female charms, but you'll remain faithful if your wife gives you oceans of emotional support and steadily builds your self-esteem. Not the take-over type, you need constant stroking and reassurance. However, the woman who imposes her will on you or tries to control you will find you slip through her fingers. If she can strike the right balance of strong support and gentle stroking, you'll be an appreciative, sensual, and romantic lover for life!

# The Pisces Woman: The Romantic Heroine

The Pisces woman is likely to have a life story worthy of a novel. She embodies a combination of glamour, talent, and empathy that seems to attract dramatic scenarios. The most receptive, compassionate, imaginative sign of the zodiac, Pisces often dives beneath the waters of the emotions. You are attracted to the underdog. One of your paradoxes is that by helping the sick or needy, you miraculously gain prestige, power, and financial stability for yourself—if you don't become so involved in the troubles of others that you actually absorb them. Many Pisces, like Elizabeth Taylor and Drew Barrymore, come out of the depths of difficult experiences to emerge victorious and stronger than ever.

Your symbol, the Fish swimming in opposite directions while tied together, gives clues about your contradictions. You are really many women in one, and what fascinating characters you all are! Here is the ravishing beauty who swears like a dockworker, the socialite who runs off with her bodyguard, the sophisticated talk-show hostess with half a dozen children, the wholesome former Miss America dethroned by past scandal who reemerged a popular star, the desperately impoverished teenager who became an ambassador. Never predictable, Pisces hides much strength and resourcefulness under an ultrafeminine exterior. Deceptively fragile and vulnerable, you're really quite capable of fending for yourself and reinventing yourself after fate has dealt you a blow.

One Pisces challenge is to use your great compassion and sensitivity in a productive way. Your sympathy encompasses everyone who is suffering, and you'll often champion causes that others reject as too controversial, such as Elizabeth Taylor's work on behalf of AIDS. But you must learn to discriminate in order to protect yourself against those who would play upon your sympathies. By building up your own self-esteem, and by learning to discern the really needy from those who merely drain your energy, you can truly help others and reward yourself with a feeling of accomplishment.

It is especially important for Pisces to find an outlet for your powerful emotions, preferably one that rewards your self-expression with financial security. Gloria Vanderbilt, once the poor little rich girl, made her own fortune after forty as a fashion designer. Model and spokeswoman Cindy Crawford is another Pisces who capitalized on her beauty and talent. Extremely compassionate, you can enter and absorb a role, which makes you an excellent actress. Pisces women also do well in sports (Jackie Joyner-Kersee), where they can lose themselves in physical activity.

Along with success stories are the inevitable tearjerker tales of Pisces whose scandalous ups and downs, marriages, and bouts with alcohol and drugs are chronicled in the tabloids. When you are drowning in your emotions, you can be easily threatened, jealous, possessive, a clinging vine. Or your feelings may get the better of you physically, creating illnesses and addictions. You become fulfilled when you can express your feelings in some artistic or creative way. This quickly puts you on the road to confidence, self-esteem, and financial independence.

## In a Relationship

Even the most liberated and independent of this sign tends to become reactive in romance. You easily perceive what your partner wants and switch into the appropriate role, often being both wife and mistress to the one you love. Because you are so willing to indulge a man's fantasies, you've been called the most dangerous "other woman" of the zodiac. However, many men prefer not to marry their Pisces paramours, choosing them as a diversion from their confining domestic life.

You need a mate who appreciates your many talents and helps you put them to constructive use. Though you may prefer to leave practical matters to your partner so you can focus on your creative talents, you have a surprisingly practical side, which is quite able to balance the budget. Negatively, you're not above using a bit of emotional manipulation, playing the martyr or victim to get your way.

## Pisces in the Family

### The Pisces Parent

Having children brings out the loving, supportive side of Pisces and can become the anchor Pisces needs to stop drifting and set goals. Your intuitive sensitivity to young children's needs and developing feelings gives them gentle, nonjudgmental support, while your creativity makes learning and playtime special. Yours is the sign most capable of unconditional love, and you are particularly nurturing to a child who is needy or handicapped in some way. Typical of the caring nature of Pisces is the story of the famous actress who chose to adopt a crippled child and help it regain health. On the negative side, you should cultivate detachment and objectivity in order to deal with the emotional ups and downs of your child. A fulfilling marriage will assure that you will not overinvest emotionally in the child and that you will be willing to let go when the time comes for independence.

## The Pisces Stepparent

In the challenging position of stepparent, Pisces has personality assets to cope with a ready-made family. As one of the most adaptable and compassionate signs, you can easily open your heart to stepchildren and empathize with their feelings. You'll be especially supportive of your mate in the period of transition and willingly give up some of your own priorities to smooth over this delicate situation. Using your natural sense of drama and glamour, you can easily fascinate this young audience and channel their feelings into creative activities. Since these children need your love and understanding, you will give it wholeheartedly. But you may also have to assert your authority from time to time to gain their respect as well as their love.

## The Pisces Grandparent

Pisces grandparents can share a magical world of fantasy with the grandchildren. When you enter their world, you become like a child again yourself. You're their special permissive playmate who never competes with parents for disciplinary rights. You are the accomplice who joins children in mischievous pranks! Through opening their minds to fantasy, you're their best teacher—the one who teaches them that it's okay to daydream and to explore their fantasies in play, for the most creative ideas happen when you're playing. You'll live in their memories because you've touched their hearts and awakened their imagination.

# CHAPTER 18

# Pisces Style: Using Pisces's Special Flair to Enhance Your Life

Are you at home in your house? Does your appearance express your real personality? Why not celebrate Pisces by living with stellar style, inspired by the colors, sounds, fashion, and living environment that suit you best. Showing off the special Pisces flair in the way you dress and live could bring more harmony into your life. You'll feel, as the French say, "at home in your skin." Even your vacations might be more fun if you tailor them to your natural Pisces inclinations. Try these tips to enhance your lifestyle and express the Pisces in you.

## The Way You Look

Pisces, the sign of glamour and illusion, understands the power of clothing to enable you to play many roles in life. Rather than limit yourself to one look, you can switch with ease from crisp, efficient office clothes to romantic evening wear or casual sporty weekend clothes. But you are most in your element when you wear glamorous clothes with a theatrical flair. Juliette Binoche, the French star of *Chocolat,* is the perfect example of the ultrafeminine Pisces style. Or Sharon Stone, who can look like a mermaid in simple sequins, or wear a Gap T-shirt to a formal party with a few diamonds added for sparkle, or play another role in tweeds.

Keep your weight down so you can wear the dramatic styles you love best.

Theatrical makeup is associated with Pisces. Many Pisces have soulful eyes, which are likely to be your best features. Use makeup cleverly to play up your lids and lashes. Experiment with false eyelashes and groom your brows carefully. If you wear glasses, have several different frames to change with your mood.

Since the feet belong to Pisces, shoes should be your special fashion indulgence. Play up your dancing feet with sexy strappy sandals or decorated pumps. Collect boots for all occasions. Since uncomfortable shoes can torture Pisces more than other signs, invest in stylish walking shoes to protect your posture. Even your glamorous evening shoes can be made more wearable with padded inserts.

Don't forget the invisible power of perfume, which should have a special place in your wardrobe, since fragrance is another Pisces specialty, especially the essential oils. Choose a signature scent and remember that the sense of smell has the longest memory.

## Pisces Colors

Complement your Pisces personality by wearing colors creatively. All the colors of the sea—iridescent fish scales, coral, sea foam green, and the deep aquamarine of tropical waters complement the dreamy side of your personality. The blue and white of the Greek islands and the elegant neutral grays of a storm-tossed sea would be good choices.

## Your Pisces Fashion Role Models

For fashion inspiration, Pisces designers Alexander McQueen, Kenzo, and Wendy Dagworthy do clothes to fantasize about. Or steal some style from Pisces supermodels: Cindy Crawford, Esther Canadas, Eva Herzigova, and Nadja Auermann. Perennial fashion icons born under

Pisces include Gloria Vanderbilt, Ivana Trump, and Lee Radziwill, while Sharon Stone, Eva Longoria, and Drew Barrymore show the Pisces theatrical style.

# Pisces Home Makeover Tips

Your home is the ideal place to express your Pisces personality. If your rooms don't suit you, you probably don't feel as comfortable as you should in your environment, which could adversely affect your health and well-being. Since solitude and security are especially important to fulfilling your Pisces creative potential, you need a safe haven to live out Pisces dreams and fantasies. Even if you share your home with others, there should be a quiet place where you can meditate, practice yoga, listen to music, and dream.

As a mutable water sign, you are very susceptible to the mood of your surroundings. If it's chaotic, you can feel jittery and unfocused. If it's too pristine, you can feel uncreative. The trick is to find the middle ground. All it takes is a beautiful rug, exotic pillows, and pools of mood lighting to do the trick. Add some mirrors and a few fabulous throws to toss over the furniture and perhaps an aquarium or small fountain to bring in your water element.

Pisces should pay special attention to comfort underfoot and the condition of your floor. Wonderful floor tiles, polished wood, and exotic carpets can make your home special as well as define each area. Pisces often shares a habitat with animal friends, so find some decorative baskets and scratch posts for your pets (and buy a powerful vacuum cleaner).

In your kitchen, provide for liquid refreshment and nourishment as well as touches of theater and fantasy. A well-stocked wine rack, a good blender or juicer, and a water purifier are important for water signs. Stock some exotic spices and delicacies to add drama to your meals. Pans suitable for cooking and serving seafood as well as decorative fish-shaped dishes could be displayed prominently.

Tap into your dreams and fantasies when you design your bedroom. Create a soothing atmosphere with water colors, ocean motifs, sensual fabrics. Go all out for a spec-tacular bed, with sumptuous coverings and piles of pillows. Pisces loves to spend time in bed and to bring work into the bedroom, which calls for cleverly hidden telephones and telecommunications lines and a table that can hold bed-side refreshment. But maintain an atmosphere of rest and relaxation when propped on pillows, tapping on your laptop.

Your bath should be a room for self-pampering, where you indulge in lotions and bubbly potions, a showerhead with multiple pulse settings, and a Jacuzzi, if possible. You're a water sign, so your bath should be therapeutic and restorative.

## Pisces Sounds

Dreamy, emotional music by Chopin or Ravel stirs your soul. Baroque music such as Handel's "Water Music" and Vivaldi's "Four Seasons" stimulates creative work. New Age meditative music and dance music, especially ballet themes, put you in a relaxed mood. Pisces voices include Seal, Nat King Cole, James Taylor, Harry Belafonte, Johnny Cash, and opera stars Kiri Te Kanawa and Renata Scotto. The mystical sounds from many lands now available as world music would be especially intriguing to Pisces, with your love of exotica.

## Pisces Getaways

You're always ready for a getaway, especially one to a mag-ical place with romance and fantasy appeal, and if the spot is near water, so much the better! Venice, Portugal, and Normandy fill the bill perfectly. Spiritual Pisces should seek out power spots such as Glastonbury, England, where King Arthur is said to be buried; the Mayan ruins of Tulum, on the coast of Mexico; the surfing beaches and mystical mountains of Hawaii. Or you might scuba dive in search of

Atlantis off the coast of Bimini. In the United States, head for the crashing surf of Monterey, the Maine coast, or the coral reefs of the Virgin Islands. Romantic Vermont is an inland Pisces-ruled place for snow lovers and ice skaters.

For an important trip, pack all your bags well in advance, when your concentration is best. The more advance planning the better when you're traveling for business. To make your trip run smoothly, tap into the Virgo side of your nature (your polar opposite) by making lists and checking them off methodically. Be sure you have double sets of directions, the proper insurance, and enough money to get you through the initial adaptation to a foreign city, when dreamy Pisces may be soaking up impressions rather than focusing on practical details. Keep a special travel folder with all your maps and papers organized together. That way you'll be free to go with the flow and truly enjoy your trip.

# CHAPTER 19

# Pisces Health and Longevity Secrets

Astrology has many ideas for keeping Pisces healthy and happy. Each sign is associated with a part of the body, which could become vulnerable in later years, and within the personality of a sign are other clues for having a long and productive life.

## The Addictive Eater

Pisces is a sign of no boundaries, therefore one of the most difficult to discipline diet-wise. You can get hooked on a fattening food like French fries (or alcohol), a habit like coffee with lots of sugar and a sweet roll, and easily gain weight. What's more, your water-sign body may have a tendency to bloat, holding extra pounds of water weight at certain times, especially around the full moon.

The key for you, as with so many others, is commitment and support. Don't try to go it alone. Get a partner, a doctor, a group, or one of the online diet-related sites to help. Since you're influenced by the atmosphere around you, choose to be with slim healthy friends and those who will support your efforts. Avoid those seemingly well-meaning diet saboteurs who say just one cookie won't do any harm. A seafood-based diet could be the right one for you. Your Pisces sisters—Queen Latifah, Liza Minnelli, and Camryn Manheim—have slimmed down, and so can you!

# Detox Your System

Health-wise, supersensitive Pisces, associated with the lymphatic system, reacts strongly to environmental toxins and emotional stress. It's no accident that we often do spring cleaning during the Pisces months. Start your birthday off right by detoxing your system with a liquid diet or supervised fast. This may also help with water retention, a common Pisces problem. Lymphatic drainage massage is especially relaxing and beneficial to Pisces.

# Don't Forget Your Feet!

The feet are Pisces territory. Consider how often you take your feet for granted and how miserable life can be when your feet hurt. Since our feet reflect and affect the health of the entire body, devote some time to pampering them. Check your walking shoes or buy ones designed specifically for your kind of exercise. If your arches are high, custom-molded orthotic inserts could make a big difference in your comfort and performance. Though you may love your sexy stiletto heels, they can take a toll on your posture and bone structure. Save them for special occasions.

Just as the sign of Pisces contains traces of all the previous signs, the soles of our feet contain nerve endings that connect with all other parts of our body. This is the theory behind reflexology, a therapeutic foot massage that treats all areas of the body by massaging the soles of the feet. For the sake of your feet, as well as your entire body, consider treating yourself to a session with a local practitioner of this technique.

# Exercise in Your Water Element

Exercise is not a favorite Pisces activity, unless it is a creative activity like dance or ice-skating, or is related to your water element, such as water aerobics or swimming. Generally, you fare best in a solo activity that is graceful and artistic. A caring coach or exercise instructor who gives you personal attention can make a difference in your motivation.

Walking regularly releases tension, gets you outdoors, and can be a way to socialize with friends away from the temptation of food and drink. If you live near the ocean or a beautiful lake, make this a place for your daily walk. If you live in a city, do local errands on foot and find a local park where you can take a daily stroll. Invite someone you love or would like to get to know better to share this time with you. Owning an active pet forces you to get out and explore the neighborhood several times a day, so why not adopt an adorable pooch from your local shelter?

# Stay Forever Young

Elder Pisces is happiest when pursuing creative activities, such as filmmaking, painting, writing, or a hobby or craft in which you can express your imagination. Fortunately, artistic talents often improve with age, allowing Pisces great fulfillment in your senior years. If traveling on vacation or planning a retirement home, choose a cruise or a location near the ocean or a scenic lake. Places near water are particularly healthful for Pisces. Water sports, especially swimming and water aerobics, can maintain your health. Avoid addictive substances, and stick to a balanced diet of organic foods, including plenty of fish. Pay special attention to the condition of your feet, which become more vulnerable as you age, and be sure to wear the appropriate shoes for each activity.

CHAPTER 20

# Pisces's Guide to a Stellar Career: What It Takes to Succeed in 2009

## Are You in the Right Career?

The right job for Pisces should have you bounding out the door in the morning, ready to take on the day. If corporate culture feels confining or the freelance world is too risk-laden, you may need to rethink your career path. If your boss gets on your nerves, or your coworkers steal your thunder, perhaps you should try a new strategy before you decide to walk out the door. Pisces has a special combination of talents and abilities that can make you a natural winner. If you develop and nurture these strengths, you'll be more likely to find a career you truly enjoy—and that's the best definition of success.

## Where to Look for Your Perfect Job

The key to Pisces success is to find a place where your sensitivity and creativity work for you rather than against you. Avoid rigid, structured companies and overbearing employers who simply exploit your talents. Office power games can sap your energy and divert your talent in unproductive directions. Instead, put your sensitive antennae to work psyching out the competition, divining the consumer mood, and understanding the hidden agendas of your coworkers.

Though Pisces-friendly jobs are usually in creative fields, that is not always the case. Pisces can use special insight in high finance, publishing, science, and medicine. Special Pisces-influenced areas are the oil, perfume, footwear, and film industries. Alcohol and drugs are also Pisces-ruled, but work in those areas will require self-discipline, as Pisces is very susceptible to alcohol and drug abuse. The caring and healing professions capitalize on your natural empathy with clients, offering many opportunities in psychotherapy, nursing, and home health care. Glamour fields of fashion and beauty, as well as theater in any form, are always Pisces havens.

# Live Up to Your Leadership Potential

The Pisces boss has uncanny intuition, the kind of instinct that can't be taught in business school. You grasp the thoughts and trends in the air as if by magic. Extremely creative, you may prefer to work alone and do your real thinking in solitude. You are very compassionate and caring of your subordinates, and oddly, they are protective of you in return, sometimes shielding you from office politics. Though they may be baffled by your unpredictable moods (sometimes your sweet temper can turn mean as a shark) and your vague sense of direction (be sure to put your orders in writing), they adore you for your caring concern and respect your outstanding talent.

Pisces's secret is your sensitivity, put to good use. It can help you psyche out the competition, divine the consumer mood, and understand the hidden agendas of coworkers. Teamed with your water sign's creativity, it's a formidable combination. There are many inspiring examples of successful Pisces, such as billionaire Michael Dell, who dropped out of college to start Dell Computers, a pioneer in direct-to-customer computer sales. At age twenty-seven, he became the youngest CEO of a Fortune 500 company in history. Steven Jobs, cofounder of Apple Computers, developed the Macintosh with an easy-to-use graphic interface that made it the first user-friendly computer. Now he has moved Apple to lead high-tech entertainment with the iPod. Sanford Weill and Walter Annenberg are legendary Pisces entrepreneurs who flourished in the worlds of finance and publishing, respectively.

## How to Work with Others

As an emotional water sign, you do your best work when you are not tied down to a routine or made to punch a time clock. This doesn't mean that you are undisciplined. You'll turn out extraordinary work in a job where your talents are appreciated and where you have creative freedom. You are not one to step on toes to get ahead, or fight to keep your position, so an atmosphere of intense competition can upset your delicate sense of balance and distract you from the work you do best. You must learn to focus on the job at hand and tune out chaotic vibrations.

Because you can adapt to many situations easily and are extremely versatile, you may take time to discover your professional potential, floating from job to job, often going far adrift of your original direction. But perceptions gained from these diverse experiences only enhance your talent and professional value. You'll amaze others with your success and stamina when you finally find a job that fully engages your abilities.

## The Pisces Way to Get Ahead

Get behind the steering wheel of your life. Use your special Pisces talents and abilities to bring you the highest return on your investment of time and energy. Look for a positive, supportive working environment with plenty of creative opportunity. Then play up these Pisces attributes:

• Creativity

- Insight
- Tact
- Charm
- Empathy
- Intuition
- Talent
- Good timing

# CHAPTER 21

# Famous Pisces Sign Mates

Over the past decade, our culture has become more fascinated than ever with the lives of celebrities. And you know how much fun it is when you find a glamorous person who shares your sun sign—and even your birthday! Maybe it's your favorite actor or someone you've long admired.

Guessing upcoming headline makers in your sign's roster is another fun activity. Who will be your sign's "It Girl" of 2009? She might be a trendy Pisces who rocks the fashion world, like Eva Longoria and Sharon Stone have done. Will there be a scandalous politician, a crusader for human rights, or a loudmouthed talk-show host in your sign's rich and powerful contenders?

As you scope your sign for the tabloid stars, why not take advantage of the fringe benefits to be gained from studying you sun-sign mates? Celebrities who capture the media's attention will reflect the planetary influences of a given time, as well as the unique star quality of his or her sun sign. You can learn from these stellar spotlight stealers what the public is responding to and what this says about our current values.

If someone intrigues you, explore his personality further by looking up his other planets using the tables in this book. Then apply the effects of Venus, Mars, Saturn, and Jupiter to his sun-sign traits. It's a way to get up close and personal with your famous friend, and maybe learn some secrets not revealed to the public.

You're sure to have lots in common with your famous sign mates. Perhaps you prefer the bohemian style of Drew Barrymore and Queen Latifah. Or you admire the way Elizabeth Taylor, Liza Minnelli, and Bruce Willis triumphed over addictions. Can you see the Pisces business savvy in Rupert Murdoch, Steve Jobs, and Michael Dell?

When you're ready to move on from the red carpet to world leaders and current newsmakers, you'll find accurate charts online at Internet sites, such as www.Stariq.com or www.astrodatabank.com. You can compare notes with other fans, including many professional astrologers who frequent the forums on these sites, and add your own insight and opinions.

# Pisces Celebrities

Smokey Robinson (2/19/40)
Prince Andrew (2/19/60)
Benicio Del Toro (2/19/67)
Gloria Vanderbilt (2/20/25)
Sidney Poitier (2/20/25)
Ivana Trump (2/20/49)
Patricia Hearst (2/20/54)
Cindy Crawford (2/20/66)
Kurt Cobain (2/20/67)
Rue McClanahan (2/21/34)
Tyne Daly (2/21/43)
David Geffen (2/21/43)
Kelsey Grammer (2/21/55)
Mary-Chapin Carpenter (2/21/58)
William Baldwin (2/21/63)
Jennifer Love Hewitt (2/21/79)
Charlotte Church (2/21/86)
Edna St. Vincent Millay (2/22/1892)
Julius Erving (2/22/50)
Kyle MacLachlan (2/22/59)
Kristin Davis (2/22/65)
Drew Barrymore (2/22/75)
Peter Fonda (2/23/39)
Michael Dell (2/23/54)
Edward J. Olmos (2/24/47)
Steve Jobs (2/24/55)
Paula Zahn (2/24/56)

George Harrison (2/25/43)
Sally Jessy Raphael (2/25/43)
Téa Leoni (2/25/66)
Johnny Cash (2/26/32)
Michael Bolton (2/26/53)
Erykah Badu (2/26/72)
Joanne Woodward (2/27/30)
Elizabeth Taylor (2/27/32)
Ralph Nader (2/27/34)
Chelsea Clinton (2/27/80)
Josh Groban (2/27/81)
Bugsy Siegel (2/28/1906)
Bernadette Peters (2/28/48)
Dinah Shore (3/1/17)
Ron Howard (3/1/54)
Esther Canadas (3/1/77)
Dr. Seuss (3/2/1904)
Desi Arnaz (3/2/17)
Mikhail Gorbechev (3/2/31)
Jon Bon Jovi (3/2/62)
Daniel Craig (3/2/68)
Miranda Richardson (3/3/58)
Jackie Joyner-Kersee (3/3/62)
Julie Bowen (3/3/70)
Jessica Biel (3/3/82)
Chastity Bono (3/4/69)
Samantha Eggar (3/5/39)
Kevin Connolly (3/5/74)
Niki Taylor (3/5/75)
Rob Reiner (3/6/47)
Stedman Graham (3/6/51)
Tom Arnold (3/6/59)
Shaquille O'Neal (3/6/72)
Willard Scott (3/7/34)
Tammy Fay Messner (3/7/42)
Michael Eisner (3/7/42)
Cyd Charisse (3/8/23)
Lynn Redgrave (3/8/43)
Camryn Manheim (3/8/61)
Kathy Ireland (3/8/63)
Freddie Prinze Jr. (3/8/76)

James Van Der Beek (3/8/77)
Raul Julia (3/9/40)
Faith Daniels (3/9/57)
Juliette Binoche (3/9/64)
Chuck Norris (3/10/42)
Sharon Stone (3/10/58)
Prince Edward (3/10/64)
Shannon Miller (3/10/77)
Lawrence Welk (3/11/1903)
Rupert Murdoch (3/11/31)
Gianni Agnelli (3/12/42)
Liza Minnelli (3/12/46)
James Taylor (3/12/48)
Neil Sedaka (3/13/39)
William H. Macy (3/13/50)
Dana Delany (3/13/67)
Albert Einstein (3/14/1879)
Michael Caine (3/14/33)
Billy Crystal (3/14/47)
Prince Albert of Monaco (3/14/58)
Fabio (3/15/61)
Mark McGrath (3/15/68)
Eva Longoria (3/15/75)
Jerry Lewis (3/16/26)
Sanford Weill (3/16/33)
Bernardo Bertolucci (3/16/40)
Kate Nelligan (3/16/51)
Lauren Graham (3/16/67)
Brooke Burns (3/16/78)
Patrick Duffy (3/17/49)
Kurt Russell (3/17/51)
Gary Sinise (3/17/55)
Rob Lowe (3/17/64)
Brittany Daniel (3/17/76)
Charley Pride (3/18/38)
Queen Latifah (3/18/70)
Vanessa L. Williams (3/18/63)
Ursula Andress (3/19/36)
Glenn Close (3/19/47)
Bruce Willis (3/19/55)
Mr. Rogers (3/20/28)

Jerry Reed (3/20/37)
William Hurt (3/20/50)
Spike Lee (3/20/57)
Theresa Russell (3/20/57)
Holly Hunter (3/20/58)

# CHAPTER 22

# Pisces's Match-Up and Mating Guide

Is your partner on your wavelength, or do you sometimes wonder if you both are living on separate planets? Did the hot chemistry of an online romance fizzle when you met in person? Relationships are full of contradictions and complexities, especially this year, when there are so many new options for meeting and flirting, from speed dating to online matchmaking.

Astrology has no magic formula for success in love, but it does offer a better understanding of the qualities each person brings to the relationship and how your partner is likely to react to your sun-sign characteristics. Knowing your potential partner's sign and how it relates to yours could give you some clues about what to expect down the line.

There is also the issue of the timing of a new relationship. From an astrological perspective, the people you meet at any given time provide the dynamic that you require at that moment. If you're a sensitive creative Pisces, you might benefit from a more objective Aquarius or a go-getter Aries companion at a certain time in your life.

The celebrity couples in this chapter can help you visualize each sun-sign combination. You'll note that some legendary lovers have stood the test of time, while others blazed, then broke up, and still others existed only in the fantasy world of film or television (but still captured our imagination). Traditional astrological wisdom holds that signs of the same element are naturally compatible. For Pisces, that would be fellow water signs Cancer and Scorpio. Also favored are signs of complementary elements, such as water signs with earth signs (Taurus, Virgo, Capricorn). In these relationships communication supposedly flows easily, and you'll feel most comfortable together.

As you read the following matches, remember that there are no hard-and-fast rules; each combination has perks as well as peeves. So when sparks fly and an irresistible magnetic pull draws you together, when disagreements and challenges fuel intrigue, mystery, passion, and sexy sparring matches, don't rule the relationship out. That person may provide the diversity, excitement, and challenge you need for an unforgettable romance, stimulating friendship, or a successful business partnership!

# Pisces/Aries

### THE ROMANCE:

Pisces love to be swept off their feet and Aries is happy to comply! Pisces is someone who can appreciate Aries dynamism without feeling the least bit threatened by Aries power. On the contrary, Aries energizes you! This sign gets Pisces moving! Aries will be number one with Pisces, who'll have wonderful, romantic ideas to contribute. Aries tempts Pisces to swim in new waters . . . to follow that dream!

### THE REALITY CHECK:

Aries wants what it wants when it wants it. And this sign doesn't care who has other plans. Supersensitive Pisces feelings can be a problem here. Pushy, bossy, or inconsiderate partners turn you into a martyr or a monster who could rain on the Aries parade. Balancing positive and negative energies is the key. Aries needs brakes to slow down and consider the consequences of their actions; in turn, Pisces needs a charge to get up and running.

Pisces Freddie Prinze Jr. and Aries Sarah Michelle Gellar

# Pisces/Taurus

**THE ROMANCE:**

You both love the good things in life and can indulge each other sensually and sexually. The Taurus focus adds stability and direction to Pisces, while your Pisces creativity is lovingly encouraged by Taurus. Taurus and Pisces are both nurturers who love to take care of each other. Your energies are complementary—there will be few fights here.

**THE REALITY CHECK:**

Taurus wants Pisces to produce, not just dream, and will try to corral the slippery Fish. Pisces can't be bossed or caged, and may leave Taurus with the dotted line unsigned!

**SIGN MATES:**

Pisces Eva Longoria and Taurus Tony Parker

# Pisces/Gemini

**THE ROMANCE:**

You both are dual personalities in mutable, freedom-loving signs. You fascinate each other with ever-changing facets. You keep each other from straying by providing constant variety and new experiments to try together.

**THE REALITY CHECK:**

At some point, you'll need a frame of reference for this relationship to hold together. Since neither likes structure, this could be a problem. Overstimulation is another monster that can surface. Pisces sensitive feelings and Gemini hyperactive nerves could send each other searching for soothing, stabilizing alternatives. The relentless socializing of Gemini could send Pisces scurrying to calmer waters.

**SIGN MATES:**

Pisces Ivana Trump and Gemini Donald Trump
Pisces soul singer Seal and Gemini supermodel Heidi Klum
Pisces Drew Barrymore and Gemini Fabrizio Moretti

# Pisces/Cancer

**THE ROMANCE:**

You both love to swim in emotional waters, where your communication flows easily. Cancer protective attention and support help Pisces gain confidence and direction. Pisces gives Cancer dreamy romance and creative inspiration. A very meaningful relationship develops over time.

**THE REALITY CHECK:**

You two emotionally vulnerable signs know where the soft spots are and can really hurt each other! Pisces has a way of slipping through the clingy Cancer clutches, possibly to dry out after too much emotion. Learn to give each other space. Find creative projects to defuse moods.

**SIGN MATES:**

Pisces Liza Minnelli and Cancer David Gest
Pisces James Taylor and Cancer Carly Simon

# Pisces/Leo

**THE ROMANCE:**

Highly sensitive Pisces admires the Leo radiant confidence. You will gain stability under the warm and encouraging protection of Leo. Leo will gain an adoring admirer in Pisces, as you easily show affection and satisfy Leo's constant craving for romance. This is a noncompetitive mutual admiration society where you promote each other enthusiastically.

**THE REALITY CHECK:**

Pisces also loves to flirt. Unlike Leo, Pisces is not basically monogamous. A stickler for loyalty, Leo may try to keep Pisces dancing attendance by strong-arm tactics. Pisces operates best in free-flowing waters—you swim off when you sense a hook!

**SIGN MATES:**

Pisces Téa Leoni and Leo David Duchovny

# Pisces/Virgo

**THE ROMANCE:**

Virgo supplies what Pisces often needs most—clarity and order—while Pisces creative imagination takes Virgo into fascinating new realms away from the ordinary. If you can reconcile your opposing points of view, you'll have much to gain from this relationship.

**THE REALITY CHECK:**

There are many adjustments for both signs here. Virgo could feel overwhelmed with your Pisces emotions and seeming lack of control and frustrated when makeover attempts fail. Pisces could feel bogged down with Virgo worries and deflated by negative criticism. Try to support, not change, each other.

**SIGN MATES:**

Pisces Antonio Sabato, Jr., and Virgo Virginia Madsen

# Pisces/Libra

## THE ROMANCE:

You're one of the most creative couples. Libra keeps the delicate Pisces ego on keel, while Pisces provides the romance and attention Libra craves. You are ideal collaborators. Pisces appreciates Libra aesthetic judgment. Libra refines Pisces ideas without dampening your creative spirit or deflating your ego.

## THE REALITY CHECK:

Pisces swims in the emotional waters where Libra gets seasick. Libra indecisiveness sends Pisces looking elsewhere for an anchor. Fluctuating moods rock the boat here, unless you find a way to give each other stability and support. Turn to calm reason, avoiding emotional scenes, to solve problems.

## SIGN MATES:

Pisces Prince Andrew and Libra Sarah "Fergie" Ferguson
Pisces Chris Martin of Coldplay and Libra Gwyneth Paltrow
Pisces Prince Harry and Libra Chelsy Davy

# Pisces/Scorpio

## THE ROMANCE:

When these two signs click, nothing gets in their way. Your Pisces desire to merge completely with a beloved is just the all-or-nothing message Scorpio has been waiting for. These two will play it to the hilt, often shedding previous spouses or bucking public opinion (like Elizabeth Taylor and Richard Burton).

## THE REALITY CHECK:

Both signs are possessive, yet neither likes to be possessed. Scorpio could easily mistake your Pisces vulnerability for weakness—a big mistake. Both signs fuel each other's escapist tendencies when dark moods hit. Learning to merge without submerging one's identity is an important lesson for this couple.

**SIGN MATES:**

Pisces Kurt Russell and Scorpio Goldie Hawn
Pisces Bruce Willis and Scorpio Demi Moore

# Pisces/Sagittarius

**THE ROMANCE:**

You spark each other creatively and romantically. Pisces imagination and Sagittarius innovation work well on all levels. Variety, mental stimulation, and spiritual understanding—plus an appreciation of exotic places—could draw and keep you together.

**THE REALITY CHECK:**

Pisces can turn from a gentle tropical fish to a vengeful shark when Sagittarius disregards tender Pisces feelings. Sagittarius goes for direct attacks, and could feel that self-protective Pisces hides truths far beneath the surface.

**SIGN MATES:**

Pisces William H. Macy and Sagittarius Felicity Huffman

# Pisces/Capricorn

**THE ROMANCE:**

Capricorn organizational abilities and worldly know-how impress, helping Pisces find a clear direction. Pisces romance, tenderness, and knowledge of the art of love bring out the gypsy in Capricorn—a fair exchange.

**THE REALITY CHECK:**

What spells security for Capricorn could look like a gilded cage to Pisces, who doesn't play by the same rules. If you both can make allowances for radical differences, you'll find you can go far together. Don't try to make each other over!

**SIGN MATES:**

Pisces Tammy Fay Messner and Capricorn Jim Bakker
Pisces Penny Lancaster and Capricorn Rod Stewart

# Pisces/Aquarius

**THE ROMANCE:**

You two neighboring signs can be best buddies. You both need plenty of space and freedom, though in different ways. You'll have great tolerance for each other's eccentricities. You can inspire each other to be original, unpredictable, and romantic. You can explore unknown waters together.

**THE REALITY CHECK:**

Intense emotions feed you Pisces Fish, but make Aquarius swim away. Aquarius detachment could cause Pisces to look for warmer seas. Pisces needs one-on-one intimacy and reassurance, while Aquarius are people who need people in groups. You'll both have to leave your elements to make this work.

**SIGN MATES:**

Pisces Joanne Woodward and Aquarius Paul Newman

# Pisces/Pisces

**THE ROMANCE:**

Who understands your inner complexity better than one of your own? Here's the psychic soul mate you've been waiting for—finally someone who's as sensitive and sensual as you are! You'll love the good life together, and you will spark each other creatively.

## THE REALITY CHECK:

This romance can sink if you both get into a negative mood at the same time. There you are, caught in the undertow without a lifeguard! Avoid escaping into alcohol or food binges. Plan a strategy to defuse black moods with light-hearted friends and shared creative projects.

## SIGN MATES:

Pisces costars Elizabeth Taylor and Rex Harrison in *Cleopatra*

# CHAPTER 23

# The Big Picture for Pisces in 2009

Welcome to 2009! This should be quite an intriguing year for you, Pisces, with more freedom to call the shots in your own life. Uranus has been in your sign since 2003, so by now you should have a pretty good grasp of the kinds of unexpected and sudden events that can happen under this transit. Uranus's job is to shake up the status quo and get you out of your comfortable ruts and routines. But it also brings excitement and new events and people into your life and will continue to do so this year.

Your ruler, Neptune, continues its transit through Aquarius, your twelfth house, and on January 5 is joined by expansive Jupiter. The combination of these two planets broadens your perspective on your own unconscious and enables you to explore who you really are in private. During the next year, you may encounter people you have known in previous lives and would benefit from meditation, yoga, or some other mind-body discipline. You may try a past-life regression or enter therapy. You'll have more opportunities to work behind the scenes in some capacity. Your compassion and idealism deepen. Synchronicities are likely to proliferate, and it's a good idea to figure out what they mean. Often, they are signs indicating that the track you're pursuing is the right one.

For most of this year, two of the slower-moving planets—Saturn and Pluto—are in earth signs. Saturn is in Virgo, your opposite sign, and could bring restrictions or delays or increased responsibilities in partnerships. On October 29, Saturn enters Libra, your eighth house, where it will be for about two and a half years. During that transit, you may have less access to a partner's or spouse's income. This person could lose his or her job or change jobs so there is a gap in earnings. It's really vital that you keep abreast of tax and insurance payments during this period.

Pluto's demotion as a planet doesn't diminish its impact in astrology. Pluto's transit through Capricorn and your eleventh house will be lengthy—until 2024. At the most profound levels, it will transform your friendships, group associations, and your wishes and dreams. Since it will be forming a beneficial angle with your sun, it should put you in the power seat in many ways. Perhaps for the first time, you will be prompted to reclaim power you have disowned over the years. As you become more aware of your identity, your talents, and your gifts, you will demand more of yourself and may be surprised when what you visualize is manifested.

If you don't have a copy of your natal chart, get one. Then look to see where Capricorn is in your chart and which house Pluto will be transiting. This will reveal quite a bit about what you can expect during this very long transit. There are a number of online sites that provide natal charts for free.

# Best Time for Romance

Look for a pleasurable time from July 31 to August 26, when Venus is in Cancer, in your fifth house. Not only will your love life improve, but so will every other area of your life. Your artistic sensibilities will be strong then too, so dive into your creative projects. If you're not involved with anyone special at the beginning of this transit, you probably will be by the time it ends. And if you're not, Venus will be attracting other positive people and experiences into your life, so it won't matter. And you'll be having too much fun to care!

Great backup dates for romance fall much earlier in the year, between January 3 and February 2, when Venus transits your sign. There will be another period when your sexuality is heightened—March 14 to April 22, when Mars is in your sign.

Another date to watch for: June 22, when a new moon in Cancer ushers in new romantic and creative opportunities.

# Best Time for Career Decisions

On your calendar, mark the dates from December 1 to 25, when Venus transits Sagittarius and your tenth house of career. This period should be absolutely great for your career and all professional activities if you've got your priorities in order. This transit also enhances the possibilities of foreign travel and dealings with educators and publishers.

Backup dates for career matters fall between October 16 to December 20, when Mars in Leo forms a harmonious angle to your tenth house. This transit energizes not only your work life, but all professional activities and relationships. Mars turns retrograde on December 20, so after that point, you'll be assimilating what you've learned.

# Mercury Retrogrades

Every year, Mercury, the planet of communication and travel, turns retrograde three times. During these periods, it's wisest not to negotiate or sign contracts, travel, submit manuscripts, or make major decisions. Granted, we can't live our lives entirely by Mercury retrogrades! However, if you have to travel during the periods listed below, then expect changes in your schedule. If you have to sign a contract, expect to revisit it. Communications are bumpy. It's easy to be misunderstood. It's a good time to revise, review, and rewrite.

During these periods, back up computer files before Mercury turns retrograde. Quite often, computers and other communication devices act up. Be sure your virus software is up-to-date too. Pay special attention to the house in which Mercury retrograde falls in your birth chart. It will tell you the area of your life most likely to be impacted. The periods to watch for in 2009 are:

**January 11–February 1:** retrograde in Aquarius, in your twelfth house. You'll be revisiting issues you thought were solved.

**May 6–30:** retrograde in Gemini, in your fourth house. This will impact your home and family life.

**September 6–29:** retrograde in Libra, in your eighth house, resources you share with others.


# Eclipses

Every year, there are four eclipses, two solar and two lunar. This year, there are six.

Solar eclipses trigger external events that allow us to see something that eluded us before. When an eclipse hits one of your natal planets, it's especially important. Take note of the sign and house placement. Lunar eclipses bring up emotional issues related to the sign and house into which they fall. If you have your birth chart, check to see if the eclipses hit any natal planets. If they do, pay special attention to events that occur for up to six months after the eclipse.

Here are the dates to watch for:

**January 26:** solar eclipse at six degrees Aquarius, in your twelfth house.

**February 9:** lunar eclipse at 21 degrees Leo, in your sixth house, health and work.

**July 7:** lunar eclipse at 15 degrees Capricorn, in your eleventh house of friendships.

**July 22:** solar eclipse, 29 degrees Cancer, in your fifth house of romance and creativity.

**August 6:** lunar eclipse in Aquarius, in your twelfth house again!

**December 31:** lunar eclipse in Cancer, in your fifth house again!

# Luckiest Days in 2009

Every year, Jupiter forms a beneficial angle with the sun, usually a conjunction, when both planets are in the same sign. In 2009 it happens early in the year—between January 23 and 25, with the exact conjunction on January 24. It occurs in your twelfth house, so expect luck and serendipity concerning everything that happens behind the scenes.

Now let's take a look at what 2009 has in store for you, day by day.

# CHAPTER 24

# Eighteen Months of Day-by-Day Predictions: July 2008 to December 2009

*Moon sign times are calculated for Eastern Standard Time and Eastern Daylight Time. Please adjust for your local time zone.*

## JULY 2008

***Tuesday, July 1 (Moon in Gemini)***    Mars enters Virgo and your seventh house. This transit lasts until August 19 and can trigger impatience and anger at other people or bring a project to a successful culmination. Mars symbolizes energy, and when it's opposed to your sun, your life always is filled with activity. Whether the activities are positive or negative depends on you.

***Wednesday, July 2 (Moon in Gemini to Cancer 3:54 a.m.)***    You may get ready for guests for the long weekend. Try not to stress yourself out. Just have fun and go with the flow. Your love life should pick up over the next two days, and your muse stands by, ready to assist!

***Thursday, July 3 (Moon in Cancer)***    You may be in the mood to redecorate your home—new floors, new furniture, fresh paint, no telling where this urge can take you. But if you're on your way out of town for the long weekend—or people are coming to your place—satisfy the urge to redecorate by simply rearranging furniture.

*Friday, July 4 (Moon in Cancer to Leo 4:16 a.m.)*
Think back to last month, when the moon was in Leo. What events occurred? How did you feel? Look for the common emotional patterns. You're onstage whether you want to be or not.

*Saturday, July 5 (Moon in Leo)*     Even though it's Saturday, you've got obligations with employees or coworkers that must be met. Touch base through e-mail and the phone. On other fronts, you and your visitors may head to a new restaurant for dinner.

*Sunday, July 6 (Moon in Leo to Virgo 7:04 a.m.)*     You may be involved in contract negotiations through e-mail. It's a good time for this, since Mercury is moving direct and won't be retrograde again until September 24. Tie up loose ends so you can return to work fresh tomorrow.

*Monday, July 7 (Moon in Virgo)*     Since you tend to be such a romantic, indulge yourself and your partner. Do something special together that honors your partnership. Make memories by the way you live together.

*Tuesday, July 8 (Moon in Virgo to Libra 1:32 p.m.)*     You lend a helping hand today to an elderly person or someone who needs additional aid. It may be something as complex as helping the person fill out Medicare forms or as simple as moving some furniture around. You never turn away someone in need.

*Wednesday, July 9 (Moon in Libra)*     You lend a helping hand to a neighbor or friend. And while your focus is elsewhere, you're aware of something mysterious building in the air around you. Perhaps tomorrow, when the moon enters Scorpio, you'll have a clearer sense of what it is.

*Thursday, July 10 (Moon in Libra to Scorpio 11:35 p.m.)*     Mercury enters Cancer, joining Venus here for two days before Venus moves on. Take advantage of the next two days, when your mind and your heart are in complete agreement. Your creative adrenaline is at a very nice high.

*Friday, July 11 (Moon in Scorpio)*     Intense emotions run fast and furious. Rather than keeping it bottled up inside, write it all out. Or confide in a trusted friend or family member. Not only is it healthier to do that, but your imagination won't run as wild.

*Saturday, July 12 (Moon in Scorpio)*     Venus enters Leo and your sixth house and remains there until August 5. This transit may bring an office relationship to a whole new level. It also portends generally smooth sailing in your work routine. You may want to change your appearance in some way.

*Sunday, July 13 (Moon in Scorpio to Sagittarius 11:50 a.m.)*     You feel the subtle shift from a water-sign moon to a fire-sign moon. It isn't nearly as comfortable for you. However, the Sagittarius moon brings some opportunities in your career, so pay attention.

*Monday, July 14 (Moon in Sagittarius)*     A professional issue demands emotional flexibility on your part. You can easily bring yourself to see the other person's point of view. You're as camouflaged as a chameleon, able to fit in anywhere.

*Tuesday, July 15 (Moon in Sagittarius)*     You link up with your support group. Whether your group consists of writers or actors, bridge players or computer enthusiasts, it gives you the emotional support you need to pursue your creative dreams and life plans.

*Wednesday, July 16 (Moon in Sagittarius to Capricorn 12:20 a.m.)*     There are some things that you do for money; other things that you do strictly for love. The question is whether your current projects are done out of love or for money. Or is it both?

*Thursday, July 17 (Moon in Capricorn)*    You're good at prioritizing. And whether you're prioritizing your own needs and obligations or someone else's, the result is the same. You intuitively recognize the patterns, and these patterns explain what must be done. You would be hard-pressed to explain your technique to someone else.

*Friday, July 18 (Moon in Capricorn to Aquarius 11:41 a.m.)*    Get organized for the week ahead. Be methodical and thorough. Keep in mind that you're building a base for a creative future. Stay focused. Try not to scatter your energies.

*Saturday, July 19 (Moon in Aquarius)*    With the moon in your twelfth house, retreat for the day. Find a quiet place somewhere and work behind the scenes. Relations with the opposite sex can be difficult. Keep your feelings secret. Stuff from your past that makes you feel uncomfortable could surface.

*Sunday, July 20 (Moon in Aquarius to Pisces 9:09 p.m.)*    Accept what comes your way, but don't start anything new. Clear up odds and ends. Look beyond the immediate. Let go of preconceived notions about any limitations. And this evening, when the moon enters your sign, you're ready to take on the world.

*Monday, July 21 (Moon in Pisces)*    It's your power day. The moon is in your sign, and life is looking very sweet. So define your territory today, get down to work—or go out and play! The universe supports whatever you do.

*Tuesday, July 22 (Moon in Pisces)*    Your dream recall is excellent. Experiment with requesting dreams on particular concerns. Be sure to have a notebook next to your bed. Or set the alarm for the middle of the night and then record whatever it is you've been dreaming. The techniques take practice, but you shouldn't have any trouble with it all. Dreams and imagination are where you navigate without any trouble at all.

***Wednesday, July 23 (Moon in Pisces to Aries 4:23 a.m.)***
When the moon moves into Aries, your attention turns to
your finances. You may be worried that you don't earn
enough money. Worry never does anyone any good, so take
steps to rectify the situation.

***Thursday, July 24 (Moon in Aries)***   You're the leader
of the pack. Actually, you may be so far out in front of
the rest that they're eating your dust. Watch yourself while
driving—don't speed! And definitely don't get behind the
wheel if you're angry.

***Friday, July 25 (Moon in Aries to Taurus 9:15
a.m.)***   You feel stubborn about an issue that could involve a relative or a neighbor. Don't back down. Stick to
what you believe; don't hesitate to speak your mind. On
the other hand, if you know you're wrong, admit it and
move on.

***Saturday, July 26 (Moon in Taurus)***   Mercury enters
Leo and joins Venus in your sixth house. You're so primed
for working on your nutrition and health that there's no
stopping you. The difference from times in the past is that
you're serious and committed.

***Sunday, July 27 (Moon in Taurus to Gemini 11:56
a.m.)***   Issues surface concerning your home and family.
Someone in your family needs advice, and they come to
you, expecting you to provide guidance. Even if you don't
have a clue about what to say, make sure that whatever
you say is positive and upbeat.

***Monday, July 28 (Moon in Gemini)***   Information and
news are the hallmarks. Your sources include—but aren't
limited to—books, the Internet, movies, other people, and
your own innate wisdom. Be alert for signs in the oddest
places—for example, a tune on the radio that holds personal significance for you.

***Tuesday, July 29 (Moon in Gemini to Cancer 1:12
p.m.)***   You awaken with creative adrenaline coursing

through you. You're on fire with ideas. If your creative work is not how you earn your daily bread, is there any chance you can take the day off to indulge your muse?

*Wednesday, July 30 (Moon in Cancer)*     The moon forms a harmonious angle with Saturn in your seventh house and with your sun. Saturn brings structure and form to the areas of your life where you need them.

*Thursday, July 31 (Moon in Cancer to Leo 2:22 p.m.)*     The moon joins Mercury and Venus in Leo, your sixth house. Not only are you on display, but your heart, mind, and emotions work in tandem to support your endeavors. The areas are work and health.

## AUGUST 2008

*Friday, August 1 (Moon in Leo)*     The solar eclipse in Leo, your sixth house, triggers external events that allow you to see a work- or health-related issue clearly. In two weeks, there's a lunar eclipse in Aquarius, your twelfth house, and on August 30, a new moon in Virgo, your opposite sign. Stay tuned!

*Saturday, August 2 (Moon in Leo to Virgo 4:59 p.m.)*     As the moon enters Virgo and your seventh house, you become detail-oriented and perhaps emotionally discerning. In real life, this can translate as self-criticism or criticism of others. Watch yourself!

*Sunday, August 3 (Moon in Virgo)*     You and your partner work together on a project that is a labor of love. In the near future, it may prove to be lucrative for both of you. You may want to consider going into business together. Brainstorm for ideas. With Saturn in your seventh house, you have the diligence to make the abstract practical.

*Monday, August 4 (Moon in Virgo to Libra 10:28 p.m.)*     You're in a social mood, but may have obligations that you need to tend to—like taxes, insurance forms, or wills. Can any of it be put off for a couple days? You should get together with friends this evening and enjoy yourself!

**Tuesday, August 5 (Moon in Libra)**     Venus enters Virgo and your seventh house. This transit lasts until August 30 and should spice up your relationship with your partner. If you're not involved, you may be before this transit ends. Another manifestation of this transit is that it favors contracts and friendships.

**Wednesday, August 6 (Moon in Libra)**     It's a great day for romance. Plan something special with your partner. If you're not involved, be sure to keep your options open. Don't be a hermit!

**Thursday, August 7 (Moon in Libra to Scorpio 7:27 a.m.)**     You find the bottom line concerning a business expansion overseas or something to do with publishing or higher education. If you're considering college or graduate school, be very clear about what you seek. Be organized about test dates and scholarship submissions.

**Friday, August 8 (Moon in Scorpio)**     With the moon in a fellow water sign, you're in the flow and loving it. Areas of focus? Education, publishing, your worldview, and overseas travel and individuals. Any research or investigations are successful.

**Saturday, August 9 (Moon in Scorpio to Sagittarius 7:11 p.m.)**     Be careful that you don't have a confrontation with a boss or some other authority figure. You may feel edgy and could blurt out something that will come back to haunt you!

**Sunday, August 10 (Moon in Sagittarius)**     Mercury enters Virgo and joins Venus in your seventh house. The nice combination of these two planets makes you precise and detailed about what you're looking for in a relationship—

or in a contract negotiation. Make good use of the next twenty days, before Venus enters Libra.

**_Monday, August 11 (Moon in Sagittarius)_**    Pace yourself. Otherwise, you may feel overwhelmed with all the demands on your time and energy. Young people are the source of excellent ideas that you can use in some way in your career.

**_Tuesday, August 12 (Moon in Sagittarius to Capricorn 7:43 a.m.)_**    Complete outstanding projects. You clear space in your life for new contacts who will support your dreams and efforts. It's all something of a mystery, but intuitively you sense you're on the right path.

**_Wednesday, August 13 (Moon in Capricorn)_**    Whenever the moon joins Jupiter in Capricorn, you feel grounded, and you are able to bring imaginings into concrete reality. Use this lunar energy to make long-range plans.

**_Thursday, August 14 (Moon in Capricorn to Aquarius 6:57 p.m.)_**    Cooperation and team work are called for on a project you're involved in. You and a partner or close friend discuss the larger questions of life. Why are you here? What are you supposed to be doing with the time you have? This type of metaphysical discussion is exactly what your soul craves.

**_Friday, August 15 (Moon in Aquarius)_**    You recharge your batteries, rest up, and get ready for when the moon enters your sign the day after tomorrow. Work in solitude if you can. This evening, get out into nature and appreciate everything you see.

**_Saturday, August 16 (Moon in Aquarius)_**    The lunar eclipse in Aquarius falls in your twelfth house. An issue that you've buried or perhaps some past-life memory surfaces. Your emotional reaction is powerful, and the insights you gain are valuable.

*Sunday, August 17 (Moon in Aquarius to Pisces 3:47 a.m.)*   You've come full cycle. The moon is in your sign, an invitation to romance and adventure. The opportunities arrive from the most unlikely sources. Be prepared for a whirlwind.

*Monday, August 18 (Moon in Pisces)*   You and a partner or friends may attend a concert or the opening of a museum or art exhibit. Your artistic sensibilities and creative power are the focus.

*Tuesday, August 19 (Moon in Pisces to Aries 10:11 a.m.)* Mars enters Libra and your eighth house, and before the month ends, Mercury and Venus will join Mars. Pay attention to the subtle shift in rhythms and patterns in your life. You may tend to income tax matters—perhaps by setting up an IRA or college fund.

*Wednesday, August 20 (Moon in Aries)*   Don't make impulsive investments or financial decisions. You feel like you just have to take care of the issue, but wait until the moon enters Taurus tomorrow. You need that sort of stability.

*Thursday, August 21 (Moon in Aries to Taurus 2:38 p.m.)*   By early this afternoon, you feel you must resist certain changes, perhaps with a long-standing tradition in your community. Resistance to what you sense is wrong is the correct thing to do. A neighbor or sibling has news for you.

*Friday, August 22 (Moon in Taurus)*   The moon is in your third house. Expect one or more short trips on your agenda. You'll probably have to deal with a troubling situation concerning a relative. You'll need to stay in control of your emotions. Allow your intuition to lead the way in this situation.

*Saturday, August 23 (Moon in Taurus to Gemini 5:49 p.m.)*   By this afternoon, you're ready to retreat to your couch and chill out with a book or magazine. And when you get bored doing that, rent a movie.

**Sunday, August 24 (Moon in Gemini)**   The moon is in your fourth house. Retreat to a private place. Work at home or enjoy the day off. Work on a home-repair project. In other words, the world won't collapse if you allow yourself some downtime!

**Monday, August 25 (Moon in Gemini to Cancer 8:19 p.m.)**   With Mars in Libra in your eighth house until October 3, apply for mortgages and loans. Mercury turns retrograde on September 24, so get all the paperwork done before then.

**Tuesday, August 26 (Moon in Cancer)**   Be yourself. You're possessive of loved ones, more involved with kids and animals. You may feel particularly protective about them. It's a day that favors any kind of creative work.

**Wednesday, August 27 (Moon in Cancer to Leo 10:51 p.m.)**   This evening, the moon enters Leo and your sixth house. You'll feel the need to help someone else. Set up a schedule for tomorrow that includes doing that. Be a good Samaritan.

**Thursday, August 28 (Moon in Leo)**   Mercury enters Libra, joining Mars in your eighth house. Together, these two planets make your communications forceful and clear. Call the bank to check on the status of your mortgage or loan application.

**Friday, August 29 (Moon in Leo)**   Strut your stuff and don't be shy. Whether you present a paper or audition for a part, try to sell a manuscript or simply spell out policies at your company, you're onstage and you've got an audience.

**Saturday, August 30 (Moon in Leo to Virgo 2:19 a.m.)**   Venus enters Libra and joins Mercury and Mars in your eighth house. There are all kinds of possibilities when these planets link up. Romance could be one of the things involved, but so could loan and mortgage applications, taxes, legacies, and inheritances. It all works in your favor.

**Sunday, August 31 (Moon in Virgo)**    Be helpful and diplomatic with anyone giving you a hard time. You may need to make a domestic adjustment, which will work out for the best. Do a good deed for someone, but avoid scattering your energies.

# SEPTEMBER 2008

**Monday, September 1 (Moon in Virgo to Libra 7:45 a.m.)**    Your organizational skills are top-notch. You examine budgets—your own or your company's—and initiate changes that bring your expenses in line with your revenue. Taxes and insurance issues are part of the activities.

**Tuesday, September 2 (Moon in Libra)**    Your artistic side shines through. Your imagination is already stellar, but the Libra moon urges you to express that imagination in photography, dance, art, or writing. You need to define your deepest passion.

**Wednesday, September 3 (Moon in Libra to Scorpio 4:03 p.m.)**    Journey into the unknown to investigate, research, and explore. Avoid confrontations and conflicts. Your imagination and intuition are deepened with the Scorpio moon, but that can lead to a rigid stance that you're right and everyone else is wrong.

**Thursday, September 4 (Moon in Scorpio)**    The moon forms a beneficial angle to your sun; you're in the driver's seat. Publishing and education issues are highlighted. Make your travel plans while the deals are hot and Mercury is moving direct. Don't travel between September 24 and October 15.

**Friday, September 5 (Moon in Scorpio)**    This moon helps to eliminate indecisiveness and puts you on track toward career success. But you need to stay alert and read the invisible signs all around you. Only you can tune in on these signs with such finesse and certainty.

*Saturday, September 6 (Moon in Scorpio to Sagittarius 3:12 a.m.)* Travel connected with professional matters is a possibility. If you speak to a group, the goal is to inspire and encourage others to see the big picture of their own career goals. In doing this, you grasp your own place in the cosmic scheme.

*Sunday, September 7 (Moon in Sagittarius)* Jupiter turns direct in Capricorn, your eleventh house. Your goals and dreams for yourself are clear in your mind. And with that clarity, you imagine how you would like your life to be.

*Monday, September 8 (Moon in Sagittarius to Capricorn 3:46 p.m.)* Pluto turns direct in Sagittarius, your tenth house. As it moves toward its appointment with Capricorn on November 26, you may experience some of the same issues and situations that you've experienced since Pluto entered Sagittarius in 1995. Think of it as Pluto's last hurrah before it leaves your tenth house forever.

*Tuesday, September 9 (Moon in Capricorn)* With the moon joining Jupiter in Capricorn, a friend may need your emotional support. Even if you don't know this person well, you're pleased to help. Once Pluto enters Capricorn, where it will be until 2024, your friendships and wishes and dreams will undergo a profound change.

*Wednesday, September 10 (Moon in Capricorn)* You're building grassroots support for a political or artistic group to which you belong. You're able to plan and strategize because you can imagine outcomes better than almost any other sign.

*Thursday, September 11 (Moon in Capricorn to Aquarius 3:20 a.m.)* Retreat. If you can work out of your home, do so. You need solitude to complete a project or work out the details of a particular issue. With Neptune still in

229

your twelfth house, you need to gather all the information you can find before making a decision.

*Friday, September 12 (Moon in Aquarius)* You get ready for tomorrow when the moon enters your sign. Recharge your batteries so that if people drop by your place over the weekend, you're ready for them. Tie up loose ends so that you start with a clean slate for the weekend.

*Saturday, September 13 (Moon in Aquarius to Pisces 12:05 p.m.)* The moon is in your sign, joining Uranus in your first house. You suddenly feel good, think clearly, and look spectacular. Other people are attracted by your magnetism. There could be some unexpected events that trigger unusual emotions.

*Sunday, September 14 (Moon in Pisces)* It's another power day for you. Regardless of what you're involved in, you call the shots. With Jupiter forming a harmonious angle to your sun, options in every area of your life expand.

*Monday, September 15 (Moon in Pisces to Aries 5:39 p.m.)* You would like to purchase a big-ticket item. Resist the impulse and look beyond the immediate. Do your homework, compare prices, and then make your purchase if you can pay cash and you're sure you've found the best price.

*Tuesday, September 16 (Moon in Aries)* You're wrestling with a concept. What makes you feel emotionally secure? Is it tons of money in the bank, a happy home life, a job, friends, or a spiritual belief? Once you determine the what, you have to figure out how to get what you need.

*Wednesday, September 17 (Moon in Aries to Taurus 8:57 p.m.)* A week from today, Mercury turns retrograde in Libra, in your eighth house. So if you've applied for a mortgage or loan, call the bank and try to hurry the process along. Sign before September 24; otherwise wait until after October 15, when Mercury turns direct.

*Thursday, September 18 (Moon in Taurus)*    Your communication skills, written or verbal, are impressive. If you work in sales, get out there and really sell. It won't take much effort. People are sucked in by your charm and gift of gab.

*Friday, September 19 (Moon in Taurus to Gemini 11:17 p.m.)*    The Gemini moon feels a bit strange to you at times, but it makes you more flexible and adaptable. That's what you may need. By this evening, your priorities have shifted to your home and family.

*Saturday, September 20 (Moon in Gemini)*    The moon forms a harmonious angle to Mercury, Venus, and Mars in Libra, in your eighth house. The focus is on relationships, information, and a quest for harmony, peace, and balance. Try to nurture and attain these qualities in your daily life because very soon all the planets shift into Scorpio.

*Sunday, September 21 (Moon in Gemini)*    You may have to deal with individuals whose minds are closed up like abandoned buildings. You probably won't be able to get into minds like that, but you can at least plant seeds of information that might lead these people in new directions.

*Monday, September 22 (Moon in Gemini to Cancer 1:49 a.m.)*    Indulge your creative talents, whatever they are. Today's energies favor romance and pleasure. Get out and do something for yourself that makes you smile and laugh.

*Tuesday, September 23 (Moon in Cancer)*    Venus enters Scorpio in your ninth house and remains there until October 18. This transit favors overseas travel, intense romantic and sexual experiences, and dealings with foreign countries and individuals. If you're a writer in search of an agent or editor, this transit helps steer you toward the right individual. Back up all computer files.

*Wednesday, September 24 (Moon in Cancer to Leo 5:14 a.m.)*    Mercury turns retrograde in Libra, in your eighth

231

house. This is the last time Mercury turns retrograde this year, so you know the drill.

***Thursday, September 25 (Moon in Leo)***     If a coworker or employee is acting up, stay out of it, particularly with Mercury retrograde. This individual may need responsibility to keep him (or her) busy and focused.

***Friday, September 26 (Moon in Leo to Virgo 9:53 a.m.)*** With Mercury retrograde in your house of shared resources, you and your partner may have some misunderstandings concerning money. If you feel you can't talk honestly with your partner, write down your gripes and complaints. Have him or her do the same. Then exchange lists.

***Saturday, September 27 (Moon in Virgo)***     The moon joins Saturn in Virgo, in your seventh house. You find the proper vehicle for your emotions and use the feelings in a positive way to bring about stability in a partnership. If the partnership is related to business, you need to agree on the basics and Saturn helps you to do that.

***Sunday, September 28 (Moon in Virgo to Libra 4:06 p.m.)***     Balance is key; it may be difficult to find, particularly with Mercury retrograde in Libra. The intense and intuitive Venus in Scorpio helps you see your way clearly through challenges and obstacles, and by the end of the day, you're satisfied with your progress.

***Monday, September 29 (Moon in Libra)***     To feed your imagination, you should take in an art film, visit a museum, or get involved in the art of foreign cultures today. Get your partner or a friend to go with you. You need the feedback of others.

***Tuesday, September 30 (Moon in Libra)***     The moon joins Venus in your ninth house. Any relationship that begins under this combination should be intense, sexual, and psychic. You're connected to this person and may find that you share the same spiritual beliefs.

**Wednesday, October 1 (Moon in Libra to Scorpio 12:27 a.m.)** You entertain the idea of a trip overseas. Start planning and schedule the trip after October 15, when Mercury turns direct. You may have your eye on a foreign-born individual or could expand your business overseas.

**Thursday, October 2 (Moon in Scorpio)** Your concerns focus on foreign investments, businesses, cultures, and individuals. Your intuitive skills are best applied to research and investigation. In fact, you may be researching an alternative-health treatment or a skin or hair product.

**Friday, October 3 (Moon in Scorpio to Sagittarius 11:15 a.m.)** Mars enters Scorpio, a sign it corules, and joins Venus in your ninth house. This is a surefire recipe for an affair, particularly if you're traveling overseas. But even if you're at home, Venus and Mars in passionate Scorpio promise an exciting, perhaps even karmic romance.

**Saturday, October 4 (Moon in Sagittarius)** Even though it's a weekend, travel for business is a possibility. Try to get home by tomorrow when the moon will be in a compatible earth sign and you'll feel more like yourself. Stay witty and keep your distance from troublemakers.

**Sunday, October 5 (Moon in Sagittarius to Capricorn 11:49 p.m.)** You're in the mood for people who think as you do. You may get together with a group of friends or with the members of a group to which you belong. You need the emotional support this group provides.

**Monday, October 6 (Moon in Capricorn)** With the moon and Jupiter hooking up in your eleventh house, you build on a new advertising or promotional campaign that is larger than anything you've done before. Get out into the public and be seen. Get the word out. Use your network.

**Tuesday, October 7 (Moon in Capricorn)** Mercury retrograde may be causing some communication glitches at work. If possible, write things out first. This gives you the opportunity to mull over what you want to say. You may decide to keep your thoughts private until after October 15.

**Wednesday, October 8 (Moon in Capricorn to Aquarius 12:03 p.m.)**   Whenever the moon is in Aquarius, you feel an urge to retreat. If possible, you may want to work from home. Be sure to get out for some exercise.

**Thursday, October 9 (Moon in Aquarius)**   Your cutting edge ideas are ready to be implemented as soon as Mercury turns direct. Keep notes. Try some dream recall tonight to clarify your ideas.

**Friday, October 10 (Moon in Aquarius to Pisces 9:31 p.m.)**   Save time for special events and activities. Or schedule for challenges that you know you'll have to face—a presentation, a dental appointment, or a talk with a loved one. You're in the driver's seat!

**Saturday, October 11 (Moon in Pisces)**   Charisma, magnetism, and sex appeal—these words describe you when the moon is in your sign. You're on. Your intuitive judgment is nearly infallible. It may be difficult to make decisions because Uranus is also in your sign and its energy is always unpredictable.

**Sunday, October 12 (Moon in Pisces)**   Your dream recall is remarkable. Request dreams on particular issues or situations and marvel at what your dreams bring up. Your understanding of your own dream symbolism is good, so start compiling your personal dream dictionary.

**Monday, October 13 (Moon in Pisces to Aries 3:07 a.m.)**   When the moon enters Aries, you begin to feel restless and impatient, and you may worry about your finances. Instead of letting this worry gnaw away at you, do something about it. Start by making a realistic budget.

**Tuesday, October 14 (Moon in Aries)**   Isn't it time to ask for a raise? If your present employer won't give you a raise—and you know you're deserving—then perhaps it's time to send out résumés and network to find a better-paying job that meets your inner criteria.

**Wednesday, October 15 (Moon in Aries to Taurus 5:31 a.m.)**    Mercury turns direct, and you don't have to worry about another retrograde of this planet for the rest of the year. So make your Christmas travel plans. Sign your contracts.

**Thursday, October 16 (Moon in Taurus)**    You glean pleasure from beauty. That beauty comes disguised in various forms. It could be in the first hint of autumn in the air. Or it could be the face of the one you love.

**Friday, October 17 (Moon in Taurus to Gemini 6:26 a.m.)**    Expect lots of activity around your place. Neighbors may drop in unexpectedly, you could run errands before and after work, and there could be people around the house doing renovations. Consider hiring a professional cleaning service to step in tomorrow.

**Saturday, October 18 (Moon in Gemini)**    Venus enters Sagittarius and your tenth house. This very nice transit should benefit your career. Everything hums along smoothly, the opposite sex is helpful, and there could be a flirtation or romance with a peer or boss. Be careful that hearts don't get broken!

**Sunday, October 19 (Moon in Gemini to Cancer 7:41 a.m.)**    In the wake of Venus's entrance to your tenth house, the moon sails into your fifth house, so you are in a very romantic mood. If you're not involved, get out this evening and be seen!

**Monday, October 20 (Moon in Cancer)**    Pleasure and romance are on your agenda. You have so many interests and talents that it may be difficult to narrow your pleasures down to one or two. As for romance, if you're like many Pisces, there's no shortage of interested parties!

*Tuesday, October 21 (Moon in Cancer to Leo 10:36 a.m.)* The hired help has quit. Or they haven't shown up. And if they haven't shown up, they haven't bothered calling. Try not to obsess about it. Just dismiss the thing as unimportant and get on with the rest of the day.

*Wednesday, October 22 (Moon in Leo)* Services that you perform for others, without thought of compensation, are like karmic brownie points. Those brownie points are earned by helping out an employee or coworkers. You help out of compassion, not out of hope for compensation, which is the true Pisces way.

*Thursday, October 23 (Moon in Leo to Virgo 3:41 p.m.)* The moon joins Saturn in Virgo, in your seventh house. You should have a clear sense of what happens when the moon and Saturn link up. But the mix is quite different because Mars is in fellow water sign Scorpio, Venus is sitting at the top of your chart, and Mercury is in your eighth house. In other words, there's stability in your closest partnership and smoothness in your career, and you are itching to travel.

*Friday, October 24 (Moon in Virgo)* Tend to work details so that you can enjoy your weekend! You and your partner or a couple friends may get a jump on holiday shopping. Buy personal gifts rather than generic gifts.

*Saturday, October 25 (Moon in Virgo to Libra 10:48 p.m.)* If this is one of those days when you feel you don't measure up, try to overcome these feelings by substituting negative thoughts with more positive thoughts. Otherwise, you may draw experiences that reinforce negativity.

*Sunday, October 26 (Moon in Libra)* The moon joins Mercury in Libra, adding an intuitive flow to your conscious thoughts. You may feel as if you have to please everyone around you, and at some point in the day, it drives you nuts. Do something for yourself first, and then deal with everyone else.

*Monday, October 27 (Moon in Libra)*    Social activities and relationships of all kinds take center stage. Cooperation is the key to success. Listen to what other people say, weigh their words against your inner wisdom, and then make your decision. You may tackle some esoteric topics—reincarnation, ghosts, or life after death.

*Tuesday, October 28 (Moon in Libra to Scorpio 7:48 a.m.)*    Perseverance is the rule. It may involve signing up for a workshop or sending queries to magazines and publishers. Try to stay focused and resist the urge to do everything at once.

*Wednesday, October 29 (Moon in Scorpio)*    Your researching and investigative skills are top-notch. Use them to dig into some long-standing riddles concerning your spiritual beliefs. Since Mars is in Scorpio, you've got plenty of psychic energy to zone in on other people's motives.

*Thursday, October 30 (Moon in Scorpio to Sagittarius 6:41 p.m.)*    Unless you have a natal moon or rising in a fire sign, you're rarely confrontational. Someone could push your buttons; if possible, just walk away. Someone close to you may renege on a promise or obligation.

*Friday, October 31 (Moon in Sagittarius)*    Happy Halloween! Don your costume for the office party or for trick-or-treating with your kids. Get out there and have some fun! The Sagittarius moon always loves a good party.

## NOVEMBER 2008

*Saturday, November 1 (Moon in Sagittarius)*    Neptune goes direct in your twelfth house. Scrutinize your ideals and decide how you can integrate them into your daily life. This transit should be very good for all spiritual and creative work.

*Sunday, November 2—Daylight Saving Time Ends (Moon in Sagittarius to Capricorn 6:13 a.m.)*    A professional issue may surface that requires your immediate attention. It may involve a power struggle between two people with whom you work. You may delay making a decision until tomorrow, when the moon is fully in compatible Capricorn.

*Monday, November 3 (Moon in Capricorn)*  The moon moves into your eleventh house, joining expansive Jupiter. Focus on your dreams and wishes and figure out how you might best achieve them. Remain goal-oriented. Make sure that your goals are still an expression of who you really are.

*Tuesday, November 4 (Moon in Capricorn to Aquarius 7:02 p.m.)*  Mercury enters Scorpio, joining Mars in your ninth house. Talk about an intuitive combination. You may be downright psychic. This trend continues until Mars leaves Scorpio on November 16.

*Wednesday, November 5 (Moon in Aquarius)*  You may want to kick back and tend to your own business. Get a jump on the Thanksgiving holidays by figuring out where you're going or who you're having over or how you're going to spend that day. Planning and foresight never hurt!

*Thursday, November 6 (Moon in Aquarius)*  A Gemini or a Libra figures into your day. This person has information or insights that help you make an important decision. Make a symbolic act—cleaning your attic or garage, perhaps—that shows the universe you're clearing space for new experiences and opportunities.

*Friday, November 7 (Moon in Aquarius to Pisces 5:44 a.m.)*  Lovely, isn't it, when you wake with the moon in your sign? You may feel so good that you'll want to just lounge around the house. Do some of that, or indulge yourself with a visit to a spa.

*Saturday, November 8 (Moon in Pisces)*  Enjoy the festivities, whatever they are, and let your imagination roam free. You may want to carve out some time for your creative projects or, if you earn your living through the arts, to do some serious work!

*Sunday, November 9 (Moon in Pisces to Aries 12:27 p.m.)*    Balance your checkbook and stay on top of your finances, particularly as you enter the holiday season. Resist impulsive spending unless you are absolutely certain that you can afford what you want to buy!

*Monday, November 10 (Moon in Aries)*    The pioneer spirit is alive and well. It's got you feeling restless, perhaps even edgy, but you can't pinpoint the problem or the source. So don't try to identify it. Follow your impulses and hunches and see where they lead you. Make it an adventure.

*Tuesday, November 11 (Moon in Aries to Taurus 3:06 p.m.)*    By this afternoon, you feel grounded and stable. You and a relative or neighbor may get together, and you'll feel better about this relationship than you have in a while. The Taurus moon always urges you to make the abstract practical.

*Wednesday, November 12 (Moon in Taurus)*    This is where your love life gets interesting. Venus joins Jupiter in Capricorn, your eleventh house. It's possible that someone you meet through a group or whom you have thought of as a friend becomes something much more. Jupiter always seeks to expand whatever it touches.

*Thursday, November 13 (Moon in Taurus to Gemini 3:13 p.m.)*    With Venus and Jupiter on very friendly terms, your circle of friends expands like crazy. You could commit yourself to more groups than you really have time for, but you'll get the idea soon enough.

*Friday, November 14 (Moon in Gemini)*    You've got things to say to someone in your family. Write down your gripes, complaints, feelings, and thoughts. Try not to be cruel or mean, but get it all out. Then clear the air face-to-face.

*Saturday, November 15 (Moon in Gemini to Cancer 3:53 p.m.)*    If you have children, take them holiday shopping.

239

They may shop for their teachers or other friends, but you can notice what they touch and admire and make mental notes about which gifts you'll get for them.

**Sunday, November 16 (Moon in Cancer)**     Mars enters Sagittarius, and on November 23, Mercury will follow. The Mars transit energizes your career and all professional matters. Mars only goes through this house every two years, so look back to this time roughly two years ago for possible events and situations that may surface.

**Monday, November 17 (Moon in Cancer to Leo 4:08 p.m.)**     There's always some chaos when the moon changes signs. But by this afternoon, it's pretty clear that drama and flamboyance are what this moon is about.

**Tuesday, November 18 (Moon in Leo)**     You get an excellent work evaluation. Is a raise in your future? A coworker may be somewhat jealous about your good fortune and could spread gossip about you. Laugh it off and get back to work.

**Wednesday, November 19 (Moon in Leo to Virgo 8:13 p.m.)**     If there's any chance that you can take a few days off before Thanksgiving, do it. Get out of town with your partner or a group of friends. The point is to break up your routine. Even though you may feel somewhat vulnerable emotionally, try not to take every little thing personally. Just go with the flow.

**Thursday, November 20 (Moon in Virgo)**     Avoid self-criticism and picking on the people around you. It's easy to do when the moon and Saturn link up in Virgo. Look for a positive vehicle into which you can pour your criticisms.

**Friday, November 21 (Moon in Virgo)**     If you have a copy of your birth chart, look for the planets you have in the seventh house. If you have one or several, chances are you can make friends of your enemies. If you have no natal planets in your seventh house, transits become all the more important. Be informed.

*Saturday, November 22 (Moon in Virgo to Libra 3:20 a.m.)*   With the moon entering Libra, balance becomes important. If you do yoga, for instance, you would benefit from any kind of balance postures.

*Sunday, November 23 (Moon in Libra)*   Mercury enters Sagittarius, joining Mars in your tenth house. A very nice combination for grasping the big picture concerning your career. It's also a great combination for sales, for pitching your ideas and agenda, and for winning the support you need to advance a project. The one thing you have to watch out for is appearing boastful.

*Monday, November 24 (Moon in Libra to Scorpio 12:54 p.m.)*   You'll feel the urge to work on your own creative projects. Regardless of who is visiting you or where you're visiting for the holidays, leave time for your own creative expression.

*Tuesday, November 25 (Moon in Scorpio)*   Resist the urge to get even with someone under this transit. Instead, look for the deeper issues. What does your relationship to the person teach you? What are you learning from it? Once you know that, the need for vindication will pass.

*Wednesday, November 26 (Moon in Scorpio)*   After retrograding back into Sagittarius for much of the year, Pluto enters Capricorn until 2024. This transit will be an important one for you, transforming your friendships, wishes, and dreams.

*Thursday, November 27 (Moon in Scorpio to Sagittarius 12:14 a.m.)*   Happy Thanksgiving! And what a nice day for Uranus to turn direct in your sign. You're able to enthusiastically embrace all the abrupt changes in your personal life. In fact, such change seems exciting.

*Friday, November 28 (Moon in Sagittarius)*   With the moon, Mercury, and Mars in your tenth house, you've got an opportunity to actively pursue your career goals. You gain an elevation in prestige. Bosses pay attention. You're responsive to the needs of a group and the public in general.

**Saturday, November 29 (Moon in Sagittarius to Capricorn 12:48 p.m.)**    Clear up odds and ends. Discard preconceived notions as you visualize your future. Expansive Jupiter in this sign and house helps you to expand your inner vision, which translates as external and positive change in your life. Complete projects and plan, but don't start anything new.

**Sunday, November 30 (Moon in Capricorn)**    Take an honest look at your goals. You prepare for your resolutions. Make sure that what you're striving for is a true expression of who you really are. You could join a group of like-minded individuals; you'll benefit from the association.

# DECEMBER 2008

**Monday, December 1 (Moon in Capricorn)**    You never lack for friends; things run very smoothly. You may join a group whose members think very much like you do. Focus on your wishes and dreams.

**Tuesday, December 2 (Moon in Capricorn to Aquarius 1:45 a.m.)**    You wake this morning with a kind of peacefulness settled into your bones. You're ready for some solitude, introspection, and brainstorming with your muse. By afternoon, you're stir-crazy, so you head out to the mall for holiday shopping.

**Wednesday, December 3 (Moon in Aquarius)**    Your sights are set high; you always strive to realize the best of your talents. You beat up on yourself when you think you've failed to meet the mark. Start there in your self-analysis.

**Thursday, December 4 (Moon in Aquarius to Pisces 1:24 p.m.)**    The shift in energy is tangible. By early afternoon, you feel strong, confident, and sexy. The moon has linked up with direct-moving Uranus in your sign. Expect the unusual and the exciting.

**Friday, December 5 (Moon in Pisces)**    You may feel somewhat nostalgic for the old days. This nostalgia is part of a process that takes you back through your life, then forward. Think of it as a shamanic journey.

**Saturday, December 6 (Moon in Pisces to Aries 9:45 p.m.)**    There are certain times when you know you're in your element. That's what most of today is like. This evening, there's a shift in energy. Instead of feeling anxious, strive to retain that place within yourself where everything is exactly right.

**Sunday, December 7 (Moon in Aries)**    Venus enters Aquarius, your twelfth house, where it will be through the end of the year. One of the possible manifestations of this transit is a secret romance. If such a relationship begins under this transit, it will be unusual, exciting, and based on mutual communication. It won't remain secret very long!

**Monday, December 8 (Moon in Aries)**    You get a tip on a hot new investment. If it seems too good to be true, don't plop down your money until you've done some research. And even then, don't act until the moon enters Taurus.

**Tuesday, December 9 (Moon in Aries to Taurus 1:53 a.m.)** Take a close look at yesterday's hot tip and weigh the information against your instincts. Talk to an expert in the field. A relative or neighbor may have expertise you need.

**Wednesday, December 10 (Moon in Taurus)**    Make your decision about that hot new investment. On other fronts, you and a relative discuss the holidays.

**Thursday, December 11 (Moon in Taurus to Gemini 2:34 a.m.)**    The moon enters your fourth house. To save yourself from chaos, gather together anyone who is at home and go shopping. Visit a bookstore and try to satisfy that itch for information.

***Friday, December 12 (Moon in Gemini)***    Mercury enters Capricorn, joining Jupiter and Pluto. Before the end of the year, there will be a lineup of planets in your eleventh house. But with just these three planets, the focus is definitely on group activities that somehow expand your concepts of what is possible.

***Saturday, December 13 (Moon in Gemini to Cancer 1:41 a.m.)***    Each month, the moon transits the same signs and houses. As an astute observer of the patterns in your own life, you know which transits are positive for you. This Cancer moon triggers deep feelings about your family and home.

***Sunday, December 14 (Moon in Cancer)***    Your mother or another nurturing female in your life gets in touch. It could be about the holiday celebrations, but this person may just need your company, and the holidays are the excuse.

***Monday, December 15 (Moon in Cancer to Leo 1:23 a.m.)***    This close to the holidays, you may not be very interested in work, but today a situation calls for your attention. An employee or coworker may act up, and it's up to you to put a stop to the annoying behavior.

***Tuesday, December 16 (Moon in Leo)***    Unless you have a natal moon or rising in a fire sign, you probably find the Leo moon irritating. It may put you on edge. But it's forming a nice angle with Mars in Sagittarius, so you're likely to be warm and friendly toward people, even those who bother you.

***Wednesday, December 17 (Moon in Leo to Virgo 3:36 a.m.)***    You and your partner go holiday shopping. This can be disastrous or great fun, depending on whether you and your partner have similar views on how much to spend. Be sure you know this before you head out.

***Thursday, December 18 (Moon in Virgo)*** Schedule appointments with dentists and doctors. But unless you've got an emergency, schedule the appointments for early next year so you don't get caught up in the holiday crunch.

***Friday, December 19 (Moon in Virgo to Libra 9:23 a.m.)*** You and your spouse or partner may look for end-of-the-year tax breaks. Consult with your accountant or a tax specialist to find out how much you need to cut down your tax bill. You've got until April 15, 2009, to open a tax-free IRA or similar account.

***Saturday, December 20 (Moon in Libra)*** Balance is required concerning someone with whom you share resources—a business or romantic partner, a spouse, even a child or parent. You may give this person too much of your time and energy. Make the necessary adjustments.

***Sunday, December 21 (Moon in Libra to Scorpio 6:37 p.m.)*** Every planet is moving in direct motion, which means each is functioning at maximum capacity. So with the moon forming a harmonious angle to Jupiter, Pluto, and Mercury, all in Capricorn, in your eleventh house, you should feel on top of the world. At the same time, this moon forms a great angle to your natal sun, to Uranus in your sign, and to Saturn in Virgo. All this positive energy continues through the end of the year.

***Monday, December 22 (Moon in Scorpio)*** Goodwill toward others—isn't that what the holiday season is really about? If you can practice that in your daily life, you're well on your way toward making the world a better place. After all, change begins with just one person. And the Scorpio moon reminds you of these small, intimate truths.

***Tuesday, December 23 (Moon in Scorpio)*** You may dash out to buy some last-minute gifts for tomorrow's office party. The gifts don't have to be expensive; just tailor them to the individuals. Give some thought to your resolutions.

*Wednesday, December 24 (Moon in Scorpio to Sagittarius 6:14 a.m.)*     You've got your finger on the pulse of the holidays, what they really mean and how you can celebrate spiritually with the people around you. There could be some ups and downs in your mood, but by tomorrow, you're in high spirits.

*Thursday, December 25 (Moon in Sagittarius)*     Merry Christmas! With every planet moving direct, this should be a wonderful day of celebration and gratitude. Whether you spend it with friends or family, strive to create great memories for everyone.

*Friday, December 26 (Moon in Sagittarius to Capricorn 6:57 p.m.)*     By tomorrow, seven out of ten planets will be in signs compatible with your own. Even when the moon moves on into Aquarius, that leaves six out of ten planets in compatible signs. So for this last week of 2008, use this positive energy in positive ways. There will be a special emphasis astrologically on Capricorn, in your eleventh house. This highlights friends, groups, and your wishes and dreams.

*Saturday, December 27 (Moon in Capricorn)*     Mars joins Pluto, the moon, Jupiter, and Mercury in your eleventh house. Talk about energy! Everything centers around friends—who are your closest friends, why are they your closest friends, and how can you nurture these friendships?

*Sunday, December 28 (Moon in Capricorn)*     Take a look at your wishes and dreams. Where would you like your life to be in six months or a year? Lay out your goals and start figuring a strategy on how to attain them.

*Monday, December 29 (Moon in Capricorn to Aquarius 7:44 a.m.)*     If you're making party plans, keep in mind that on New Year's Eve, Saturn turns retrograde. It won't be enough to mess up your plans, but it could put a damper of some kind on the celebrations.

*Tuesday, December 30 (Moon in Aquarius)*     Take a little time for yourself. Chill out, take a nap, spend time with your kids or your pets—whatever it is that recharges your batteries. Not only are you preparing for New Year's Eve, but also for the moon's entrance into your sign.

*Wednesday, December 31 (Moon in Aquarius)*     Saturn turns retrograde in your seventh house. This movement will impact your partnerships, but the effects unfold over the next few months. There could be some delays or restrictions with a business or romantic partner. Best advice? Don't worry. Proceed with goodwill in your heart.

### HAPPY NEW YEAR!

### JANUARY 2009

*Thursday, January 1 (Moon in Aquarius to Pisces 4:05 a.m.)*     Mercury enters your twelfth house, increasing the likelihood that until February 1 you'll be working behind the scenes on some sort of communication or writing project. But for the next two days, the moon is in your sign, which puts you in the power seat. So start the New Year off on the right foot. Begin implementing your 2009 resolutions!

*Friday, January 2 (Moon in Pisces)*     Your intuition and imagination are remarkable today, right on the money. So if you feel torn, with your head urging you to move in one direction and your heart urging you to move in the opposite direction, allow your intuition to guide you. A Scorpio or a Cancer is helpful.

*Saturday, January 3 (Moon in Pisces to Aries 4:50 a.m.)* Until February 2, Venus will be transiting your sign, making this one of the most romantic and creative periods for you all year. Other people—friends, business clients, family members—are attracted to your ideas and ideals and lend their emotional support to whatever you're doing.

*Sunday, January 4 (Moon in Aries)*     With Venus in your sign and the moon in Aries, your second house, your finances may be on the upswing. This news is especially good if holiday bills are now coming due. You could be looking for investment opportunities. Don't leap in without checking out the company first.

*Monday, January 5 (Moon in Aries to Taurus 10:46 a.m.)* Jupiter enters Aquarius, your twelfth house, for a yearlong transit. During this time, you will be actively exploring your own unconscious in ways that are comfortable for you. You may try therapy or meditation. You may take workshops or seminars that help illuminate topics that interest you. Foreign travel could be on your agenda, but as a kind of spiritual quest.

*Tuesday, January 6 (Moon in Taurus)*     The moon enters your third house. This transit sweetens your resolve to say what you think and feel and not beat yourself up about it if someone around you doesn't like what they hear. You may dig your heels in about an issue involving a relative or a neighbor.

*Wednesday, January 7 (Moon in Taurus to Gemini 1:12 p.m.)*     With the moon entering your fourth house, activity at home picks up. You or a family member could be gathering information, perhaps in anticipation of a move. If you're looking at other neighborhoods and towns for this move, you may want to schedule the move around the new moon in Gemini on May 24.

*Thursday, January 8 (Moon in Gemini)*     You're apt to be in a talkative mood, eager to share your thoughts and feelings with a family member or a close friend who is like family. There could be a lot of running around. You may feel, in fact, that you're frittering away your time, but you aren't. Networking is a good thing.

*Friday, January 9 (Moon in Gemini to Cancer 1:14 p.m.)*     With the moon entering fellow water sign Cancer, your fifth house, your love life begins to heat up. At the same time, Mars is in your sign, so your sexuality is heightened and others find you enormously attractive. You're in a very nice groove, so make the most of it!

**Saturday, January 10 (Moon in Cancer)**    The full moon in Cancer, in your fifth house, highlights a romantic relationship, a creative issue, or a relationship with a child. Both Saturn and Uranus form beneficial angles to this moon, indicating that events unfold suddenly, that you find the proper venue for creative expression, and that there's plenty of excitement. Sounds like good news! Mercury turns retrograde tomorrow, so be sure to back up computer files.

**Sunday, January 11 (Moon in Cancer to Leo 12:41 p.m.)**    Mercury turns retrograde in Aquarius. Until February 1, follow the usual rules for a Mercury retrograde—revise, review, and reevaluate. In addition, if you have to travel, remain flexible because your schedule is likely to change. Don't sign contracts. Issues from the past that you thought were resolved crop up.

**Monday, January 12 (Moon in Leo)**    Your work routine and health are highlighted. You may be out in front of the public more than usual. Employees and coworkers are pleased with your ideas, and your presence somehow boosts the spirits of everyone with whom you come into contact.

**Tuesday, January 13 (Moon in Leo to Virgo 1:33 p.m.)**    The moon joins Saturn in your seventh house. There could be a kind of heaviness to events. Thank Saturn for that. It's moving retrograde, in your seventh house of partnerships. So you may be feeling somewhat burdened by a partnership. Talk it out.

**Wednesday, January 14 (Moon in Virgo)**    If you feel somewhat vulnerable, you may need to boost your vibrational energy by conjuring joyous thoughts and visualizations. Think back to a time when you were very happy. Imagine the details, the smells, and the textures. Capture that emotional high; then bring it up inside. Then step back and watch your mood rebound!

***Thursday, January 15 (Moon in Virgo to Libra 5:31 p.m.)*** The moon enters your eighth house, shifting your emotional focus to resources you share with others. Your partner's income could be an issue. Try not to argue. You're seeking balance in relationships.

***Friday, January 16 (Moon in Libra)*** You may mediate a dispute. Try not to take sides. Instead, listen impartially and then offer your best advice. And if neither party is satisfied with that advice, make it clear they will have to find a solution on their own. You could be delving more into esoteric areas.

***Saturday, January 17 (Moon in Libra)*** With Mercury retrograde in your twelfth house, old issues are surfacing. These issues may be connected to old friends. What's unresolved? If you aren't sure, meditate on it.

***Sunday, January 18 (Moon in Libra to Scorpio 1:21 a.m.)*** Despite this moon's emotional intensity, it's probably more comfortable to you because it's a water sign. This moon enables you to probe deeply into your worldview. Your beliefs should mesh nicely with those of your partner.

***Monday, January 19 (Moon in Scorpio)*** You may be researching spots for an overseas trip. Be as wild and outrageous as you want as long as you're just virtual traveling. Figure out the realistic stuff later. Plan your trip after February 1, when Mercury turns direct again. Keep in mind that the next Mercury retrograde period falls between May 6 and 30.

***Tuesday, January 20 (Moon in Scorpio to Sagittarius 12:31 p.m.)*** Your emotional focus shifts to career matters and professional relationships and agendas. Mars forms a great angle to this moon, giving you the jolt that you may need to accomplish whatever your agenda is. You may be feeling flirtatious and someone who interests you takes notice.

*Wednesday, January 21 (Moon in Sagittarius)*   You grasp a larger emotional picture concerning a professional relationship. This relationship could be with a colleague, a boss, or someone else in your business with whom you must deal. There are repercussions if you don't handle this issue diplomatically. You may want to wait until Mercury is moving direct before making a decision.

*Thursday, January 22 (Moon in Sagittarius)*   Travel could be indicated when the moon is in Sagittarius. It may be related to work, but it will certainly be enjoyable, despite Mercury's retrograde. Venus is still in your sign, which adds to your sex appeal and self-confidence. Romance on the road? Sounds like it could be intriguing.

*Friday, January 23 (Moon in Sagittarius to Capricorn 1:19 a.m.)*   The moon enters earth-friendly Capricorn, your eleventh house, shifting your emotional focus to friends. Promote and publicize your product or your company's. People will be receptive, and getting out among people will bolster your self-confidence.

*Saturday, January 24 (Moon in Capricorn)*   Plan for the long term. Where would you like to be in six months? Take any area of your life that you would like to improve or enhance and figure things out. Then get out of the way, and let the universe do its magic!

*Sunday, January 25 (Moon in Capricorn to Aquarius 1:57 p.m.)*   Visualize, imagine, and brainstorm with a partner or close friend. With the moon in your twelfth house, you're in the mood to hunker down, chill out, and do mental work. You're equipped for this kind of work. Let your intuition and imagination do the hard stuff!

*Monday, January 26 (Moon in Aquarius)*   The solar eclipse in Aquarius is like a double new moon. Opportunities for working behind the scenes, for exploring your own unconscious, and for encountering people you have known in previous lives surface. Meditation, past-life regressions, and yoga—all of these activities are part of this solar-eclipse picture.

**Tuesday, January 27 (Moon in Aquarius)**     Clear up old projects, fulfill obligations, and tie up loose ends. You're preparing the way for the moon entering your sign tomorrow. Whenever the moon is in your sign, it's a power day. Your head and heart will be in complete agreement.

**Wednesday, January 28 (Moon in Aquarius to Pisces 1:13 a.m.)**     The moon is in your sign, and you're in a very good place within yourself. You can pretty much call your own shots in any area you choose. You may be feeling quite sexy and flirtatious, and someone in your environment notices and takes an acute interest!

**Thursday, January 29 (Moon in Pisces)**     With both the moon and Venus in your sign, you are working from deeply intuitive levels, particularly in romance and creativity. Follow your hunches, and don't hesitate to act on impulse.

**Friday, January 30 (Moon in Pisces to Aries 10:25 a.m.)**     You may be taking time today to check through your finances. If you feel somewhat vulnerable or insecure where money is concerned, your discomfort could be the result of resistance within you about money. Are you inadvertently erecting barriers about earning more money? Examine your beliefs.

**Saturday, January 31 (Moon in Aries)**     You're fired up about a particular project, experience, or relationship. Don't be afraid to be a trailblazer. If you can imagine it, it can happen.

## FEBRUARY 2009

**Sunday, February 1 (Moon in Aries to Taurus 5:09 p.m.)**     Mercury turns direct! So pack your bags, and touch base with your clients, friends, and relatives. Hold off for another day or two before you sign any contracts.

***Monday, February 2 (Moon in Taurus)***    Venus enters Aries and your second house. This transit, which lasts until June 6, is terrific for money, earnings, and your finances. However, between March 6 and April 17, Venus will be moving retrograde, so that's a time when you shouldn't make any new investments.

***Tuesday, February 3 (Moon in Taurus to Gemini 9:15 p.m.)***    Your attention at home is required. It could be that a family member needs help or advice concerning something that involves the entire family. A move in or out of your place perhaps. Or maybe a child at college needs additional support.

***Wednesday, February 4 (Moon in Gemini)***    Mars joins Jupiter and Neptune in Aquarius, your twelfth house, a transit that lasts until March 14. During this period, you actively pursue an exploration of your own unconscious, intuition, and imagination.

***Thursday, February 5 (Moon in Gemini to Cancer 11:06 p.m.)***    This very nice transit stimulates your creative adrenaline. You're able to get into the flow of whatever you're working on, and that adrenaline just keeps on pumping. There's a nurturing quality to this moon that prompts you to reach out to others to comfort them. Or you may be comforting yourself.

***Friday, February 6 (Moon in Cancer)***    Your mother or another nurturing female in your life plays into activities. There's often an element of nostalgia associated with this moon, and you could be pining away for the good old days. Just remember that you can't go home again.

***Saturday, February 7 (Moon in Cancer to Leo 11:44 p.m.)***    You're getting ready for the week ahead, and when the moon enters Leo and your sixth house late to-night, it's all that you can think of. What do you need to do this week at work, with your family, and in your creative endeavors? Plan your time well. Things are likely to be hectic this week.

***Sunday, February 8 (Moon in Leo)***    You're on exhibit. Well, not like a piece of art, but just out in front of the public more than you usually are. A work presentation? An idea pitch? A public-relations gig? Maybe, even though it's Sunday. But it could be something as simple as lunch with friends. Be sure to look your best! Someone special will be noticing you.

***Monday, February 9 (Moon in Leo)***    The lunar eclipse in Leo brings up emotional issues related to your work or your health. Uranus in your sign forms a challenging angle to the eclipse degree, indicating you'll have to make an adjustment in your attitude before the issue is resolved.

***Tuesday, February 10 (Moon in Leo to Virgo 12:39 a.m.)*** Consider details. Whether the details concern family, a relationship, a project, your career, health, or something else, it's time to connect the dots. Your tendency is to seek the big picture. But you need to see the details.

***Wednesday, February 11 (Moon in Virgo)***    Try not to be critical of a spouse or partner. You may feel tension that will prompt you to see the other person's faults, but resist verbalizing them. Tomorrow, you'll be glad that you did. If it makes you feel better, list the other person's faults as they occur to you—and then ask yourself if you possess these same faults.

***Thursday, February 12 (Moon in Virgo to Libra 3:34 a.m.)***    You may be working on tax or insurance issues. Or maybe your credit cards are maxed out, and you're trying to figure out how to reverse the trend. Just be sure your payments are up-to-date.

***Friday, February 13 (Moon in Libra)***    Your artistic side shines like the sun. And you've got plenty of imagination to back up that creative part of you. Photography, dance, art, writing, or acting—what's your greatest passion?

*Saturday, February 14 (Moon in Libra to Scorpio 9:52 a.m.)*     Your research takes an unexpected turn. It may be connected to your spiritual and political beliefs. If you're a writer in search of a publisher, this moon makes you more aware of what the market is for what you've written and how you may have to revise somewhat. Happy Valentine's Day!

*Sunday, February 15 (Moon in Scorpio)*     Are you in the mood for a good book? Maybe a story that will appeal to your imagination and to your fascination with the hidden side of life. Or perhaps a great love story, which will appeal to the romantic that you are. Head to the store or the library, and see what you can find.

*Monday, February 16 (Moon in Scorpio to Sagittarius 7:54 p.m.)*     This evening as the moon enters your tenth house, you may be after the big picture for your professional life. You may have dealings with foreign investors or foreign individuals, or you may be trying to expand your business or product to overseas markets.

*Tuesday, February 17 (Moon in Sagittarius)*     You may need to call on the expertise of people who specialize in a field with which you aren't familiar. These individuals can help you hammer together a business plan or whatever it is that you need at this stage in your career.

*Wednesday, February 18 (Moon in Sagittarius)*     You're in an expansive frame of mind, and it shows! Other people gravitate toward your optimism, and it spills over into their lives. People enjoy being around someone as upbeat as you are. Not only does this make you feel more at home in yourself, but it helps you to garner the support you may need.

*Thursday, February 19 (Moon in Sagittarius to Capricorn 8:26 a.m.)*     Promotion and advertising are key to the day's activities. Whether you're advertising your company's product or your own business services, people are receptive to what you're selling and proposing. Friends and groups to which you belong are helpful.

*Friday, February 20 (Moon in Capricorn)*   You could be mulling over conversations you've had recently with friends concerning your long-term plans in some area. Friends may be advising one thing, but your head or heart is urging you to do something else. Weigh everything before deciding which course to pursue. This whole issue will be much clearer in a few days with a new moon in your sign!

*Saturday, February 21 (Moon in Capricorn to Aquarius 9:06 p.m.)*   This probably isn't your favorite moon. However, its purpose is to prompt you to clear up outstanding obligations, complete projects, and tie up loose ends all in preparation for the moon in your sign on February 24. This will be a new moon, which happens only once a year, so it's important to follow your impulses.

*Sunday, February 22 (Moon in Aquarius)*   Clean out your closets, your attic, and any other spot in your house or at work that is cluttered. It's a symbolic act that signals the universe you are ready for new experiences, people, and opportunities to enter your life. Old issues could crop up. Deal with them and move on.

*Monday, February 23 (Moon in Aquarius)*   Tomorrow's new moon happens just once a year, so prepare for it. Make a list of what you would like to manifest in your life during the next year. Be as specific as you want in your list, but try not to worry about how you'll get to where you want to go. Let the universe work on the fine points.

*Tuesday, February 24 (Moon in Aquarius to Pisces 8:00 a.m.)*   The new moon in your sign should usher in new opportunities in every area of your life. Pluto in Capricorn forms a wide and harmonious angle to this moon, indicating that you're in the driver's seat. You can make anything

256

happen—not just today, but throughout the year. It's all a matter of intention and focus.

***Wednesday, February 25 (Moon in Pisces)*** Whatever challenges you encounter are easily overcome with your wit and imagination. If you're involved with someone, then your partner is easily convinced that a weekend out of town together is a terrific idea. And it definitely should be just the two of you. With both Venus and Mars still in Aquarius, transiting your twelfth house, the stars support your privacy!

***Thursday, February 26 (Moon in Pisces to Aries 4:24 p.m.)*** You have the urge to spend. Just be sure that the checks have cleared and that the money is in your account already. You may still be dealing with holiday bills and don't want to add to your debt.

***Friday, February 27 (Moon in Aries)*** Your values come into play, perhaps because someone in your environment criticizes a belief that you hold. It isn't worth it to get into a fight on this issue, but definitely defend your right to believe what you want. Nowhere is it written that you're obligated to go along with the pack.

***Saturday, February 28 (Moon in Aries to Taurus 10:34 p.m.)*** You may get involved with a community project of some kind. This could occur because of the prompting of a neighbor or sibling. The only question is whether you can afford the time this project may take. Your schedule is busy.

## MARCH 2009

***Sunday, March 1 (Moon in Taurus)*** Whether it's your home or your office, your mind or your heart, you're taking active steps to get rid of negativity and beautify your surroundings and yourself. In a sense, this is like weeding a garden. You're clearing space for more positive experiences and people to enter your life.

***Monday, March 2 (Moon in Taurus)***   In a relationship with a relative or a neighbor, you're especially stubborn. It may be exactly what the situation requires. You are sometimes too flexible, too willing to change, and others may perceive it as indecisiveness. You simply don't like hurting anyone's feelings.

***Tuesday, March 3 (Moon in Taurus to Gemini 3:00 a.m.)***   Your home life may suddenly be the spot for a social event. It could be due to an influx of kids, if you have them, or simply that your place is the friendliest and most convenient for the people who are gathering. Information is key to the day's events.

***Wednesday, March 4 (Moon in Gemini)***   In about ten days, Mars enters your sign, and that transit will energize your personal life. So if at all possible, schedule important appointments and meetings between March 14 and April 22. The outcome will be much better.

***Thursday, March 5 (Moon in Gemini to Cancer 6:08 a.m.)***   You certainly do enjoy the Cancer moon. It shifts your emotional focus to romance, creativity, and what you do for fun and pleasure. Play for all you're worth. Tomorrow, Venus turns retrograde in Aries, so your love life could get a bit bumpy.

***Friday, March 6 (Moon in Cancer)***   There's a nurturing quality to this moon that speaks to the more compassionate side of your personality. Your nurturing, in fact, may be toward yourself. If so, treat yourself to a day a spa, a weekend trip to a spot you've never visited before, or an art exhibit. The idea here is to awaken and deepen your nurturing side.

***Saturday, March 7 (Moon in Cancer to Leo 8:26 a.m.)***   You may go into the office to paint the walls, rearrange furniture, or enhance the surroundings in some way. You want to make your work environment more pleasing and aesthetic.

*Sunday, March 8—Daylight Saving Time Begins (Moon in Leo)*     Mercury enters your sign, and on March 14, Mars will join it. This transit lasts until March 25 and deepens your intuition as it relates to your daily life. Your communication skills are sharpened, so if you have to pitch an idea or sell a product, or if you are a writer, take advantage of this transit!

*Monday, March 9 (Moon in Leo to Virgo 11:35 a.m.)*     With the moon entering Virgo, your opposite sign, you could be short-tempered with a business or romantic partner or overcritical of that person. The best use of this lunar energy is to perfect the details of a project or relationship, but without being overcritical or -analytical.

*Tuesday, March 10 (Moon in Virgo)*     The full moon in Virgo highlights a partnership. Saturn is closely conjunct to this moon, indicating that whatever you feel emotionally finds the proper vehicle for expression. Full moons often symbolize the culmination or completion of something— a project, relationship, job—so there can be some tension involved. Saturn's presence in this picture indicates a need to fulfill obligations.

*Wednesday, March 11 (Moon in Virgo to Libra 2:47 p.m.)*     Your focus is on balance in all areas of your life, but particularly in relationships. You're in a social mood, and the day's festivities could shed light on a situation that has become uncomfortable for you. Part of this feeling is due to Venus's retrograde, which makes relationships bumpy until April 17.

*Thursday, March 12 (Moon in Libra)*     Venus's retrograde in Aries, your second house, could be playing havoc with your finances. But more than likely, there is a physical discomfort involved. Perhaps an appliance goes on the fritz, and this creates discomfort in your living situation.

*Friday, March 13 (Moon in Libra to Scorpio 8:23 p.m.)*     Your day is iffy until early this evening, when the energy suddenly shifts in your favor. You may be investigating or researching a particular spiritual or political belief. This research could tie in with a trip overseas—a kind of spiritual quest in which you're searching for answers that traditional religions can't supply.

**Saturday, March 14 (Moon in Scorpio)** Mars enters Pisces, joining Mercury in your first house. The combination of these two planets gives you the physical and mental jolt that you need. You can tackle anything or sell anything to anyone, and you generally feel on top of the world—all of this despite the Venus retrograde!

**Sunday, March 15 (Moon in Scorpio)** Whether you're traveling for real or just virtual traveling, you're looking for a spot that appeals to the artist in you. Your nomadic tendencies are urging you to explore new places.

**Monday, March 16 (Moon in Scorpio to Sagittarius 4:22 a.m.)** A professional issue that should be dealt with quickly comes up. Your first instinct may be to ignore it or deal with it another day, but if you do that, the issue will simply be exacerbated. You may have to travel in the next few days for business. A conference, perhaps?

**Tuesday, March 17 (Moon in Sagittarius)** You're an emotionally complex individual, and the complexities deepen. You're not sure about the career path you have chosen, but you don't know which way to turn. How can you change what you do for a living? Well, the first step is to ask yourself what you enjoy most of all. Is there any way you can make your living at it?

**Wednesday, March 18 (Moon in Sagittarius to Capricorn 5:19 p.m.)** Focus on your wishes and dreams. Be as outrageous as you want. And don't listen to the naysayers who tell you your ideas aren't practical. If you can remain goal-oriented, you'll attain whatever you desire.

**Thursday, March 19 (Moon in Capricorn)** Promotion and publicity are part of the agenda. Whether you're promoting your product or the services of your company, people are warm and receptive. You come away from these experiences with new advertising ideas. You also gain clarity on your long-term goals.

*Friday, March 20 (Moon in Capricorn)*    You're conscientious about spending, probably due to Venus's retrograde in the financial sector of your chart. Rather than approaching this money issue from a perspective of lack, imagine your bank account filling up with the green stuff. Create a spread sheet where you fill in the numbers that you want.

*Saturday, March 21 (Moon in Capricorn to Aquarius 6:07 a.m.)*    Fortunately, you probably will be sleeping when the moon changes signs; that transition can be something you're sensitive to. The moon favors sleeping late or chilling out. Your dreams could be vivid, or if you meditate, you may reach deeper levels than you do ordinarily.

*Sunday, March 22 (Moon in Aquarius)*    Clean out closets, attic, and garage. As you're cleaning out these places, you're also cleaning out the detritus in your head and heart concerning old emotions, experiences, and relationships. In this way, you're preparing the way for the moon entering your sign tomorrow afternoon.

*Monday, March 23 (Moon in Aquarius to Pisces 5:08 p.m.)*    The moon enters your sign. So how are you going to use this power day? Have you planned it out? Or are you just going to take off and enjoy yourself? Whatever you decide, the universe supports your decision.

*Tuesday, March 24 (Moon in Pisces)*    This is the last day that Mercury, Mars, Uranus, and the moon are in your sign. This combination is powerful and boosts your intuition, self-confidence, sex appeal, energy, and imagination. Don't fritter the day away!

*Wednesday, March 25 (Moon in Pisces)*    Mercury enters Aries, joining Venus in your second house. You may be working longer hours, but you're loving it. There could be

261

a romantic flirtation in this picture. The person isn't necessarily someone with whom you work, but is definitely someone who shares your values about what's important.

***Thursday, March 26 (Moon in Pisces to Aries 1:03 a.m.)***    Along comes a new moon in Aries, accentuating and supporting Mars and Venus in the same house and sign. This new moon should attract opportunities with money—a raise, a second job, investments. But since Mars and Venus are both in the same sign, a sure indication of romantic and sexual chemistry, this new moon could also usher in opportunities for relationships.

***Friday, March 27 (Moon in Aries)***    You're off on a new adventure of some kind. Whether you skip work or hit the office on time, the adventure unfolds. Wherever the adventure leads you could be fodder for a creative project that you're involved in or will be involved in. Better bring your digital camera, your laptop, and some extra cash.

***Saturday, March 28 (Moon in Aries to Taurus 6:10 a.m.)***    The Taurus moon suits you. It makes you more aware of how to ground your ideas and use your imagination in a focused, directed way; and it convinces you of the validity of your intuition. All you have to do is follow your own advice. Listen closely to your hunches.

***Sunday, March 29 (Moon in Taurus)***    If you enjoy puttering—at home, in stores, at the office, or in a garden—do it. In fact, you may end up antiquing, and you may uncover some unique treasures.

***Monday, March 30 (Moon in Taurus to Gemini 9:37 a.m.)***    Your emotional focus shifts to information and networking, perhaps with some larger plan in mind. This networking may take place in your home office, through the Internet chat rooms or e-mail.

***Tuesday, March 31 (Moon in Gemini)***    You may be planning a family vacation. Remember not to travel while Mercury is retrograde. The next one falls between May 6 and 30. Other than that, the summer looks free and clear. A family member may be pushing for a trip to a particular locale. Be sure everyone agrees.

# APRIL 2009

**Wednesday, April 1 (Moon in Gemini to Cancer 12:31 p.m.)**    Your muse is up close and personal. The urge to work on a creative project may be so strong, in fact, that if you're still working at a day job, you take off early. This creative endeavor could be something you're doing with a child or a partner.

**Thursday, April 2 (Moon in Cancer)**    Even if you're not involved, there's romance in the air. But if you are involved, the day is just that much sweeter, filled with lots of calls and e-mails from that special person, who may be so smitten that, for him or her, it's Valentine's Day all over again!

**Friday, April 3 (Moon in Cancer to Leo 3:33 p.m.)**    Feeling flashy? Blame that Leo moon! You're eager to show off the result of your diet or your gym workouts. You may be in a cycle of redoing yourself from the inside out.

**Saturday, April 4 (Moon in Leo)**    Pluto turns retrograde in Capricorn, your eleventh house. Since Pluto moves so slowly, the impact of this move won't be readily noticeable. However, over the course of the next several months, you'll be taking a deeper look at what you would like to find in friendships. Are your current friends genuine?

**Sunday, April 5 (Moon in Leo to Virgo 7:02 p.m.)**    If you have a copy of your natal chart, look to see where Pisces and Virgo fall in your chart. Pisces will be where your sun is, and Virgo should be on the cusp of the opposite house. This will tell you the area of your life that demands your concentration. Details—that's what you need to deal with for the next two days.

*Monday, April 6 (Moon in Virgo)*     You're the type of person who can make friends with just about anyone—even your enemies! You may have a chance to do exactly that. There may be someone in your environment who is jealous or resentful of you for some reason. You manage to turn the relationship around with just your natural tact and diplomacy.

*Tuesday, April 7 (Moon in Virgo to Libra 11:23 p.m.)*     Late this evening, your intuition takes a decided turn for the esoteric. Your dreams could be filled with insights, precognitive visions, and even information about past lives. Be sure to keep a notebook handy.

*Wednesday, April 8 (Moon in Libra)*     There is always emphasis on relationships and aesthetics when the moon is in Libra. You may feel a need to connect in a more meaningful way with a partner, a friend, or even a family member. Cultivate the art of listening, and that connection will happen more quickly!

*Thursday, April 9 (Moon in Libra)*     The full moon in Libra should be enormously pleasurable for you. Expansive Jupiter forms a harmonious angle to this moon, so the insights you gain concerning relationships and resources you share with others will expand your life in some way. Mercury also enters Taurus, a transit that lasts until April 30. During this time, your communication skills will attract all the support you need in any area of your life where you focus.

*Friday, April 10 (Moon in Libra to Scorpio 5:23 a.m.)*     The moon enters your ninth house, opposite Mercury. This particular angle is sure to deepen your intuition, fire up your passions, and perhaps even fuel some jealousy. You may feel particularly antsy to get out of town for the weekend. So do it!

*Saturday, April 11 (Moon in Scorpio)*     Your worldview may be undergoing subtle changes. It's all part of your evolution as a spiritual being living a physical existence. Pay close attention to hunches and impulses.

**Sunday, April 12 (Moon in Scorpio to Sagittarius 2:01 p.m.)**    Even though it's Sunday, today is a career day. You could be touching base with clients, figuring out your schedule for the coming week, or e-mailing employees or customers. If you feel rushed and impatient, take some time for yourself. You've earned it!

**Monday, April 13 (Moon in Sagittarius)**    You're looking for the big picture concerning your career. But you may get bogged down in tax details. Hopefully, you've already mailed off your return. In the event that you haven't, check and recheck the figures; if you have an accountant do your taxes, be sure to sign and date the forms.

**Tuesday, April 14 (Moon in Sagittarius)**    Fire signs are integral to your day. Sagittarius, Leo, and Aries—all of these people have qualities that you may need to complete a project or assignment. In return, you have that wonderful imagination and intuition that they may need someday soon. It all evens out in the end.

**Wednesday, April 15 (Moon in Sagittarius to Capricorn 1:28 a.m.)**    Whether you're setting goals or simply planning for the future, the Capricorn moon grounds your imagination and makes your ideas practical. Don't worry. You're not losing anything. You're just making your ideas accessible to other people.

**Thursday, April 16 (Moon in Capricorn)**    You spend time with your support group. Whether it's a group of writers, actors, or artists or a union to which you belong, you come away from the gathering energized and buoyant. Such is the power of the collective spirit!

**Friday, April 17 (Moon in Capricorn to Aquarius 2:20 p.m.)**    Venus turns direct! This is terrific news for your love life and your creative endeavors. It also indicates that you may get a financial break. Or, if things have been stalled financially, that trend reverses itself.

**Saturday, April 18 (Moon in Aquarius)**    Hidden issues surface. They are certainly emotional issues, with roots in the past. The past, though, could be very distant, as in past lives. You benefit from therapy, meditation, a past-life regression, or even a discussion with a close friend or a trusted member of your family.

**Sunday, April 19 (Moon in Aquarius)**    You've got a million ideas rushing through your head. How can they serve you creatively? Wait until the moon enters your sign before you seek the answer.

**Monday, April 20 (Moon in Aquarius to Pisces 1:56 a.m.)**    The moon enters your sign. Welcome to another power day. If there are any hurdles or challenges at all, you overcome them easily. So easily, in fact, that it's wise to remember how you feel emotionally so that, on down days, you can conjure the feeling again.

**Tuesday, April 21 (Moon in Pisces)**    Tie up contracts, travel plans, and computer purchases before Mercury turns retrograde on May 6. Today is the last day Mars will be in your sign for another two years. And since the moon is also in your sign, you're a powerhouse of activity. Make good use of the energy!

**Wednesday, April 22 (Moon in Pisces to Aries 10:10 a.m.)** Mars enters Aries, your second house, energizing your finances. You're pursuing money in a major way. Perhaps you're being more aggressive about money in anticipation of quitting your job and pursuing something you love.

**Thursday, April 23 (Moon in Aries)**    The moon joins Mars in your second house. Follow your hunches. Your emotions may be volatile, and you could feel impatient and restless. But just the same, your intuition is right on the money.

*Friday, April 24 (Moon in Aries to Taurus 2:47 p.m.)*     Today's new moon in Taurus is in your third house. It should attract opportunities for community involvement, in communication and writing, and in the way you conduct your daily life. If you're moving, don't hesitate to enlist the help of relatives and friends.

*Saturday, April 25 (Moon in Taurus)*     Feeling stubborn? Good. It's needed. Someone may be trying to enlist you in a project you really don't have time for or which you really don't want to work on. Rather than getting sucked in by a sob story, dig in your heels and politely turn down the request.

*Sunday, April 26 (Moon in Taurus to Gemini 5:03 p.m.)*     This moon is square to your sun, but Gemini is the only sign besides your own represented by two of something. So expect your desires to be torn in many directions. Don't even try to make a decision. Wait until the moon enters Cancer.

*Monday, April 27 (Moon in Gemini)*     Gather your facts. Tap experts in the field. Collect all your data. Then weigh the pros and cons, and write down what you're really looking for. Make your final decision when the moon enters your sign.

*Tuesday, April 28 (Moon in Gemini to Cancer 6:39 p.m.)*     The Cancer moon is one of the universe's monthly gifts to you. The focus is on you. It's about romance, creativity, and what you feel and think about both and how you attract opportunities in both areas into your life.

*Wednesday, April 29 (Moon in Cancer)*     Someone you're interested in is reciprocating. You initially feel— what? Panic? Doubt? Those feelings symbolize some sort of resistance deep inside of you. Just try to go with the flow.

*Thursday, April 30 (Moon in Cancer to Leo 8:56 p.m.)*     Mercury enters Gemini. Until May 6, your home

267

life is a hotbed of activity, discussions, and people coming and going at all hours. On May 6, Mercury turns retrograde until May 30. That will impact your home and family life.

## MAY 2009

**Friday, May 1 (Moon in Leo)**    Your emotional focus shifts to your daily work routine and health. You may be more aware of your appearance and could take measures to enhance yourself in some way. You might hire a trainer, for instance, so you can be disciplined about a gym work-out. Or perhaps you find a friend or partner for a yoga class or a daily run.

**Saturday, May 2 (Moon in Leo)**    You may be going along with one eye on the small imperfections around you. Resist that urge. Instead, use this lunar energy to perfect yourself or something in your environment. Pay attention to the details.

**Sunday, May 3 (Moon in Leo to Virgo 12:37 a.m.)**    You and a partner may take the day off and head out for parts unknown. Schedule time together to re-connect. Mercury turns retrograde in three days, so be sure to make a note to back up computer files on May 5. The retrograde will be in Gemini, your fourth house. You may want to check appliances to make sure they are all function-ing smoothly. Don't make any major purchases under this retrograde.

**Monday, May 4 (Moon in Virgo)**    In a business partner-ship, be sure you and the other person are on the same page. It's important that you not only have the same goals, but have a similar philosophy about running the business, about people's respective jobs, and how it all fits together. If you're too picky about it all, it may drive you and your partner apart.

**Tuesday, May 5 (Moon in Virgo to Libra 5:52 a.m.)**    Your spiritual beliefs come into play. It could be

268

related to a discussion you had with a friend or partner. If you feel you have to defend your beliefs, that's fine. But don't get into an argument about it. Back up computer files and finalize travel plans. Mercury turns retrograde tomorrow.

***Wednesday, May 6 (Moon in Libra)*** Mercury turns retrograde in Gemini. You know the drill. Take in an art exhibit or a new film, or help someone else whose resources may be faltering. You're seeking balance in your life; one way to find it is to do something for someone else without thought of compensation.

***Thursday, May 7 (Moon in Libra to Scorpio 12:48 p.m.)*** Your intense feelings midday sweep over you suddenly. They concern a relationship or situation about which you feel passionately. This moon enables you to see past disguises, into the true motives behind a relationship or situation.

***Friday, May 8 (Moon in Scorpio)*** Use your passion and intense emotions to transform some area of your life where you seek improvement. Bring this energy to bear against challenges, and watch the obstacles fall away. That's one of the best uses of the Scorpio-moon energy.

***Saturday, May 9 (Moon in Scorpio to Sagittarius 9:50 p.m.)*** The full moon in Scorpio lights up your ninth house. You gain insights into your spiritual and political beliefs. Saturn forms a wide but harmonious angle with this moon, indicating that you're able to use your insights in a constructive way.

***Sunday, May 10 (Moon in Sagittarius)*** You usually aren't that fond of this moon—too much fire for your water-sign sun! However, it enables you to see the big picture of your life. Even if you can't connect the dots yet, you're on the right track.

***Monday, May 11 (Moon in Sagittarius)*** There could be discussions under way about an overseas trip related to business. If your company is seeking to expand its services or product overseas, you could be tapped to do the groundwork. You may find that you like the country you visit and wouldn't mind moving there!

**Tuesday, May 12 (Moon in Sagittarius to Capricorn 9:10 a.m.)**    You and a group of friends may be launching a new Web site or project that will require some very focused time. Be sure to clear your schedule so that you don't get caught up in a time crunch that has you running around like a person possessed.

**Wednesday, May 13 (Moon in Capricorn)**    This moon actually suits you. It helps to ground your ideas and urges you to plan for the long term. You're better able to lay down strategy, to clarify your goals, and to bring your imagination into the realm of the real world without losing any of that special magic.

**Thursday, May 14 (Moon in Capricorn to Aquarius 10:03 p.m.)**    Cooperation and teamwork are the hallmarks. You and a partner or friend could be discussing the big issues in life. What makes the world tick? What's at the core of most political systems? What role does religion or your spiritual beliefs play in your lives?

**Friday, May 15 (Moon in Aquarius)**    With the moon in your twelfth house, you have easy access to your own unconscious. Your dreams may provide insights and clues to issues in your life or to questions you have. You're recharging your batteries in preparation for the moon entering your sign Sunday morning.

**Saturday, May 16 (Moon in Aquarius)**    Saturn turns direct in Virgo, your opposite sign. The effects will be subtle, but over the course of the next several months, your partnerships will function smoothly. Your emotions will find a more appropriate venue for expression. If you're involved in business with another person or group of people, you may be shouldering a lot of responsibility. But your efforts pay off down the line.

*Sunday, May 17 (Moon in Aquarius to Pisces 10:18 a.m.)* Another power day. Your artistic sensibilities are up front and center, and may lure you to an art exhibit, an antiques fair, a gardening exhibition, or even a photography exhibit. Or you may just dive into your own creative work with renewed vigor and self-confidence.

*Monday, May 18 (Moon in Pisces)* Your relationships hum along at a pleasant pitch. You may still be working longer hours to make ends meet or to earn extra money to stash away from something special. But you really don't mind the hours because you enjoy what you do.

*Tuesday, May 19 (Moon in Pisces to Aries 7:31 p.m.)* The moon joins Mars in Aries, your second house. This combination brings your focus to security matters. Is it a certain amount of money in the bank? A happy home life? A secure and satisfying job and career?

*Wednesday, May 20 (Moon in Aries)* An investment pays off. It could be a financial investment, but could just as easily be an emotional or spiritual investment. You're a pioneer venturing into emotional terrains that you may shy away from when the moon is in a different sign.

*Thursday, May 21 (Moon in Aries)* You're clearing the way for a new chapter in your creative endeavors. You have the will and the energy to stick with whatever you're implementing and to see it through to the end.

*Friday, May 22 (Moon in Aries to Taurus 12:41 a.m.)* Over the weekend, you may be taking a short trip, perhaps to visit a relative. Or you may be looking at neighborhoods in anticipation of a move. If you're just in the early stage of looking for a new home, try looking on days when the moon is in an earth sign—Taurus, Virgo, Capricorn. Or in your own sign.

*Saturday, May 23 (Moon in Taurus)* There may be some sort of community event that you attend. But until

271

then, be methodical and organized in whatever you do, even if it's just cleaning out closets! You may have accumulated a lot of stuff you don't need, so start tossing and giving away.

**Sunday, May 24 (Moon in Taurus to Gemini 1:34 a.m.)** The new moon in Gemini occurs in your fourth house. So if you're looking for a new home, this moon could attract just the place you want. Opportunities related to home and family are a given.

**Monday, May 25 (Moon in Gemini)** Retreat to a private place and spend the day reading, surfing the Internet, or doing whatever you want. If you feel really ambitious, spiff up your home.

**Tuesday, May 26 (Moon in Gemini to Cancer 1:58 a.m.)** Strive for emotional honesty. If you're not involved yet but have met someone who interests you, emotional honesty has to be a part of the equation for you. Be yourself. If you're a protective nurturing sort, express that.

**Wednesday, May 27 (Moon in Cancer)** You're so in the flow of your creativity that you simply can't hold back. If you still have your day job, you may want to start taking steps to cut back on your hours or to find a part-time job so that you have more time to pursue what you love.

**Thursday, May 28 (Moon in Cancer to Leo 3:45 a.m.)** Neptune turns retrograde in Aquarius, your twelfth house. The effects of this movement are subtle. However, until November 4, when Neptune turns direct, you'll have ample opportunities to figure out how to integrate your idealism into your life more effectively.

**Friday, May 29 (Moon in Leo)** The key event is a service that you perform for someone else. Then get out there and strut your stuff! You're open, honest, and even impulsive—all part and parcel of the Leo moon, which loves to be applauded and recognized.

*Saturday, May 30 (Moon in Leo to Virgo 6:18 a.m.)*
Finally! Mercury turns direct. But before you run out and buy those tickets for Europe, sign contracts, or send off all those e-mails to clients, wait another day or two for Mercury to stabilize. In the meantime, tend to details.

*Sunday, May 31 (Moon in Virgo)*     Mars enters Taurus and your third house and doesn't move on again until July 11. During this transit, your energy is poured into neighborhood and community projects and relationships with relatives. This transit energizes you physically.


# JUNE 2009

*Monday, June 1 (Moon in Virgo to Libra 12:17 p.m.)*     Since it's almost summer—or winter if you live south of the equator—you should consider planning to celebrate a ritual that marks the change of seasons in a few weeks. Also, you may have to research or investigate something that's going on in your environment. Secret meetings may be involved.

*Tuesday, June 2 (Moon in Libra)*     Emotions could get intense as you and your partner discuss money and resources. Back off, take a deep breath, and tackle this whole situation later in the month. You may be launching a journey or quest into the unknown.

*Wednesday, June 3 (Moon in Libra to Scorpio 7:45 p.m.)*     You're ready for the intense Scorpio moon. You know exactly how to use this energy so that it benefits you. You deviate from your usual routine and dive into something that fascinates you. It could be a course you take on psychic development or a seminar on remote viewing. However this manifests for you, your intuition deepens.

*Thursday, June 4 (Moon in Scorpio)*     If you're feeling restless or impatient, get on the Internet and do some virtual traveling. This isn't just a great way to plan a trip—

273

it's educational as well. If you can afford it, get away for a long weekend. The travel will settle your soul.

**_Friday, June 5 (Moon in Scorpio)_**    Passions run high. Your intuition is heightened and right on the money. Forget your left brain. Trust your hunches and feelings. Control issues may surface; how you deal with these may determine how you spend your weekend!

**_Saturday, June 6 (Moon in Scorpio to Sagittarius 5:25 a.m.)_**    Venus enters Taurus, your third house, and remains there until July 5. Love and romance may be as close as your backyard. You may meet a special person through a relative, or this person could be your neighbor. This transit also favors all communication and writing endeavors.

**_Sunday, June 7 (Moon in Sagittarius)_**    The full moon in Sagittarius highlights a professional issue or career matter. Jupiter forms a wide but beneficial angle with this moon, suggesting that the insights you gain somehow expand your career options. Uranus in your sign forms a wide but challenging angle to this moon (but not to your sun), so events unfold quickly, unexpectedly.

**_Monday, June 8 (Moon in Sagittarius to Capricorn 5:01 p.m.)_**    Your attitude determines everything. So keep your mood upbeat, believe that anything is possible, and be sure to associate only with positive individuals. You're prone to absorbing the moods of people around you, so it's doubly important to be sure that the company you keep is in line with your best intentions.

**_Tuesday, June 9 (Moon in Capricorn)_**    Insist on obtaining all the information you need, instead of just bits and pieces. You're entitled to the full picture, so don't hesitate to ask for what you're entitled to. Friends and acquaintances are helpful. In particular, a Virgo, a Capricorn or a Taurus proves vital.

**_Wednesday, June 10 (Moon in Capricorn)_**    Focus on your wishes and dreams. You may attend a meeting with a

274

group of people whose interests and passions support your own.

**Thursday, June 11 (Moon in Capricorn to Aquarius 5:53 a.m.)**    Be generous with your time. Even if you feel like taking off by yourself, fulfill an obligation first, or extend a helping hand to someone in need. Your unconscious attitudes can create challenges.

**Friday, June 12 (Moon in Aquarius)**    You should keep your thoughts, opinions, and beliefs to yourself. Others either wouldn't understand or might violate your trust. Just try not to deceive yourself about the actual situation in a relationship. Things will look much better tomorrow, when the moon is firmly in your sign.

**Saturday, June 13 (Moon in Aquarius to Pisces 5:33 p.m.)**    You come into your own late this afternoon. You may be looking to free yourself from certain restrictions; perhaps that's where your focus is. How can you extricate yourself from whatever is restricting your freedom of movement?

**Sunday, June 14 (Moon in Pisces)**    If you're feeling moody, it's just that tendency to flit back and forth between what your head wants and what your heart wants. Or you may be around someone negative whose energy you're absorbing. You're a psychic sponge.

**Monday, June 15 (Moon in Pisces)**    Jupiter turns retrograde in Aquarius, your twelfth house. This simply means that the planet goes into a kind of dormant state until October 12. During this period, you will be giving a lot of thought to the larger canvas of your life. It's possible that you'll meet people you have known in previous lives.

**Tuesday, June 16 (Moon in Pisces to Aries 4:52 a.m.)**
With the moon entering Aries and your second house, and both Venus and Mars in Taurus, you're looking for a relationship with stability. You would like someone who is will-

ing to take risks, but who also understands the value of commitment.

**Wednesday, June 17 (Moon in Aries)**     Your values assume greater meaning. This could come about as a result of a conversation with someone you trust, or it could just be your mood. But the bottom line is that you identify emotionally with your deeper values, and you're comfortable with them. If someone challenges you about what you believe, stand up for your beliefs, but don't get into a prolonged debate.

**Thursday, June 18 (Moon in Aries to Taurus 11:21 a.m.)**     The moon joins Mars and Venus in Taurus, your third house. If you're a writer or in any facet of the communication business, this trio of planets really sharpens your skills. If you're in the travel business, business picks up. You may be spending more time than usual with a relative or even with neighbors.

**Friday, June 19 (Moon in Taurus)**     There's an element of mysticism involved with Taurus. And with three planets in that sign, it could be that you're going to take a seminar or workshop in some sort of psychic development or self-improvement course that uses visualization and intention.

**Saturday, June 20 (Moon in Taurus to Gemini 2:01 p.m.)**     If you're looking for a new home, the search heats up. You're gathering information and lighting up with ideas; your search may broaden beyond neighborhoods you have currently targeted. In fact, you may be moving farther than you anticipated.

**Sunday, June 21 (Moon in Gemini)**     With the moon stirring up activity at home, you may be running around like the proverbial chicken without a head. Take a few deep breaths, detach from the situation, and get off by yourself to recharge. One of your parents may need additional help.

**Monday, June 22 (Moon in Gemini to Cancer 2:12 p.m.)**     This beautiful new moon in Cancer occurs in your fifth house. This moon should usher in opportunities in romance and creative endeavors, with your kids and with everything you do for fun and amusement. It's possible that power plays surface with this moon, but otherwise, it should be enjoyable for you.

**Tuesday, June 23 (Moon in Cancer)**    Relationships have emotional depth. You may feel somewhat possessive in a relationship or with a child. If possessiveness is the more prominent emotion, back off a little, and remember that smothering love may drive the person away.

**Wednesday, June 24 (Moon in Cancer to Leo 1:51 a.m.)** Diplomacy is called for in a work relationship or with a work-related issue. Even if an employee or coworker is nagging at you or pestering you for something, diplomacy will get you farther than outright confrontation. Avoid being judgmental.

**Thursday, June 25 (Moon in Leo)**    Your personal health needs attention. You may be trying out a new diet or nutritional program or getting back into the swing of regular exercise. Your business dealings go well, even though the other people may be demanding more than you're willing to give.

**Friday, June 26 (Moon in Leo to Virgo 2:47 p.m.)** Your emotional focus shifts to partnerships, both business and romantic. Personal relationships take on new meaning, and you gain insights in business partnerships. Allow your intuition the freedom it needs to bring in new information.

**Saturday, June 27 (Moon in Virgo)**    Make appointments with doctors, dentists, or anyone else who helps you maintain your health. You may be seeking out health-related books or Web sites in a search for an alternative treatment of some kind.

**Sunday, June 28 (Moon in Virgo to Libra 6:25 p.m.)**    Your diplomacy proves to be a valuable asset. You're dealing with shared assets and resources and emotions could turn intense. Insurance and joint investments also come into play.

**Monday, June 29 (Moon in Libra)**    You feel a definite physical attraction to a special person in your life. This individual also appeals to your artistic side, perhaps because his or her creative interests are similar to your own. Other issues that may surface: sexuality, taxes, or insurance.

**Tuesday, June 30 (Moon in Libra)**    Balance is key to success. Whether you're balancing responsibilities in various areas of your life, or whether someone else is after balance, the end result to you is the same. Confusion. Guests may be arriving early for the July Fourth weekend.

## JULY 2009

**Wednesday, July 1 (Moon in Libra to Scorpio 1:20 a.m.)**
Uranus turns retrograde in your sign. The impact of this movement is subtle, but over the next few months, you'll be taking a closer look at your personal life. Where have you become habitual in your responses or beliefs? Strive for change.

**Thursday, July 2 (Moon in Scorpio)**    Your personal beliefs in several areas are highlighted. If you happen to be traveling overseas, your trip isn't strictly for pleasure. You're on a quest of some kind.

**Friday, July 3 (Moon in Scorpio to Sagittarius 11:12 a.m.)**
Mercury enters Cancer until July 17. During the next two weeks, you and partners will be discussing the finer details of your relationship. Also, there will be a lot of conversation about a creative project. If you're a writer, this transit brings a quick flow to your endeavors.

**Saturday, July 4 (Moon in Sagittarius)**    You've got the big picture concerning a career issue or professional relationship. Even though it's the July Fourth weekend, you may sneak off to tend to some work project. Your sense of humor definitely saves the day!

**Sunday, July 5 (Moon in Sagittarius to Capricorn 11:08 p.m.)**     Venus enters Gemini, your fourth house, where it will be until July 31. This transit should add pizzazz to your love life at home. You may also feel compelled to beautify your surroundings in some way. If you're not involved, you probably will be by the time Venus finishes its transit of Cancer and your fifth house. That transit begins on July 31 and ends on August 26.

**Monday, July 6 (Moon in Capricorn)**     Take a close look at your goals. Are they an expression of who you really are or have you adopted them because of peer or parental pressure? It's important to be true to yourself. Don't fall for a sob story!

**Tuesday, July 7 (Moon in Capricorn)**     The lunar eclipse in Capricorn triggers emotions related to friends and your own wishes and dreams. Saturn forms a close and harmonious angle to this moon, so you find the proper vehicle for expressing what you feel. The event to watch for comes on July 21, with a solar eclipse in your sign.

**Wednesday, July 8 (Moon in Capricorn to Aquarius 12:04 p.m.)**     If you're ready for a new relationship, put out your intention to the universe. List the qualities you're seeking in a close relationship. Be focused, but don't worry about how it will happen.

**Thursday, July 9 (Moon in Aquarius)**     Keep your feelings to yourself. When the moon is firmly in your sign on Saturday, you'll be ready to broadcast what you feel and think. Work behind the scenes is emphasized. You're getting recharged right now, so relax.

**Friday, July 10 (Moon in Aquarius)**     Early tomorrow, the moon enters your sign, signaling a busy couple days ahead of you. You're prepped and ready for whatever the next few days bring. Listen to others, but make your own decisions.

**Saturday, July 11 (Moon in Aquarius to Pisces 12:44 a.m.)**
Mars enters Gemini, joining Venus in your fourth house, and the moon joins Uranus in your sign. These combinations of planets should lead to an exciting day, although there could be some stress involved too. It depends on how well you respond to change and the quick flux of events.

**Sunday, July 12 (Moon in Pisces)**    Whenever Venus and Mars are in the same sign and house, as they are now, your love life and your sexuality are heightened. If you're not involved, you will be soon, if that's what you want.

**Monday, July 13 (Moon in Pisces to Aries 11:40 a.m.)**
Keep a lid on your temper. Don't fight or argue with others even if there's disagreement. With any conflict, say what you have to say, and then walk away. Show your appreciation for the parts of your life that are running smoothly. The more you cultivate appreciation, the greater the chances that you attract more to appreciate.

**Tuesday, July 14 (Moon in Aries)**    Take care of your bills; don't procrastinate. You're working up to the solar eclipse in your sign on July 21, which will be like a double new moon. So clear the clutter from your desk and closets, and clean out the cobwebs in your own mind. These gestures signal the universe that you're ready for all the opportunities the solar eclipse will bring.

**Wednesday, July 15 (Moon in Aries to Taurus 6:30 p.m.)**    Assimilate yesterday's events and emotions, and get on with business. You may get together with siblings or neighbors, perhaps for some sort of community project. You may be hurrying to meet a deadline pertaining to a research paper or project or to a book or novel that you're writing.

***Thursday, July 16 (Moon in Taurus)***    You resist what you must and insist on doing things your way. It's exactly what is needed in this situation, so don't apologize or back-pedal. Remain firm and committed to your own path. If the issue involves a relationship, you may want to be more flexible and really listen to what your partner says.

***Friday, July 17 (Moon in Taurus to Gemini 11:42 p.m.)***    Mercury enters Leo, your sixth house. Until August 2, you're involved in conversations and discussions concerning work. This could involve bargaining with employees, planning some sort of trip or project with coworkers, or working on a writing project.

***Saturday, July 18 (Moon in Gemini)***    A situation at home may need your attention. Perhaps a parent or a child needs help with something. If you're part of the sandwich generation—with young children at home and also responsible for elderly parents—you may be the one who needs help! Enlist the advice of experts.

***Sunday, July 19 (Moon in Gemini)***    Take things a step at a time. By early tomorrow, the moon will be in a fellow water sign, and you'll feel more positive about everything. You may be completing a home-improvement project.

***Monday, July 20 (Moon in Gemini to Cancer 12:52 a.m.)***    The moon joins Mars in Cancer, your fifth house. This powerful combination brings romance, love, and sexuality together in one very nice package! If you're not involved, this energy could find expression in creative endeavors or in just plain ol' fun!

***Tuesday, July 21 (Moon in Cancer)***    The solar eclipse in Cancer promises excitement. Even though one relationship or creative project may be ending, the solar eclipse should attract opportunities in romance and creativity, and with children. In fact, if you have been wanting to start a family, this eclipse could make it happen.

*Wednesday, July 22 (Moon in Cancer to Leo 12:28 a.m.)*    You're the star at work. Be sure to dress for success and to act decisively and with self-confidence. Even if you may not feel particularly self-confident, others will perceive you that way because you speak with authority.

*Thursday, July 23 (Moon in Leo)*    Strive for diplomacy in your dealings with others. With Jupiter still in your twelfth house, you probably have a clear idea of other people's motives—as well as your own—so don't use that knowledge against anyone. File the information away, and deal with what is visible.

*Friday, July 24 (Moon in Leo to Virgo 12:24 a.m.)*    If the devil lies in the details, today should be dedicated to details. Whether you're dealing with a professional or a personal issue, your path to understanding the situation lies in what may not be obvious. While you're tending to details, make appointments with health-care professionals for the maintenance of your physical well-being.

*Saturday, July 25 (Moon in Virgo)*    If you've finished a project already, take another look and, revise, review, and rewrite. Be as picky as you want in your scrutiny. Better to turn in something you love than to turn in something toward which you only feel lukewarm.

*Sunday, July 26 (Moon in Virgo to Libra 2:26 a.m.)*    It's wise to draw on the expertise of the people around you. While your knowledge is impressive, you may not be an expert in what you're dealing with. Let your intuition loose; it will bring you the people you need.

*Monday, July 27 (Moon in Libra)*    Take the lead. It could be that the people around you are locked in indecisiveness or simply not available. Approach everyone with forthrightness. It will make things easier in the long run, and the others involved will appreciate your honesty.

*Tuesday, July 28 (Moon in Libra to Scorpio 7:57 a.m.)*    Research and investigative work are your strong points. You're trying to get to the bottom of a situation or relationship, and once you turn your intuition loose on this issue, you find what you need.

**Wednesday, July 29 (Moon in Scorpio)** In a couple days, Venus enters Cancer and your fifth house, signaling the beginning of the most romantic and creative time for you this year. You may be feeling the effects of this impending transit already. Someone new could show up in your life tomorrow, and you'll suddenly be looking at the world through the eyes of an innocent.

**Thursday, July 30 (Moon in Scorpio to Sagittarius 5:10 p.m.)** You may be too flexible, too willing to bend to other people's wishes and demands. This issue involves your career or a professional relationship. Tread carefully.

**Friday, July 31 (Moon in Sagittarius)** Venus enters Cancer and your fifth house and stays there until August 26. This transit brings opportunities in romance, with creative endeavors, and with activities that make your heart sing. Your self-confidence and sex appeal soar.

# AUGUST 2009

**Saturday, August 1 (Moon in Sagittarius)** With the moon in your tenth house, you're planning for the week ahead. You socialize at some point and strive to maintain your broader perspective about your career and path in life. Venus and Mercury are still in Leo, your sixth house, so there's a lot of flirtation going on with someone special.

**Sunday, August 2 (Moon in Sagittarius to Capricorn 5:09 a.m.)** Mercury enters Virgo, your seventh house and remains there until August 25. During this period, you have numerous discussions with romantic and business partners. You tend to be more detail-oriented too, even when it irritates you to be so.

*Monday, August 3 (Moon in Capricorn)*  The moon joins Capricorn in your eleventh house. You may be conscious about spending and power issues related to money and friends. For every dollar you spend, stash another dollar into your savings.

*Tuesday, August 4 (Moon in Capricorn to Aquarius 6:08 p.m.)*  You may be planning a trip for your family or with a group of friends. Check out the usual travel search engines and pick a spot on the globe. Then see what kinds of fares are being offered and figure out the cheapest way of getting there.

*Wednesday, August 5 (Moon in Aquarius)*  The lunar eclipse in Aquarius brings up emotional issues related to the past. You gain insights into your own unconscious, and your insights expand and broaden your life in some way. Mars forms a harmonious angle to this moon, suggesting lots of activity around this date.

*Thursday, August 6 (Moon in Aquarius)*  What would you like to be doing tomorrow when the moon enters your sign? Rather than thinking in terms of obligations and what you should be doing, go with the flow of your emotions and see where it leads.

*Friday, August 7 (Moon in Aquarius to Pisces 6:35 a.m.)*  You feel the shift in energies as soon as you wake up. You may feel a visceral tug toward a particular person or experience. Rather than rationalize the feeling, go with it. Resistance isn't on your agenda.

*Saturday, August 8 (Moon in Pisces)*  If you have an encounter with an animal, think about the deeper meaning. What is the animal's behavior? What myths and fairy tales and legends surround this animal? What are its mating habits? All of this information may hold clues about what the encounter means on a deeper level.

*Sunday, August 9 (Moon in Pisces to Aries 5:24 p.m.)*  If you're having financial troubles, try visualizing yourself with a check for whatever sum you want. Back the visualization with emotion. Create a spread sheet where you enter that amount of money. Experiment. Have fun. Then get out of the way, and let the universe bring you the money you want.

**Monday, August 10 (Moon in Aries)**    You may pursue something that you know should be left alone. Perhaps it's the result of a feeling of jealousy, possessiveness, or passion. Back off, and think things over. Tomorrow, you'll be glad that you did.

**Tuesday, August 11 (Moon in Aries)**    Pioneering is something you probably did a lot of in previous lives. And when you trailblaze, it feels familiar, as if you know the terrain. You're forging new emotional synapses in your love life.

**Wednesday, August 12 (Moon in Aries to Taurus 1:51 a.m.)**    Aesthetic pleasure is the hallmark. You appreciate being surrounded by beauty, so wherever you are, that's what you strive to do. Seems as if your choices are widen open.

**Thursday, August 13 (Moon in Taurus)**    Yesterday's revisions are today's new ideas. You may want to spend a few minutes grounding yourself. Whether it's through meditation or some other technique, it enables you to get in touch with your most genuine feelings and desires.

**Friday, August 14 (Moon in Taurus to Gemini 7:27 a.m.)**    Indulge your restlessness by changing your routine in some way. There are a million ways to do something or to think about a given topic. Explore your options.

**Saturday, August 15 (Moon in Gemini)**    You're into body language—not your own, but that of a family member. What the person says with his or her body reveals just about everything you need to know. You're so intuitive that you don't need a repeat performance.

*Sunday, August 16 (Moon in Gemini to Cancer 10:14 a.m.)* One of the best ways to understand the patterns that operate in your own life is to take note of how lunar transits affect you. When the moon enters Cancer, for example, how do you feel? What kinds of experiences do you have? Does your love life pick up? Does your creative adrenaline really get going?

*Monday, August 17 (Moon in Cancer)* You're in the mood for creating. Ideas flow fast and furiously, and you have to be sure you capture all of them. Ideas are like books that you save for rainy days. Have a file for them on your computer that you can consult when your creativity seems flat.

*Tuesday, August 18 (Moon in Cancer to Leo 10:57 a.m.)* The day after tomorrow there will be a new moon in Virgo, your sixth house. Prepare for it now by listing the opportunities and experiences related to your work routine and health you would like to have. A new job? Include it. More pay? Include it. You get the idea.

*Wednesday, August 19 (Moon in Leo)* You could be challenged at work. Someone annoys you or pesters you in some way. You react with hostility, and from there, of course, things only snowball. Or, at any rate, that's one version of events. But if you're aware of what the energy is, you can change it and the situation by toning down your reaction.

*Thursday, August 20 (Moon in Leo to Virgo 11:01 a.m.)* The new moon in Virgo should attract opportunities related to work, health, and interactions with the larger world. Mars forms a harmonious angle to this new moon, indicating a lot of activity that ushers in opportunities. Travel could be involved too.

*Friday, August 21 (Moon in Virgo)* The moon in your seventh house usually may lead to some sort of tension between you and a partner. It's not serious, but it should

286

be addressed as soon as it happens. If you just let it slide, the tension may fester, and the repercussions will multiply.

**Saturday, August 22 (Moon in Virgo to Libra 12:12 p.m.)** Activities revolve around balance, relationships, and socializing. You may have to revise the terms of a mortgage or loan, perhaps through refinancing. You could be delving into areas like reincarnation and communication with the dead.

**Sunday, August 23 (Moon in Libra)** Can you put off making a decision for a few more days? Wait until the moon is in a fellow water sign. In fact, Tuesday would be the day to make your decision. Mars enters Cancer that day, galvanizing everything you do for fun and amusement.

**Monday, August 24 (Moon in Libra to Scorpio 4:17 p.m.)** This afternoon, the moon enters fellow water sign Scorpio, and you're after the absolute bottom line. And if you can't get that, you're not interested. Your business interests may be expanding to overseas markets.

**Tuesday, August 25 (Moon in Scorpio)** Mercury enters Libra, your eighth house, and Mars enters Cancer. The first transit brings taxes and insurance matters up front and center in your life until October 28. During this period, Mercury will be retrograde from September 6 to 29. So sign contracts and travel on either side of that date. The transit of Mars lasts until October 16 and heightens your sexuality, your creative drive, and romance.

**Wednesday, August 26 (Moon in Scorpio)** Venus enters Leo, your sixth house, where it remains until September 20. During this period, your work life should run smoothly, and an office flirtation could launch a relationship. But be careful about mixing business with pleasure.

**Thursday, August 27 (Moon in Scorpio to Sagittarius 12:16 a.m.)** The moon enters your tenth house and fire signs figure prominently in events. An Aries, a Leo, or a

Sagittarius is helpful in career matters. Someone in your family shares ideas that you can use professionally.

*Friday, August 28 (Moon in Sagittarius)*     The day calls for greater flexibility on your part. It's due to a career matter that may not be going quite as you hoped. The situation is easily rectified, by adjusting your attitude and seeing things from the other person's point of view.

*Saturday, August 29 (Moon in Sagittarius to Capricorn 11:45 a.m.)*     You may hook up with your support group. Whether it's a group of writers, actors, artists, or people who follow a particular political and spiritual belief, you come away refreshed and recharged. You have the creative inspiration and drive to pursue your dreams.

*Sunday, August 30 (Moon in Capricorn)*     You have a lot of friends and even more acquaintants, part of your network. The party may be at your place today. So go all out. But don't overdo it. Tomorrow is a workday.

*Monday, August 31 (Moon in Capricorn)*     Hidden issues surface. They involve your own motives or those of someone else. If you don't like what you discover, strive to change it by focusing your intentions on what you want to happen.

# SEPTEMBER 2009

*Tuesday, September 1 (Moon in Capricorn to Aquarius 12:43 a.m.)*     Yesterday's hidden issues become today's conversation. You're trying to puzzle through what you learned and may need some help figuring it all out. Ask an air sign for help—a Gemini, a Libra, or an Aquarius.

*Wednesday, September 2 (Moon in Aquarius)*     You rarely lack for ideas. How can you make them practical? How can you implement them in your life and work? Tomorrow, when the moon has moved into your sign, you'll gain clarity on this issue.

*Thursday, September 3 (Moon in Aquarius to Pisces 12:59 p.m.)* A relationship that begins this close to the full moon in your sign will be unusual, to say the least. However, if you're involved already, tomorrow's full moon simply brings clarity to your feelings. Today, the person you meet is someone you have known in previous lives.

*Friday, September 4 (Moon in Pisces)* The full moon in your sign may require an attitude adjustment on your part in terms of a romantic relationship. You gain insight and clarity into a personal issue. Events probably unfold without warning, taking you by surprise.

*Saturday, September 5 (Moon in Pisces to Aries 11:15 p.m.)* Money is your focus. You may be trying to earn more of it and feel somewhat frustrated by your lack of progress. Focus on the abundance in your life, whatever form it takes. And nurture the art of appreciation. Mercury turns retrograde tomorrow in Libra. Back up your computer files!

*Sunday, September 6 (Moon in Aries)* Mercury turns retrograde in Libra and stays that way until September 29. Don't apply for mortgages or loans under this retrograde. In fact, don't make any investment decisions. Just lie low financially.

*Monday, September 7 (Moon in Aries)* You'll feel like going on a spending spree. Instead, hit the thrift shops. Keep your expenses low. At the end of the month, you'll be glad you did. If your values are attacked by someone, just turn around and walk away.

*Tuesday, September 8 (Moon in Aries to Taurus 7:19 a.m.)* Try not to become trapped by your own perceptions. Just because you think you're right doesn't mean that you are. Listen to another person's point of view. Then make up your mind later this month.

*Wednesday, September 9 (Moon in Taurus)* You may be tapped to work on a neighborhood beautification project. You'd like to volunteer, but time may be a factor. Before you commit, consider this. A relative may figure into activities.

***Thursday, September 10 (Moon in Taurus to Gemini 1:18 p.m.)*** The moon enters your fourth house, stirring up activity and emotions, and triggering a need for more information. You and one of your parents iron out differences in your relationship.

***Friday, September 11 (Moon in Gemini)*** Pluto turns direct in your eleventh house. You'll feel the impact over time, as issues with friends begin to straighten out. This transit, though, is a very long one, so don't expect immediate effects. You may have to compromise to reach an agreement with a family member.

***Saturday, September 12 (Moon in Gemini to Cancer 5:20 p.m.)*** The moon joins Mars in Cancer, in your fifth house. This combination of planets should really rev up your creative adrenaline. Time to get serious about doing what you love and making your living at it. This combo also heightens your sexuality, and you're actively seeking love and romance.

***Sunday, September 13 (Moon in Cancer)*** Intuitively, you're in very high gear. So go with your hunches and don't allow your left brain to shout over what you know to be true. Since it's the weekend, get out and do what you love. Another water sign may be part of the picture—a Cancer, a Pisces, or a Scorpio.

***Monday, September 14 (Moon in Cancer to Leo 7:40 p.m.)*** There's something a bit different about the day. As the moon makes its transition from Cancer to Leo, you can feel the shift in energies. You're suddenly feeling more flamboyant, showy, ready to strut your stuff.

***Tuesday, September 15 (Moon in Leo)*** Let the air fill your senses, and then take your goodwill out into the larger world. There are gaps in other people's lives that beg to be filled. Today is about service to others. Figure out where you can be of help, and then volunteer.

**Wednesday, September 16 (Moon in Leo to Virgo 8:56 p.m.)**    If you feel you're being taken advantage of, speak up. Whether it involves a business or personal partnership, you're entitled to your opinion. Don't hold in what you feel. Deal with things as they are, not as you wish things to be.

**Thursday, September 17 (Moon in Virgo)**    You may want to plan something special for this weekend for your partner, especially with tomorrow's new moon in Virgo coming up. If you're not involved, do something special for yourself!

**Friday, September 18 (Moon in Virgo to Libra 10:26 p.m.)**    The new moon in Virgo attracts business and personal partners. If you're not involved, you will be soon. If you're involved already, this new moon indicates the relationship may be taken to a higher level. In business, you attract exactly the right person you need at this point in time.

**Saturday, September 19 (Moon in Libra)**    Your spiritual or political beliefs take center stage. You may feel conflicted about your beliefs in some way, and this conflict attracts a confrontation that forces you to clarify what you believe.

**Sunday, September 20 (Moon in Libra)**    Venus enters Virgo, your seventh house, a transit that lasts until October 14. This should be a very romantic and even creative period for this year. If you're involved, this transit may have the two of you moving in together or getting married. If you're not involved, hold on to your hat. Things are about to get very interesting!

**Monday, September 21 (Moon in Libra to Scorpio 1:52 a.m.)**    This moon sharpens your edges and gives you penetrating insight into other people's motives and agendas. Your intense feelings toward someone deepen. You're a seeker of truth.

***Tuesday, September 22 (Moon in Scorpio)*** With Mercury still retrograde, you may be scrambling to set things right with a partner, family member, or friend. You might consider putting everything in an e-mail. Sometimes, it's helpful to get your feelings on paper.

***Wednesday, September 23 (Moon in Scorpio to Sagittarius 8:44 a.m.)*** It's a career day, and you are prepped and ready. There may be travel related to your career and work. But you're even ready for that, with your bag packed and Mercury retrograde. Just remain flexible. Your schedule will change.

***Thursday, September 24 (Moon in Sagittarius)*** You're in an expansive, buoyant mood, and it spills over, infusing people around you. Suddenly, you're the center of attention, with colleagues and bosses clamoring for you. People figure you have the answers!

***Friday, September 25 (Moon in Sagittarius to Capricorn 7:19 p.m.)*** You enjoy this earth-sign moon. It helps to ground your ideas, to make you more practical in your approach to life and living. It also helps to solidify your relationship with a particular group of friends.

***Saturday, September 26 (Moon in Capricorn)*** You hook up with your support group. This could be just a group of friends with whom you meet periodically for lunch or a group of writers, actors, or political activists—whatever your passion is.

***Sunday, September 27 (Moon in Capricorn)*** If your dreams and goals are in flux, fine-tune them. You may want to look back over the past five years to see how far you've come. If you're not satisfied with where you are, make a one-year plan.

*Monday, September 28 (Moon in Capricorn to Aquarius 8:07 a.m.)* Tomorrow, Mercury turns direct. You'll start feeling the energy—a kind of difference in your communications with people. You may retreat for a while to do research and creative work.

*Tuesday, September 29 (Moon in Aquarius)* Mercury turns direct. This is always cause for celebration, but today it really is. You can move forward with your holiday travel plans. Touch base with clients and friends. Get ready for the moon to move into your sign tomorrow.

*Wednesday, September 30 (Moon in Aquarius to Pisces 8:27 p.m.)* You're ready for a power day. You may attract the attention of another water sign and feel a deep tug of attraction, particularly if this person is a Scorpio. It's safe to apply for that mortgage or loan.

# OCTOBER 2009

*Thursday, October 1 (Moon in Pisces)* To enhance this power day, consider conducting some sort of ritual to celebrate who you are. You may want to meditate for a few minutes at some point just to underscore your intuitive nature and to find out where your imagination may take you.

*Friday, October 2 (Moon in Pisces)* Your dream recall is terrific. Whether it's an afternoon nap or your regular sleep at night, keep a notebook and pen handy. Your dreams are likely to provide insights into issues that concern you, they may cough up visions of the future, and they could even take you straight into a past life.

*Saturday, October 3 (Moon in Pisces to Aries 6:21 a.m.)* Finances are your top priority. You're anticipating a large expense in some area, and you may be stashing away money for that purchase. But with the holidays rapidly approaching, you may have to dig into your savings for a gift for someone special in your life.

*Sunday, October 4 (Moon in Aries)*     The full moon in Aries clarifies a financial issue. It also may have you feeling pretty restless, perhaps even directionless. That feeling won't last long.

*Monday, October 5 (Moon in Aries to Taurus 1:34 p.m.)*     It's a communication day. Whether you're writing or talking, you're very clear and precise in what you say. Others appreciate your ability to express yourself. You may be digging in your heels about something related to your neighborhood or community.

*Tuesday, October 6 (Moon in Taurus)*     You can sell anything to anyone. Even if you're not in sales, you can sell an idea or concept. You'll surprise yourself!

*Wednesday, October 7 (Moon in Taurus to Gemini 6:47 p.m.)*     This evening, home will be your focus. Plan something special with your family, even if it's just a dinner out. Your parents could be a part of this scenario. On some level, you're collecting information that you'll use later this month.

*Thursday, October 8 (Moon in Gemini)*     Yesterday, you dealt with foundations. Today you deal with what you can see, hear, and feel. Things are up close and personal, and your imagination fills in the gaps. Before you jump to any conclusions, open the group to discussion.

*Friday, October 9 (Moon in Gemini to Cancer 10:48 p.m.)*     Tonight, you don't have to dig very far for inspiration. Your muse is close enough to whisper in your ear. But you have to commit to the time. Take advantage of this energy for the next two days. You might be able to finish your manuscript or portfolio, or you might land the audition of your dreams!

*Saturday, October 10 (Moon in Cancer)*     You're especially sensitive to the moods of others. If you have kids, you'll have to resist smothering them with love and attention, especially if they're teens. Mars is in Cancer for another six days. The combination creates an intuitive flow that you can dip into whenever you want.

**Sunday, October 11 (Moon in Cancer)**   Your impulses lead you in important directions creatively. You may want to brainstorm with a partner or friend, or write down your ideas. Get them down so that on days when you don't feel as creative, you can use them.

**Monday, October 12 (Moon in Cancer to Leo 2:03 a.m.)**   Jupiter turns direct in Aquarius, your twelfth house. It will now be easier for you to integrate your worldview and spiritual beliefs into your life. And you'll start with your work routine. How can you improve this situation?

**Tuesday, October 13 (Moon in Leo)**   You and your partner can enjoy each other's company without petty differences intervening. In fact, you may want to get off together this evening for some activity you both enjoy.

**Wednesday, October 14 (Moon in Leo to Virgo 4:46 a.m.)** Venus enters Libra, your eighth house, and doesn't move on again until November 7. During this period, applications for mortgages and loans go well. You could get a break on tax or insurance matters. If a relationship begins under this transit, balance will be key to its success.

**Thursday, October 15 (Moon in Virgo)**   You may be more self-critical or critical of others. It's vital that you back off on the criticism. It will only create discord and unhappiness. Instead, practice the art of appreciation.

**Friday, October 16 (Moon in Virgo to Libra 7:30 a.m.)** Mars enters Leo and your sixth house, where it will be through the end of the year. It will be retrograde from December 20 on into 2010. During this transit, your work routine will undergo change. You may be more concerned about your appearance.

*Saturday, October 17 (Moon in Libra)*    You're happiest when harmony prevails. So don't do anything to rock the boat. Keep your criticism to yourself, and focus on self-perfection. Your artistic interests take center stage later in the day.

*Sunday, October 18 (Moon in Libra to Scorpio 11:23 a.m.)*    The new moon in Libra ushers in opportunities in social relationships, mortgages, taxes, and insurance. You could have the chance to explore the deeper questions in life too—something at which every Pisces excels.

*Monday, October 19 (Moon in Scorpio)*    Try not to over-react. Even though your emotions are intense, and you could be somewhat jealous or taken aback by a partner's actions or words, don't let things get out of hand. Tomorrow, as they say, is another day. Even better, wait until the moon is in Capricorn to get things off your chest.

*Tuesday, October 20 (Moon in Scorpio to Sagittarius 5:50 p.m.)*    The gregarious Sagittarius moon has you focused on career matters, but with great humor and optimism. Your mood spreads throughout the office like a beneficial virus, and makes the day far more enjoyable to everyone in your environment.

*Wednesday, October 21 (Moon in Sagittarius)*    You gain prestige and support just when you need it. Colleagues are behind you a hundred percent. Bosses are paying close attention. Some travel may be involved in the day's events—something other than your regular commute.

*Thursday, October 22 (Moon in Sagittarius)*    Your love life should be moving full speed ahead, with Mars in Cancer making you more aware of the importance of roots, family, and stability. Start submitting manuscripts and portfolios, and scheduling auditions.

*Friday, October 23 (Moon in Sagittarius to Capricorn 3:40 a.m.)*    In your research, insist on getting the full picture, not just bits and pieces. This may require some intensive investigation over the Internet. If you need other facts and figures, consult an expert in the field.

*Saturday, October 24 (Moon in Capricorn)*    There is power within a group of individuals coming from the same place. Whether the group's interest is politics or spirituality or something else altogether, you stand united. Change begins when it gathers momentum.

*Sunday, October 25 (Moon in Capricorn to Aquarius 3:08 p.m.)*    A kick-back kind of day. You may want to get off by yourself. If it's fall where you are, take a hike, a walk, or a bike ride. If it's warm where you are, head to the pool or the beach, if that's possible. You need to recharge by relaxing.

*Monday, October 26  (Moon in Aquarius)*    You could be virtual traveling, in preparation for a trip. With Mercury entering Scorpio and your ninth house on October 28, your destination could be overseas. Find out what you can about the country you're going to visit. A traveler is never overprepared.

*Tuesday, October 27  (Moon in Aquarius)*    You and a partner spend the day together. Regardless of where this together time takes place, it renews your spirits and your relationship. Sometimes, you simply have to get out of the routine of your ordinary life and rediscover the magic you are certain exists beneath the surface.

*Wednesday, October 28 (Moon in Aquarius to Pisces 3:46 a.m.)*    Mercury enters Scorpio and remains there until November 15. During this time, your emotional focus shifts to your belief system. It may be that you've absorbed beliefs from family and friends. Untangle the web.

*Thursday, October 29 (Moon in Pisces)*    Saturn enters Libra—a major transit that lasts for about two and a half years. Since the moon is in your sign, you may be too caught up in your own stuff to realize the importance of this transit.

*Friday, October 30 (Moon in Pisces to Aries 1:57 p.m.)* If you find yourself in a blue funk, it may be because you're absorbing the energy of people around you. Turn in early so you can save energy for the weekend ahead.

*Saturday, October 31 (Moon in Aries)* Happy Halloween! You could be shopping to show your appreciation for someone you love. Be sure to make the gift specific to that person. A generic gift just won't cut it.

# NOVEMBER 2009

*Sunday, November 1—Daylight Saving Time Ends (Moon in Aries to Taurus, 7:45 p.m.)* Conversations with relatives are likely today; perhaps they'll concern the upcoming holidays. Whose house will the celebrations be at this year? Behind the scenes, there may be some soul-searching going on concerning a relationship.

*Monday, November 2 (Moon in Taurus)* The full moon in Taurus brings insights concerning a relative, a communication project, or your neighborhood and community. Your beliefs may come up against those of someone close to you. News is also possible, particularly if you're a writer or in the communication business.

*Tuesday, November 3 (Moon in Taurus to Gemini 11:53 p.m.)* Get organized. You'll need to as the moon enters Gemini late tonight. Persevere to get things done. You're in the right place at the right time, but you have to believe you are. Without that underlying belief in yourself, it's all just words.

*Wednesday, November 4 (Moon in Gemini)* Neptune turns direct in Aquarius. Once again, the effects of this movement are subtle because Neptune crawls through the zodiac. But you should be in a much better spot now to integrate your ideals and idealism into your life. Remember, too, that Jupiter is also in the same sign and house, expanding your inner world.

*Thursday, November 5 (Moon in Gemini)*    After your organization spree, you may want to take time to retreat. Maybe you take the day off from work and usher the family out of town for a long weekend. You're dealing with the foundation of who you are.

*Friday, November 6 (Moon in Gemini to Cancer 2:43 a.m.)*    The moon represents feminine yin energy, the mother, your emotional security. Your emotional security lies in two primary areas: your creative output and your love life. Your mother or another nurturing female plays a role in activities.

*Saturday, November 7 (Moon in Cancer)*    Venus enters Scorpio, your ninth house. During this transit, which lasts until December 1, romance abroad is likely. And if you're not traveling overseas, you could meet someone from another country who interests you. If you're involved already, you and your partner may head overseas for a trip that has some deeper purpose. Sounds like the beginning of a quest.

*Sunday, November 8 (Moon in Cancer to Leo 5:23 a.m.)* Look beyond the immediate. Nurture yourself in the same way that you nurture others. Set your goals, and get to work. Mars is also in Leo and your sixth house, galvanizing you to achieve and accomplish.

*Monday, November 9 (Moon in Leo)*    It's a service day. You're taking care of your own business, but you also may be doing a good deed for someone else. This is the sort of thing you do because you are moved by the other person's situation or plight.

*Tuesday, November 10 (Moon in Leo to Virgo 8:31 a.m.)*    The moon enters your opposite sign, shifting your emotional focus to a business or romantic partnership. It's wise to pay attention to the kind of details you might miss ordinarily because they seem mundane. But the mundane is the day's saving grace!

**Wednesday, November 11 (Moon in Virgo)**    You have the ability to make friends with anyone, even people who don't like you. It's not just your charm and wit, but your ability to reach inside other people and extract their innate goodness. Put this skill to work.

**Thursday, November 12 (Moon in Virgo to Libra 12:23 p.m.)**    Relationships are the focus. You may need balance in this area of your life, but aren't sure how to achieve it. Enlist the help of a Gemini, a Libra, or an Aquarius. They're great with ideas, and ideas are exactly what you need now.

**Friday, November 13   (Moon in Libra)**    A romance blossoms. And while that's going on, you may sign up for a seminar in an esoteric topic that interests you.

**Saturday, November 14 (Moon in Libra to Scorpio 5:25 p.m.)**    Here's that intense Scorpio moon. But you're ready for it. Your creative adrenaline is pumping fast and furiously, you're on top of the holiday preparations, and you've got your activities lined up.

**Sunday, November 15 (Moon in Scorpio)**    Mercury enters Sagittarius, your tenth house. During this transit, which ends on December 5, you'll have ample opportunities to pitch your ideas and gather support for your pet projects. You may even be traveling for work. Even if your focus isn't on your professional life, use this transit to push forward in your career.

**Monday, November 16 (Moon in Scorpio)**    Today's new moon in Scorpio ushers in opportunities related to education, overseas travel, or an expansion of your business interests overseas. You may be doing more research and investigative work of some kind. Neptune forms a close and challenging angle to this new moon, suggesting that you should be careful about deceptive scams.

*Tuesday, November 17 (Moon in Scorpio to Sagittarius 12:23 a.m.)*    The moon joins Mercury in Sagittarius, your tenth house. The combination of energies makes this the ideal day to pitch ideas, submit manuscripts, schedule auditions, or put the finishing touches on a portfolio. Your security lies in your satisfaction with your career.

*Wednesday, November 18 (Moon in Sagittarius)* You're very responsive to the needs of colleagues and co-workers. You're more in the public view, perhaps due to travel or public relations or even public speaking. Your relationship with a boss goes well.

*Thursday, November 19 (Moon in Sagittarius to Capricorn 10:01 a.m.)*    Conclude projects and reflect on how to expand your base. Your friends may hold vital clues to how you can do this. Perhaps it's simply a matter of broadening your network.

*Friday, November 20 (Moon in Capricorn)*    Capricorn excels at long-range planning, so use the unar energies to examine your goals. How can you best attain these goals? Do you need more education or greater opportunities? Would it be in your best interest to move to a different area?

*Saturday, November 21 (Moon in Capricorn to Aquarius 10:11 p.m.)*    The moon joins Neptune and Jupiter in your twelfth house. This trio of planets heightens everything you do behind the scenes. Your understanding of your own unconscious is broadening and deepening.

*Sunday, November 22 (Moon in Aquarius)*    Time to ease up on your routine. Kick back with a favorite book or movie, or get together with a group of friends and celebrate the upcoming holidays early. Tomorrow you'll have plenty of time for your Thanksgiving preparations.

*Monday, November 23 (Moon in Aquarius)*    Keep your feelings to yourself. Tomorrow, you'll be glad that you did. You're working on uncovering your own motives and inhibitions. Your imagination and intuition are valuable guides in this area. Tomorrow, the moon enters your sign, so you're preparing for another power day.

*Tuesday, November 24 (Moon in Aquarius to Pisces 11:08 a.m.)*    With the moon entering your sign this morning, you're feeling physically vital and upbeat. Approach everything with an unconventional attitude. Don't hesitate to think outside the box. Unconventional thinking takes you much farther than the status quo.

*Wednesday, November 25 (Moon in Pisces)*    Your Thanksgiving preparations are done, and you're ready to rock and roll! Whether the festivities are at your place or someone else's, you've got the food prepared, you're in the proper frame of mind for appreciation, and you're ready to enjoy yourself.

*Thursday, November 26 (Moon in Pisces to Aries 10:11 p.m.)*    Happy Thanksgiving! Your values certainly come into play. You look around at the people with whom you share your life and realize that the outer world is a perfect expression of your inner world. So, if the day is great for you, how can you attract more of this good feeling into your life?

*Friday, November 27 (Moon in Aries)*    It's the biggest shopping day of the year in the U.S. So when someone suggests going to the local mall for a jump on holiday shopping, you may want to think twice about it—unless you love crowds.

*Saturday, November 28 (Moon in Aries)*    You're on a mind trip that could take you into unexplored terrains. It's as if you're aware of the invisible world that moves to the right and left of you, but your eyes are straight ahead. Live in the moment.

*Sunday, November 29 (Moon in Aries to Taurus 5:35 a.m.)*    You tackle a community or neighborhood project. This could include writing or some other type of mass communication, perhaps through a Web site.

**Monday, November 30 (Moon in Taurus)**   As you get ready to enter the last month of the year, take stock of where you have been this year and where you would like to be next year. Lay down your goals. It's not too early to think about New Year's resolutions!

# DECEMBER 2009

**Tuesday, December 1 (Moon in Taurus to Gemini 9:24 a.m.)**   Venus enters Sagittarius and your tenth house, and Uranus turns direct. Even if you're not fully into professional matters, this Venus transit, which lasts until December 25, is fantastic for your career. Travel could also be involved. For romance, it may indicate a relationship with a colleague or someone you meet through work. Uranus's movement should help straighten out your personal life!

**Wednesday, December 2 (Moon in Gemini)**   The full moon in Gemini brings lot of activity at home. You gain insight into a family issue. With both Mars and Saturn forming wide but harmonious angles to this moon, your insights are funneled into the proper structure.

**Thursday, December 3 (Moon in Gemini to Cancer 11:01 a.m.)**   The moon stirs up your emotions concerning a relationship or a creative endeavor. Use the emotions in a positive way, and then you're on a roll. You could feel somewhat possessive about kids or loved ones. You may have to back off some.

**Friday, December 4 (Moon in Cancer)**   You could be feeling somewhat nostalgic for a relationship, a certain time in your life, a parent, or a place that you lived. These feelings can be transformed into creative fodder. You may want to spend some time with your kids. You've earned the time off!

*Saturday, December 5 (Moon in Cancer to Leo 12:08 p.m.)* Mercury enters Capricorn, your eleventh house. This transit, which ends on December 25, should bring plenty of invites for holiday festivities. You may be involved in some sort of group activity that has a long-range plan too.

*Sunday, December 6 (Moon in Leo)* Your health and how to maintain it occupies you. Maybe it's time to hit the gym, take that yoga class you've been promising yourself, or join an aerobics class. If you shop, it's with the new you in mind!

*Monday, December 7 (Moon in Leo to Virgo 2:07 p.m.)* The moon enters your opposite sign. Now that Saturn has finally moved out of Virgo and into Libra, there's a lightness in most of your partnerships that has been absent the past few years. Enjoy it.

*Tuesday, December 8 (Moon in Virgo)* Women play an important role—anyone from friends to a female relative. Don't allow others to manipulate your feelings. You know who you are and where you're going and what you feel right this second.

*Wednesday, December 9 (Moon in Virgo to Libra 5:48 p.m.)* The moon joins Saturn in your eighth house. There's a certain heaviness to this combination, but it also provides the right structure for the exploration of metaphysics.

*Thursday, December 10 (Moon in Libra)* Romance with a coworker could blossom. If you're involved already, you and a partner may undertake a project together. Think back to a time when you felt really happy and buoyant. Then try to conjure those emotions if you feel low.

*Friday, December 11 (Moon in Libra to Scorpio 11:32 p.m.)* The highlights involve publishing and education. If you're headed for college next year, you may be prepar-

304

ing to take SATs or GREs, or you may be involved in extracurricular activities that look good on applications.

***Saturday, December 12 (Moon in Scorpio)*** Your research is taking unexpected turns, but you're anticipating the adventure. It's like a treasure hunt, and even if you don't find the treasure, the search and the journey are what matter.

***Sunday, December 13 (Moon in Scorpio)*** Whatever you learn is something you can put to work immediately. It may be connected to your deeper beliefs and how those beliefs create your reality from the inside out.

***Monday, December 14 (Moon in Scorpio to Sagittarius 7:25 a.m.)*** You may feel somewhat conflicted. You have obligations at home and at work. Given the upcoming holidays, your best bet is to take the day off and finish up your holiday shopping. Then play catch-up with clients and colleagues by phone or e-mail.

***Tuesday, December 15 (Moon in Sagittarius)*** Tomorrow's new moon in Sagittarius will set the stage for your career in the New Year. So start thinking about what you would like for yourself professionally over the next year. Take steps to set a plan into action at work.

***Wednesday, December 16 (Moon in Sagittarius to Capricorn 5:32 p.m.)*** The new moon in Capricorn ushers in opportunities for career options. You may find a new job, get a raise or a promotion, or move to another location within your company. It's also possible that you'll become self-employed. It all depends on what you want.

***Thursday, December 17 (Moon in Capricorn)*** You do some things for money, and other things for the love of it. Today it's a combination of those energies. But you may be wondering how you can earn money doing what you love. Ask a Taurus.

*Friday, December 18 (Moon in Capricorn)*     Until December 20, every planet is moving in direction motion. That means they're all functioning the way they should be. So for this weekend, take advantage of that energy, and do something special with the special people in your life.

*Saturday, December 19 (Moon in Capricorn to Aquarius 5:39 a.m.)*     You're finalizing your holiday plans. Whether you're going out of town or having the festivities at home, there are plenty of details to tend to. In addition, your inner world continues to expand, offering insights into issues that concern you.

*Sunday, December 20 (Moon in Aquarius)*     Mars turns retrograde in Leo. The timing on this is probably good, what with the holidays taking your mind off work. But until mid-March, when Mars turns direct, you may be revisiting work issues and situations that you thought were resolved.

*Monday, December 21  (Moon in Aquarius to Pisces 6:42 p.m.)*     With the moon entering your sign, you're in high spirits, and with good reason. People are either arriving at your place, or you and your partner and family are leaving town. If you're single or uncommitted, you've got plenty on your plate.

*Tuesday, December 22 (Moon in Pisces)*     Your thoughts and feelings are in alignment. That angst you often feel is blessedly absent. Your physical vitality is strong; your intuition is right on target. Take time to listen to others. There are plenty of stories to hear!

*Wednesday, December 23 (Moon in Pisces)*     If someone you know has a birthday, be sure that person isn't celebrating alone. Bring the person to your place, or have a surprise party. In a sense, this is your holiday gift for the person— you're helping her or him to create memories that will last.

*Thursday, December 24 (Moon in Pisces to Aries 6:40 a.m.)*     The spotlight is on independence. You're on fire with ideas and plans. You may want to keep them to yourself. You sometimes puzzle the people around you, and these plans will have them totally baffled.

*Friday, December 25 (Moon in Aries)* Merry Christmas! Venus enters Capricorn and your eleventh house, making it likely that in 2010, you'll have plenty of social invitations coming your way. Some may be from friends you haven't seen for a while.

*Saturday, December 26 (Moon in Aries to Taurus 3:27 a.m.)* Mercury turns retrograde in Capricorn. This movement may change your New Year's Eve plans, so remain flexible and open, and don't be surprised if a party gets canceled at the last minute or if someone tosses a party at the last minute.

*Sunday, December 27 (Moon in Taurus)* The moon enters your third house, and you know the score on this moon! It's stubborn, it likes to have its own way, and it doesn't give in easily. But that's exactly what're required from you. Dealings with relatives may be getting a bit more challenging.

*Monday, December 28 (Moon in Taurus to Gemini 8:15 p.m.)* The moon enters your fourth house, stimulating your home and family life. There could be some miscommunications, particularly with Mercury moving retrograde. Be sure everyone is on the same page before you attempt a dinner discussion!

*Tuesday, December 29 (Moon in Gemini)* The gathering and dissemination of information is at the top of your agenda. There's no telling what the information is about—with your active imagination, it could be about virtually anything. But you're surrounded by your supporters.

*Wednesday, December 30 (Moon in Gemini to Cancer 9:46 p.m.)* How nice that your year will end with the moon in your fifth house of romance, creativity, and fun. It certainly is a nice send-off to 2009 and a great way to greet 2010.

***Thursday, December 31 (Moon in Cancer)*** The lunar eclipse in Cancer brings up feelings and emotions concerning romance, children, and all your creative endeavors. You may be looking back over 2009 with whoever is sharing your New Year's Eve.

## HAPPY NEW YEAR!

## SYDNEY OMARR

Born on August 5, 1926, in Philadelphia, Pennsylvania, Sydney Omarr was the only person ever given full-time duty in the U.S. Army as an astrologer. He is regarded as the most erudite astrologer of our time and the best known, through his syndicated column and his radio and television programs (he was Merv Griffin's "resident astrologer"). Omarr has been called the most "knowledgeable astrologer since Evangeline Adams." His forecasts of Nixon's downfall, the end of World War II in mid-August of 1945, the assassination of John F. Kennedy, Roosevelt's election to a fourth term and his death in office . . . these and many others are on the record and quoted enough to be considered "legendary."

## ABOUT THE SERIES

This is one of a series of twelve *Sydney Omarr® Day-by-Day Astrological Guides* for the signs of 2009. For questions and comments about the book, go to www.tjmacgregor.com.